Mutsu Munemitsu
and
His Time

Mutsu Munemitsu
and
His Time

Okazaki Hisahiko

Translated by

Noda Makito

Japan Publishing Industry Foundation for Culture

Translation Note

All Japanese names appearing in this book are written in traditional Japanese order, with the family name first. In addition, all Japanese words have been romanized in accordance with the Hepburn system, and macrons have been applied to indicate long vowels wherever deemed appropriate. Furthermore, the kanji for proper nouns is also displayed alongside the romanized text where deemed appropriate by the author.

Unless otherwise specified, all citations and references have been translated from the original Japanese text.

Mutsu Munemitsu and His Time
Okazaki Hisahiko. Translated by Noda Makito.

Published by
Japan Publishing Industry Foundation for Culture (JPIC)
3-12-3 Kanda-Jinbocho, Chiyoda-ku, Tokyo 101-0051, Japan

First English edition: March 2018

Copyright © 2003 by Hisahiko Okazaki
All rights reserved.
Originally published in Japanese language by PHP Institute, Inc. in March 17, 2003.
English publishing rights arranged with PHP Institute, Inc.
English translation copyright © 2018 by Japan Publishing Industry Foundation for Culture

This book, based on the original English translation by Noda Makito and carried out by the Okazaki Institute, is an updated and revised edition by JPIC.
The original English translation is based on the paperback version of *Mutsu Munemitsu to sono jidai*, published by PHP Institute, Inc. in 2003; first published in hardcover by the same publisher in 1999.

Jacket and cover design: Senō Hiroya
Front and cover photo of Mutsu Munemitsu: National Diet Library

As this book is published primarily to be donated to overseas universities, research institutions, public libraries and other organizations, commercial publication rights are available. For all enquiries regarding those rights, please contact the publisher of the English edition at the following address: japanlibrary@jpic.or.jp

Printed in Japan
ISBN 978-4-86658-025-8
http://www.jpic.or.jp/japanlibrary/

CONTENTS

CHAPTER VI

BURNING THE MIDNIGHT OIL AGAIN
Study during Imprisonment

CHAPTER VII

BURNING THE MIDNIGHT OIL A THIRD TIME
Is a Prussian-style Constitution Appropriate?

CHAPTER
XVII

JAPAN SAILS TO VICTORY
China's Strategic Dilemma

CHAPTER
XVIII

THE FINAL PHASE OF THE WAR
A Race Against Time

CHAPTER
XIX

THE TREATY OF SHIMONOSEKI
Li Hongzhang in Japan

CHAPTER XX **THE TRIPARTITE INTERVENTION**
An Unavoidable Concession

CHAPTER XXI **MUTSU'S DEATH**
Fighting for Democracy to the Last

Mutsu Munemitsu

FOREWORD

I have long wanted to write a history of modern Japanese diplomacy.

In 1953 I was the first Japanese student to be enrolled in Cambridge University after World War II, and I had the opportunity there to read a fair number of works written in the United Kingdom during and immediately after the war. My reading made me realize how grotesquely wars can distort the objective evaluation of history.

For example, I came across the testimony of British naval officers praising the bravery shown by Japanese pilots who attacked and sank the invincible HMS *Prince of Wales* during the naval battle off Malaya. But I never saw a reference to "brave" or "patriotic" Japanese soldiers in the history books. What I found instead was remarks about "fanatical" or "atrocious" attacks.

Modern warfare since World War I has become an all-out conflict involving entire nations. One important aspect of the war effort is, therefore, the propaganda designed to indoctrinate citizens on the virtue of the war being waged. For not only soldiers and volunteers but also ordinary citizens to be induced to cooperate and participate in bloodshed, they must be convinced that theirs is a righteous cause and that the enemy is the embodiment of evil. Since wars are fought between human beings, it would be inconceivable for one side to be wholly in the right and the opponent to be wholly wrong. But it is the mission of propaganda to make people believe in this fiction.

During World War II, Japanese propaganda was more effective than that of the Allies. Since the regions that Japanese forces invaded were former colonies of Allied nations, it was natural for their inhabitants to welcome their liberation from colonial rule. Having nothing to say against this response from local residents, the Americans and the British had no recourse but to emphasize the brutal conduct of Japanese soldiers, using terms like "bloodthirsty" and "unimaginable" to describe it. Much the same language, however, was employed by the Japanese, who called their opponents "ogres" and "beasts." This is in the very nature of war, where atrocities by both sides are in fact bound to occur.

When a war is over, the propaganda of the loser usually dies out, while that of the winner remains as a record of history. Thus, while I was at Cambridge, I encountered countless examples of this in the books and magazines written in English that I picked up.

Once words are printed in history books, they are usually guaranteed a long life. The Anglo-Saxons are particularly good at writing history. It would not be an exaggeration to say that most of world history, except that of China and Japan, was written by Anglo-Saxons, including histories of Persia and India, with their long tradition of civilization. Because English is the de facto lingua franca of the world today, history written in English is bound to be adopted as the final authoritative version. I have long wished to review and revise a conception of history influenced by this predominance.

It was in the late 1970s, more than thirty years after Japan's defeat in World War II, that the so-called textbook issue erupted in Japan. This grew into a nationwide controversy over whether Japan should apologize for its conduct during the war, including the so-called Nanjing Massacre (南京大虐殺) and the comfort women issue.

Normally, memory of a war will linger for about one generation, or thirty years, beyond which it enters the realm of history. For example, for thirty years after his defeat in the Battle of Waterloo in 1815, Napoleon was the brunt of harsh personal slander and criticism of his wartime conduct. After the Revolution of 1848, however, his accomplishments became permanently fixed in French history as an exaltation of the *gloire* of France. Another example might be the criticism, which lasted no longer than ten years, of Germany's World War I conduct as unworthy of a nation of high *Kultur*.

In Japan by the late 1970s, war issues already belonged to the remote past. At that time, I was Director-General at the Defense Agency, having been seconded from the Ministry of Foreign Affairs from 1978 to 1981. While in that position, I had to answer questions in the Diet three hundred times in three years. Never once was I questioned on the issue of Japanese conduct during the war or on sentiments in neighboring Asian countries toward Japan. Neither the Nanjing Massacre nor the comfort women issue was mentioned during that time. Nor do I recall reading about these issues in newspapers or academic papers at the time, whether American, Chinese, or Korean.

It would definitely be wrong to say that such issues, along with an apology for Japanese conduct during World War II, had been left unsettled for fifty years since the end of the war. The resurfacing of these matters since the 1980s was, instead, a case of historical relics being dug up with a certain political intention under unusual politico-social circumstances. And the reverberations from a domestic situation spread to neighboring nations, creating an international issue.

The phenomenon of making a country accountable so long after the end of a war is unprecedented, and it is hard to predict how this issue will evolve. Since it was triggered deliberately and artificially, it could unexpectedly evaporate quite soon, which made me, as a historian whose writings may be read by future generations, reluctant at first to comment.

As it turns out, however, the debate could be prolonged for quite some time. After all, this has been an attempt to artificially interrupt the natural flow of history and install the issue in such media as school textbooks. The debate could also present foreign countries with a card that they may be able to play to their advantage when bargaining with Japan.

What is most worrying about the lingering of this issue is its adverse effect on future generations. I once wrote a book on the Anglo-Dutch wars of the seventeenth century, comparing them with the U.S.-Japan economic friction that was flaring up in the early 1980s. Prior to these wars, the Dutch had fought bravely against the Spaniards in their drive for independence in the late sixteenth century, which spared England, a Dutch ally in those days. The Dutch successfully blocked the Duke of Parma's massive force from joining the Spanish Armada, thus saving England from invasion by the formidable Spanish infantry and also detaining the Armada until a hurricane came.

Because the Dutch fought two consecutive wars with England, however, the latter propagated the notion that, while England was fighting a life-and-death battle with Spain, the only concern of the Netherlands was profit; England portrayed the Dutch as bloodsuckers. And after the defeat of the Dutch side in these wars, this propaganda was firmly anchored in history, erasing Dutch contributions to England's security.

When a Japanese reader of my article mentioned what he had read to some Dutch friends of his, apparently they were excited by it, saying "We've heard this story over and over again since childhood. How did the Japanese know so much about it?" Their reaction shows that the memory of their ancestors' heroic conduct a few centuries earlier is still vivid for the Dutch today, even though the episode is completely ignored by the rest of the world.

Turning back to the textbook issue in Japan, one can't help noting that what happened here was not a case of a victorious country imposing on a defeated country a distorted interpretation of events. The textbook issue was, instead, started by the biased views of a leftist element within Japan itself. The incident illustrates the danger of a people's tradition and history being expunged by their own hand.

In order to criticize or reject the inaccuracy of the textbooks currently used in schools in Japan, one must be provided with an authentic and accurate historical viewpoint. Equipped with this, there should be no need to jump into the controversy to denounce other views. All one has to do is publicize one's own view of history and quietly brush off unwarranted deviations.

If, however, those criticizing are not equipped with an authentic, accurate historical perspective, the result will be the muddle of futile debate. The problem is that Japan so far has not developed an authoritative and integrated view of its modern history.

Unfortunately, the history of modern Japan has been so distorted by biases of one sort or another that the truth of this period lies in tatters.

To begin with, in accounts of the Meiji Restoration (明治維新, 1868), the viewpoint of the victors—that is, the Satsuma and Chōshū *han* (薩摩藩, 長州藩)—naturally held sway for many years. According to this version of history, the Satsuma and Chōshū domains campaigned for the restoration of imperial rule, toppled the Tokugawa shogunate (徳川幕府), and tore down the structures of old, feudalistic Japan, clearing the way for the genesis of modern civilization.

While this account might mesh more or less with the broadest historical currents, it belittles the contribution of the civilization that the Japanese had built up over the preceding centuries. Above all, it ignores important continuities between the Meiji era (明治時代, 1868–1912) and the 260-year Edo period (江戸時代, 1603–1868), during which Japan developed an advanced and distinctive society with the world's highest literacy rate.

Most accounts of the period after World War II similarly reflect the victors' view that the Occupation ushered in the age of democracy in Japan and fail to take note of native, prewar democratic currents that manifested themselves in the Freedom and People's Rights Movement (自由民権運動) of the early Meiji era and later flourished as Taishō Democracy (大正デモクラシー) in the 1920s. It was to address such biases that I chose to describe in detail both the early years of Mutsu Munemitsu (陸奥宗光, 1844–97) in the late Edo period and the life of Shidehara Kijūrō (幣原喜重郎, 1872–1951) in the Taishō era (大正時代, 1912–26).

The demise of Emperor Meiji (明治天皇) in 1912 and ensuing political turmoil led to a period of academic and political freedom. People openly criticized the Satsuma-Chōshū oligarchs and gave expression to a wide range of ideas. They discussed Japanese history free of any prejudices, and a full gamut of historical approaches was tolerated for about two decades.

People, sadly, seem to have very short memories. Even political scientists appear too preoccupied with Nazi Germany and militaristic Japan to stretch their memories back to the 1920s, to the Weimar Republic and Taishō Democracy.

Tensions began to rise in Japan around 1930 as a result of growing international turmoil. The Great Depression of 1929 seriously affected the daily life of ordinary people. The Kuomintang (国民党, Chinese Nationalist Party) launched an intifada-like resistance movement against territorial concessions made to Japan following the Russo-Japanese War. The threat of communism became acute in the Far East as Joseph Stalin consolidated his dictatorship in the Soviet Union. And Europe saw the rise of Adolf Hitler.

These tensions encouraged a conservative, right-wing tendency in Japanese society. A more patriotic, emperor-centered, militaristic view of history came to dominate, and as the country shifted to a wartime footing, all other viewpoints were suppressed under official censorship.

Ironically, the ideologically contrasting American censorship of the Occupation that replaced it following World War II was stricter in practice and more complete. The Occupation authorities placed severe limits on freedom of expression—notwithstanding the guarantees of free speech contained in the Potsdam Declaration outlining the terms of Japan's surrender and the new constitution drafted by the U.S. authorities themselves. Any diversion from the extremely simplistic historical perspective that formed the basis of the Tokyo war crime trials and Occupation policy—namely, that from just before the Manchurian Incident (満州事変, 1931) until the end of the war, Japan was the embodiment of evil and its every move an act of aggression or tyranny—was thoroughly suppressed.

The policy of the Occupation was to eliminate Japan's war-making potential, not only materially but also morally. One important means for achieving this was to foster a popular backlash against everything related to war or the military and above all to instill in the Japanese people feelings of guilt regarding their past under a War Guilt Information Program.

However, as Cold War tensions heightened, Washington revised its policy, seeking instead to turn Japan into a reliable military partner in its global anti-communist strategy. Thus the early Occupation objective of morally disarming Japan was abandoned.

Yet because this earlier policy perfectly matched the international communist goal of keeping Japan militarily and psychologically impotent, pressure groups, mainly working with communist-led unions for school-teachers and the mass media, did their best to keep it alive even after the end of the Occupation and throughout the Cold War era. Indeed, as the Marxist propaganda offensive prevailed in Japan and around the globe, the pacifist policy gained strength, permeating Japanese academia and journalism. So it was that a seriously distorted historical outlook took root in postwar Japan.

The rise of a generation educated in this view of history from elementary school through college, and further influenced by the leftist media, resulted in the anti-American, anti-Security Treaty, and anti-government movements that raged in the 1950s and 1960s. This unrest subsided during the 1970s, but in the 1980s the frustrated left wing, with mass media in the lead, began encouraging criticism of Japan from abroad and inviting foreign interference, which led to the rise of what we might call the self-flagellating view of Japanese history.

Both South Korea and China were ready to accommodate such a view due to the concurrent emergence of nationalist sentiments in their countries. Korea in the late 1980s through the first years of the twenty-first century was shedding the pro-Japanese, pro-American, and anti-communist stance of President Park Chung-hee. And China had adopted a policy of encouraging a "patriotic movement" in the 1990s to stem growing calls for democratization, as epitomized by the 1989 Tiananmen Incident. The focus of national concern thus shifted to the "liberation" of Taiwan so as to avenge the humiliation imposed by Japan a century before. The historical perspective advanced by Japanese leftists became the prevailing view in both countries, gaining further momentum at the turn of the twenty-first century to become a source of serious political tension in the region.

All these biases of the past century have mangled the history of modern Japan to the point where compiling a reliable account may appear to be an impossible task. On the contrary, though, it is actually a very simple one. All one needs to do is strip away the added values that have distorted historical accounts until now and seek the unvarnished truth. In 1824 the German historian Leopold von Ranke prefaced his *Geschichten der romanischen und germanischen Völker* (History of the

Romantic and Germanic peoples, 1824) by saying, "You may believe that history ought to judge the past and to instruct the contemporary world as to the future. The present attempt does not aspire to that high objective. It will merely tell how it really was."

History, in other words, should be none other than the pursuit of truth based on sound understanding. In many cases it is possible to determine whether something is indeed historical fact through accurate research. The alleged massacre of 300,000 people in Nanjing, for instance, can only be said to be unrealistic. The number of Nanjing residents around the time of the Japanese occupation is estimated to have been between 200,000 and 250,000. How can there have been more people killed than actually lived there?

It is more difficult, though, to correct an overemphasis on isolated events or facts with no significant relationship to larger historical trends. Most of the distortions contained in the postwar view of Japanese history fall into this category. It is important to find a way of refuting accounts of history in which some scholars choose to ignore true historical trends, selectively highlighting those events that coincide with their own viewpoint.

Unfortunately, there are no established criteria or methods for gauging the relative importance of historical facts and events. The only criterion we have at our disposal is common sense. In earlier times great scholars respected for this quality compiled general histories to which others could refer. Recently, however, the field of historical studies has become so specialized as to make it impossible for researchers to infringe on others' areas of expertise. There has been a growing tendency in academia, moreover, to ignore established authority. As a result, there is almost no one left who is capable of writing a complete, general history.

I can't claim that my judgment in this regard is better than the next person's; in fact, I don't believe that anyone today can make such a claim. For this reason, the method I adopted was to ask scholars known for their balanced judgment to share their knowledge in private seminars four times a year in three areas of modern history—political, military, and diplomatic—with two or three such individuals from each field participating. I had them read my first draft, three chapters at a time, and listened to their comments. When they questioned the validity of a statement or mentioned historical documents that contradicted what I had written, I then rewrote my manuscript as many times as necessary until they were satisfied that I had produced a balanced piece of work. Through this process, in a way, I verified a simple axiom, embraced since the time of Socrates and Plato, that dialogue is the best method of pursuing the truth.

The product of more than five years of such seminars was an account of modern Japanese political and diplomatic history in five volumes, beginning with the original Japanese version of this book *Mutsu Munemitsu to sono jidai* (*Mutsu Munemitsu and His Time*). A condensed version of this work was later translated and published as *A Century of Japanese Diplomacy 1853–1952*, from which the current complete translation borrows rather liberally, including, most notably, this foreword. I wish to take this opportunity to express my deepest gratitude to all those who made the publication of the abridged translation possible.

In compiling the original five-volume work, I chose to build each volume around the biography of one of the representative diplomats of that era, and I have preserved that structure here, in part because I am hopeful that people who are unfamiliar with Japanese history and tradition, including the younger generations of Japanese nowadays, will find that these accounts assist them in understanding the social and educational background of their countrymen in each period. This is why I chose to begin with the formative years of Mutsu Munemitsu.

My purpose in writing this book is nothing more or less than to present, to the best of my ability, a balanced and accurate account of history. And if history is the cumulative efforts of people living in a certain era, then the natural approach to establishing the truth of history is to follow the trail of those efforts, understanding them in the context of the time in which people lived rather than judging them by contemporary standards. This is the traditional method embraced by historians since antiquity, and inasmuch as history is made by human beings, it remains the only reasonable approach. I believe that the utmost care should be taken not to view history through the lens of contemporary thinking, practice, or jargon.

Some readers may object to my uncritical discussion of the

seemingly expansionist and imperialist thinking of such figures as Itō Hirobumi (伊藤博文, 1841–1909), Mutsu Munemitsu, and Komura Jutarō (小村寿太郎, 1855–1911). These men were without doubt imperialists. Even Shidehara Kijūrō, a dyed-in-the-wool pacifist, was an imperialist who sought to augment the power and glory of the Empire of Japan (大日本帝国) through peaceful means. The difference was merely whether they adopted a tough or soft approach to pursue that objective.

However, to criticize people living in the age of imperialism for being imperialists is like attacking people of the feudal era for being feudal or premodern. It is not inaccurate, but it is irrelevant to our purpose of uncovering the truth of our past.

Okazaki Hisahiko
August 2008

I

Father and Son

At the Apex of Eighteenth-Century Culture

Cultural Setting

Mutsu Munemitsu is known as the statesman who shouldered the fate of Japan as a foreign minister during the critical years of the late nineteenth century, the period at the apex of the vicious international imperialism into which Japan plunged following the opening of its doors to the outside world.

His youth is marked by the disaster that befell his family toward the end of 1852, one year prior to the arrival of Commodore Matthew Perry's fleet at Uraga (浦賀). Mutsu's father, Date Munehiro (伊達宗広), was ousted from his position as a high-ranking official in the bureaucracy, resulting in the breakup of the Date family and extreme poverty for family members.

Let me begin Mutsu's biography by looking back at the life of his father, in an attempt to portray the political and cultural setting of the late Edo period as well as the family and intellectual environment in which Mutsu grew up.

Present-day Japanese, as well as foreign students of Japanese history, may tend to think of the Edo period as a dark, feudalistic age yet to be enlightened by the modernization of the Meiji Restoration. It should be remembered, however, that the forty years of the Bunka, Bunsei, and Tenpō periods (文化文政天保時代, between 1804 and 1843, or only twenty-five years before the Meiji Restoration) witnessed the second and final flowering of Edo culture, the first being the Genroku period (元禄時代, 1688–1703). This was a time when all academic studies, not only Confucianism but also *kokugaku* (国学, a school of Japanese philology and philosophy) and *rangaku* (蘭学, Dutch learning) too, reached their highest standard. It would also be no exaggeration to say that most of the art forms that have survived until today, including kabuki plays (歌舞伎) and ukiyo-e (浮世絵) woodblock prints, were perfected around then.

Indeed, this was the high point of the eighteenth-century culture that Japan shared with other civilized societies, before it was swallowed up by the storm of modernization.

In France, the eighteenth century was a period when the upper class indulged in an elegant lifestyle in the court of Versailles, convinced of the longevity of its social order. The politician/diplomat Charles-Maurice de Talleyrand (1754–1838), who managed to stay in power from the French Revolution through the Napoleonic years to the Bourbon Restoration, once said, "Those who have not lived before the French Revolution can never know how sweet and elegant life can be." And the same may be said of Qing China and Tokugawa Japan before their encounter with the West.

The eighteenth century had different endings in different countries. In Europe, the lifestyle of that era was forever consigned to the past as the result of the French Revolution, the subsequent Napoleonic wars, and a series of uprisings that culminated in 1848.

In North America, governance by the English monarch ended with American independence (1776). After the Civil War (1861–65), the aristocratic lifestyle of planters in the southern states also became a thing of the nostalgic past.

After the Napoleonic wars, European countries as well as the United States stepped up their colonial expansion. The movement outward reached Japan and Qing China at the far end of the Eurasian continent in the mid-nineteenth century, a half-century after the French

Revolution. The First Opium Wars of 1840 and the arrival of Perry's ships in Japan in 1853 were the evening bell tolls of eighteenth-century civilization for East Asia.

Date Munehiro, the Last of the Edo Elite

Date Munehiro was born in 1802 in the Kishū domain (紀州藩, present-day Wakayama prefecture including the southern half of Mie prefecture) and died in 1877. Thus, according to the calendar, his life span was entirely within the nineteenth century. But since the Meiji Restoration took place in 1868, Munehiro actually spent the active years of his life almost entirely in the pre-Meiji, Bunka-Bunsei-Tenpō periods in which the fully developed culture of Japan was at its peak. He also experienced the rise and fall of his fortunes in typically pre-modern, feudalistic court conspiracies.

The Date family into which Munehiro was born was a samurai clan of high rank with an annual stipend of three hundred *koku*. After repeated promotions, Munehiro became a dignitary receiving an annual stipend of eight hundred *koku* before his fall from grace in 1852. One *koku* is a unit of rice equivalent to approximately one hundred and eighty liters. While it is difficult to estimate the value of a stipend of one *koku* in today's context, we might consider the living standard of a carpenter, one of the most popular vocations for the common people of Edo. A carpenter earned an average of two *shō* (one *shō* is 1.8 liters) of rice a day, making his annual income around six *koku* if he worked for three hundred days. Given this example, one can imagine that the circumstances of a high-ranking samurai clan with an annual stipend of a few hundred *koku* must have been quite decent. It would be the equivalent of tens of millions of yen in today's terms. And the net value of this stipend must have been much larger than its face value because it was a lifetime, hereditary stipend with no tax imposed. From this, one can also ascertain how difficult it must have been for a samurai clan of low rank with a stipend of, say, thirty *koku* to keep up appearances and pay the few retainers it employed.

The income of a samurai differed according to the *han* (the domain of feudal lords) with which he was affiliated. A *han* could be as small as ten thousand *koku*, while some were as large as a million. Accordingly, while the *karō*, or chief minister, of a small *han* earned less than a thousand *koku*, the chief minister of a large *han*, such as the Kishū domain with five hundred and fifty thousand *koku*, could himself be a feudal lord with his own castle. In fact, the Kishū *han*'s chief administrator, from the Mizuno family, was the fifty thousand *koku* master of Shingū Castle (新宮城). Day-to-day administration of the Kishū *han* was the responsibility of technocrats like the Date family, whose stipends ranged from a few hundred to about a thousand *koku*.

After Hidetada (秀忠), the son of Tokugawa Ieyasu (徳川家康), founder of the Tokugawa shogunate, succeeded to the post of shogun, Ieyasu assigned three other sons of his as lords of the Owari *han* (尾張藩), Kishū *han*, and Mito *han* (水戸藩). It was decided at that time that these three branch families, referred to as the Three Houses (御三家), were to support and assist the head family of the house of Tokugawa. Should no successor to the shogun be born to the head family, a successor was to be selected from these branches.

The lords of the Three Houses were, therefore, the most prestigious among some three hundred feudal lords in the Tokugawa shogunate. The common people were required to prostrate themselves when they encountered a procession from one of the Three Houses, and a children's song still popular today refers to the splendor of the Lord of Kishū's entourage.

Of the Three Houses, the Kishū *han* was a particularly powerful domain during the second half of the Edo period. Since the eighth shogun, Tokugawa Yoshimune (徳川吉宗, 1684–1751), was from the Kishū branch of the Tokugawa clan and every shogun since Yoshimune was of the same lineage, every member of this *han*—from samurai to ordinary affiliates—acted haughtily toward people from other domains. The samurai of the Kishū *han*, particularly those of high rank, were among the elite of elites of the time, second only to direct vassals of the shogun.

A Man of Extraordinary Intellect

Munehiro was certainly expected to be a high-flier in the *han*, but he was not regarded as a prodigy or even a gifted pupil in his childhood. Education in those days began with training in the recitation of Confucian texts, called *sodoku* or, simply, reading, without any explanation of the meaning. This traditional method was based on the conviction that "repeated reading leads to real understanding." While, admittedly, the training had some merit in that it allowed students to absorb the original text without any imposed interpretation, it must have been difficult for a child with a mind of his own, such as Munehiro, to follow the rote learning that was required.

Although Munehiro was schooled in the Confucian basics four times before he was ten years old,[*1] he failed to master the texts. Surprisingly, though, he demonstrated a particular talent when he started reading the tales of Japanese and Chinese classical history available in bookstores; he was able to remember all the plots and names of characters in these books after one reading. People were puzzled by this unusual ability, which had failed to emerge in his learning of Confucian texts.

Japanese society is traditionally intolerant of this type of nonconformist, and this intolerance is cited as a reason for its failure to produce creative talents even today.

Yet, in any age, one has to survive the norms of the society in which one lives. Munehiro's mother, following this educational tradition, decided to invite tutors to their home so that she could take lessons together with the boy. She also tried to motivate Munehiro by encouraging him to make a success of his life not only in Kishū but on a wider scale.

---

*1 The equivalent of eight or nine in the West. Under the traditional age counting system in China and Japan, a person is one year old at birth and ages by one year on each New Year's Day. This system was used in Japan until reform was imposed by the American Occupation. Thus, the present author turned twenty on New Year's Day in 1949, only to become nineteen again because of the reform, and then twenty once again on his birthday in April 1950.

　Hereafter, ages will be counted according to the traditional method, since all relevant historical materials use this system, notably in connection with biographical detail. It is difficult to adjust it in the Western way unless we know the exact date of birth of each individual and the date of a relevant event. (For example, records tell us that Mutsu went to Edo when he was fifteen. In order to translate his age to the Western system, one must know both his birthday and the exact date of his arrival in Edo.)

In Confucian teaching, filial piety is the supreme virtue along with loyalty. Correspondingly, it is only natural that parents should be pleased when their children rise in the world. Following this logic, Confucianism regards advancement in life as the highest form of filial piety, deeming it a moral goal, definitely not a mere fulfillment of personal ambition.

As it happens, Mutsu, the surname that Munehiro's son Munemitsu gave himself as an ambitious young man, derives from the ancient province of Mutsu in northeastern Japan, while Date was the name of a district within this province. His choice reflects an aspiration to move up, from a district within a province to that of the province itself, and rise above his father.

With the encouragement and affection provided by his mother, Munehiro made rapid progress in his studies. As an advanced student of the Chinese classics, he developed a particular liking for Chinese poetry, and apparently reached quite a high standard in his own compositions. Munehiro himself, however, soon became aware of certain limitations.

Unique to the Chinese language is a phonological system called the "four tones"; configurations of these tones can lead to beautiful rhythms in verse. These tones do not exist in Japanese. Being fastidious, however, when absorbing foreign cultures, the Japanese created a table of the Chinese phonological system and configurations of the tones in order to help people compose Chinese poetry. Whenever educated Japanese before World War II attempted to write Chinese poetry, therefore, they had this table to assist them.

Even with the help of the table, though, there was a limit to their efforts, since the Japanese were not by birth equipped with a natural ear for the rhythms of Chinese. Realizing that no Japanese writer could ever become a first-rate Chinese poet, Munehiro decided instead to focus on *waka*, the thirty-one syllable poem that was an original Japanese form of poetry.

A person of Munehiro's disposition tends to excel in whatever he sets his mind on. It so happened that the Kishū *han* was one of the intellectual centers of *kokugaku*. While the *Man'yōshū* (万葉集, *The Ten Thousand Leaves*) was a great classic of Japanese literature and cultural resource, consisting of 4,536 poems composed in the fourth through the eighth centuries, it had been largely neglected until the late eighteenth century, due to its use of *man'yōgana* (an ancient writing system that employs Chinese characters to represent the Japanese language), making appreciation of the poems by the latter-day Japanese extremely challenging.

It was Motoori Norinaga (本居宣長, 1730–1801) of the province of Ise (伊勢), which was then part of the Kishū *han*, who for the first time succeeded in putting in order and annotating all the poems compiled in the *Man'yōshū*. This impressive work also aided in the deciphering of such classics as the *Kojiki* (古事記, *Records of Ancient Matters*), the oldest surviving history book in Japan, compiled in the early eighth century.

Munehiro studied *waka* directly under Motoori Ōhira (本居大平), Norinaga's heir. With Ōhira's guidance, he became adept in *waka* composition, so much so that the quality of his poetry was allegedly unparalleled among the thousand or so *kokugaku* scholars in the Kishū *han* even before he reached the age of twenty.

Rapid Career Ascent

Munehiro also achieved personal success as an elite bureaucrat of the Kishū *han*. When he was fifteen he was appointed *koshō* (page boy) to Lord Shunkyō (舜恭). His brilliance immediately earned the latter's favor. Lord Shunkyō at that time was the former domain lord of the Kishū *han*. Although he had been renowned for his ability, he had retired early from his position to make way for the offspring of the then shogun Ienari (家斉) and his numerous concubines. But because these designated successors died prematurely one after another and the child heir who finally survived stayed in Edo rather than move to Kishū to reign, the real power of the Kishū *han* effectively remained in Shunkyō's hands.

When he was eighteen, Munehiro was selected for promotion to the post of *kansatsu* (inspector) of the *han*. Newly appointed *kansatsu* officials were made to copy in their own hand a wide range of classified documents on historical events and precedents within thirty days of their appointment. During this first month they were also subject to traditional initiation rituals imposed by their seniors. It was customary for senior officials to congregate at the house of the newest inspector almost every night to feast and drink, forcing the host to drink as well, so that he would be unable to perform his duty as a scribe. Thus deprived of sleep and being in a constant state of inebriation, it was only natural that most of these newcomers became exhausted during the ordeal.

Munehiro, too, was no exception to the traditional initiation. Once, Ōhira visited him out of concern for his health. Munehiro showed his old teacher some three hundred *waka* he had composed during that time. When a bewildered Ōhira asked about the progress of the copying job, Munehiro coolly replied that it had long been finished. This has in it an element of the same bravura that a high-flying young businessman today might exhibit when, having completed his tasks unnoticed by others, he shows willing to participate again in games of mahjong and rounds of drinking.

It was still more than thirty years before the arrival of Commodore Perry's fleet that this episode in Munehiro's life took place, when it seemed as though the lifestyle of the Tokugawa shogunate would last forever. And the young man's future as a bureaucrat looked excellent.

Munehiro rose rapidly through the ranks of officialdom, ultimately assuming the office of *kanjō bugyō*, or finance minister—the top post in the *han* bureaucracy—at the age of forty-seven. It would be fair to say that it was Munehiro who salvaged the finances of the Kishū *han* toward the end of the Tokugawa period when most of the three hundred domains were suffering from financial difficulties. After two and a half centuries of peace, any public financial system is bound to ossify. While the standard of living continued to rise, the amount of exploitable resources was limited. Nor could much be expected from technological innovation, unlike today. Revenues showed no significant increase, as prices kept creeping up over the years.

Moreover, these were the times of a last blossoming of Edo culture, when everyone, those of high and low station alike, vied to show off in extravagance and gaiety. Because Lord Shunkyō himself was of an extravagant disposition, it was a serious challenge to manage the *han* finances.

To cope with adversity, many *han* took various measures to encourage new industries. A typical example was to encourage peasants in the domain to farm cash crops which the *han* bought up to resell to the market. This practice was adopted in many domains and was not unique to the Kishū *han*. What Munehiro proposed, however, was very different from the common initiatives seen at the time.

As a way of aiding the poverty-stricken cotton-growing villages along the Kinokawa River (紀ノ川), Munehiro encouraged the inhabitants to weave *kihachijō*, a yellow and black cloth with a striped or checkered pattern. He then threw a party, inviting businessmen from the commercial capital of Osaka. Once the guests were pleasantly drunk, they were treated to entertainment by a group of geisha and mummers, all dressed in kimono made of the same *kihachijō* cloth. Next, the whole assembly made their way to the theater, where actors performed in the *kihachijō* kimono to the accompaniment of a song whose lyrics were composed by Munehiro himself. The effect of this newsworthy event was such that *kihachijō* immediately came into fashion and thousands of bolts were sold.

An even greater contribution by Munehiro to the domain's prosperity was made by launching a *han*-managed financial business using the eighth shogun Yoshimune's donation to the Kumano Sanzan Shrines (熊野三山) as seed money. To the initial sum of fifteen thousand *ryō*,[*2] an additional eighty-five thousand *ryō* from various sources was added, the total being available as loans. Headquartered in the Edo residence of the Kishū *han* in Shiba (芝), and ornamented by a curtain with the hollyhock crest of the Tokugawa family, the Shiba Sanzan Loan Office lent money to feudal lords of above ten thousand *koku*, to temples and shrines, and to merchants and craftsmen. Although interest rates were as high as ten percent a month, the service proved convenient for such magnates even as the Kaga *han* (加賀藩) and the Satsuma *han*.

All clerical work and record keeping was taken care of by domain

---

*2   One *ryō* was a gold coin weighing approximately 37.5 grams.

officials, thus eliminating costs for rent and labor, which are normally the largest expense in a financial business. Endorsement by the shogunate assured its credibility. There were practically no bad loans because the shogunate granted the Kishū *han* the privilege of priority confiscation of assets from those who failed to repay. These factors together constituted a formula for rapid business success. Impressed by this enterprise, investors poured in, and, at one point, the scale of business expanded to the level of close to two million *ryō*, possibly the largest lending concern in the entire Edo period. Its success was undoubtedly one of the reasons why, toward the end of the period, the financial situation of the Kishū *han* was so much better than that of other feudal domains, allowing it to purchase Western-built steam vessels and weapons.

In these ways, Munehiro endeavored to expand their sources of income through financial and industrial promotions. In the tradition of the samurai government, however, the standard remedy for financial crisis was fiscal tightening and sumptuary regulation. This policy was most notably implemented by the eighth shogun Tokugawa Yoshimune, who earned respect as a principled ruler throughout the shogunate, and his grandson Matsudaira Sadanobu (松平定信, 1759–1829), who is also considered to be one of the great prime ministers in the Tokugawa period.

Nobody ever questioned the legitimacy of these remedies. It was a concurrence of economic policy, on the one hand, and samurai ethics on the other, that demanded that samurai stoically put up with hardship on the battlefield and maintain self-restraint during times of peace.

Seen in this context, it is not at all difficult to imagine that Munehiro's measures, no matter how successful they turned out to be, invited criticism, or perhaps envy, from fellow samurai, who saw it as demeaning for a member of their class to do so much just for money.

Munehiro's Downfall

Since the Tang dynasty, poetic cameos of a nobleman mounted on a white horse with a silver-ornamented saddle being feted by the demimonde—something akin to the world of *La Traviata*—had been featured in Oriental literature. Munehiro was a bit of "a lion of the salon" himself, particularly with his tremendous financial success, and left behind a long poem permeated by *Man'yō*-like free-spiritedness, describing the pleasures he had enjoyed in the Gion (祇園) entertainment area of Kyoto. Staunch believers in traditional samurai values must have found the tone of this *chōka* (a long poem) very objectionable.

Times were quickly changing. The uninhibited, pleasure-loving lifestyle Munehiro enjoyed at the peak of his career continued only through the dying glow of eighteenth-century glory. The short-lived and unsuccessful Tenpō Reforms (1841–53), which were the last attempt at a tightening of official discipline in the shogunate, marked the end of the apogee of Edo culture.

The international environment was also undergoing drastic changes. While the Japanese elite might be indulging in eighteenth century-style refinements, the nineteenth century, filled with revolution and gun smoke, was just around the corner. Munehiro's fall from grace occurred ten years after the First Opium War in China and one year before Commodore Perry's arrival in Uraga. By that time, the culture of "demimonde sophistication" had already begun to fade in people's minds, and, instead, stirrings of a new zeitgeist could be felt.

The official reason given for Munehiro's downfall was overindulgence. He was accused of embarrassing old guard men of integrity by forcing them to make some contribution to an evening's entertainment, failing which they would be excluded from future revelries. While today this conduct would hardly constitute a crime, in samurai society it must have been conduct that deserved to be condemned.

The true reason for Munehiro's fall, however, was a power struggle in which he was the loser. This had involved contention between the home domain faction centered around Lord Shunkyō and the Edo faction focused on the child heir; and the death of Lord Shunkyō triggered the purge of the former side.

Munehiro's punishment was cruel. He was exiled to the Tanabe region in Wakayama, and his family was deprived of its stipend and forced out of the domain. The Date clan lost its wealth and power overnight, and the family was scattered in exile.

Mutsu was only nine years old when this happened. Apparently the boy, on hearing the news, was incensed and, grabbing an ancestral sword, made to dash outside, only to be stopped by family members. Repeated attempts to reprimand and calm the child did not work; Mutsu wouldn't stop arguing and challenging his family. When tears slowed him down, he went to wash his face, then returned to remonstrate. It is said that, even after this outburst subsided, he repeatedly swore to avenge the humiliation someday.

The Driving Motive of Mutsu's Later Life

This calamity was a determining factor in his life. Naturally, his immediate reaction must have been a longing to redress the wrong done to his family by the Kishū *han*. More importantly, the incident also seems to have implanted in the boy a lasting determination to make something of himself.

The kind of misfortune experienced by Mutsu's family would leave a deep scar in anyone, but particularly in someone of that age, who found himself absolutely powerless in the face of it. In some people it might lead to a slide downhill, while others might find resolve and inspiration in it.

To use a modern metaphor, Mutsu seems to have faced his life after this incident with the "hungry" ambition of an athlete. His eldest son, Mutsu Hirokichi (陸奥広吉), said, "A lot of people thought that my father was a brilliant person, but that wasn't all. It seems to me that with that degree of hard work and diligence even quite an ordinary man could have gotten as far as he did.... One thing I learned from him was to take advantage of sleepless nights to focus on one thing and think it over, because it would prove useful later. My father always followed this precept as a matter of course."

In a letter to his wife in 1881 while he was serving five years in a Sendai prison for treason, Mutsu wrote, "Since the year before last, I have spent every day reading, from eight o'clock in the morning until twelve at night, never missing a day. I have found it so interesting and enjoyable that even spring days seem short to me; nor have the nights

I spent sleeping alone struck me as the least bit long. I am never bored."
("Spring days" were conventionally described in classical Japanese literature as being long, as were "nights spent sleeping alone.") Even in a
prison cell, he never wasted a moment.

In 1882, Mutsu's younger cousin, Okazaki Kunisuke (岡崎邦輔, 1854–
1936) remembered, "He used to say to us youngsters 'I want you to
keep up with me. I don't like dawdlers.'" In another memoir, Okazaki
also said, "Hardly anyone could in fact keep up with him, he walked
so fast. Even in old age, his escort on long walks would seldom go the
whole way."

Mutsu earned the reputation of a man of *saigaku sōzen*, or "talent and
learning in equal measure." This expression comes from the saying *saishi
manabazu, manabu mono wa sai ni toboshi* (Those who are talented don't
study, and those who study lack talent.) Had Mutsu not been faced at
the age of nine with an incentive to succeed, it wouldn't have been surprising if he had turned out to be the sort of student who bluffs his way
through his work on the strength of innate talent and laughs at "grinds."
By a whim of fate, a person to whom application by no means came
naturally willingly applied himself to learning. So it was that a rare combination of cleverness and erudition was born. It must have been with
the insight he acquired through his studies that Mutsu turned himself
into a man of conviction who was later instrumental in bringing about
parliamentary democracy in Japan.

As it happened, during his childhood, he met the owner of a book-
store who was visiting Wakayama. The man was from Yamato-Gojō
(大和五条), a territory under direct control of the Tokugawa shogunate.
Amused by the boy's repeated vows of revenge, he said to Mutsu, "Master, if you want to take revenge on the Kishū clan, I recommend that you
become a local magistrate of a region like mine, administered directly
by the Tokugawa government." Taking him up on this suggestion, Mutsu
became his house guest in Yamato-Gojō where, among other subjects,
he read textbooks on civil administration, which may well have formed
the basis for his later proposal on land-tax reform that would facilitate
Japan's modernization.

This reading can't have been much fun even for a grownup. As an indication of the intensity that a young mind brought to his quest, it is reminiscent of the numerous old tales of vengeful samurai honing their skills at swordsmanship.

Leaving Yamato-Gojō, Mutsu returned to keep his mother company in a life of impoverished isolation, as described in his autobiography, until he decided to study in Edo at the age of fifteen. Not having enough traveling money, he became the servant of an old priest who was going there along the Ise (伊勢路) and Tōkaidō (東海道) roads. Mutsu's immediate destination was the office of the Kōyasan Temple (高野山) in Isarago (伊皿子), Edo, where he was to become a temple manservant. As he set out, he wrote the following Chinese poem:

> I have read the classics and works of literature
> And reached the age of fifteen
> I am adrift like a shipwrecked vessel
> But one day I will triumph and grow giant wings
> To burst through the clouds
> And soar across the heavens.

It was an ambition he faithfully lived up to throughout his life.

Meanwhile, Mutsu's father, Munehiro, had been sent into exile in the Tanabe region, his heart aching for his scattered family. In his memoir he wrote, "When Lord Shunkyō, who had been my great benefactor, passed away, I was entrusted with his funeral. It was during my humble preparations for the dead lord that the overthrow occurred, which resulted in my exile to a place called Tanabe within the Kishū *han.* Transported there in a bamboo cage like a common criminal, I felt as if a mountain wind had blown me, an autumn leaf, down to the bottom of a dark valley."

A ship adrift, a fallen leaf; both father and son found similar images to describe the dislocation of their lives.

DATE MUNEHIRO IN EXILE (JITOKU-Ō)

Intellectual Pilgrimage of an Edo Dignitary

Lament and Despair

Munehiro left an account of his days as an outcast entitled *Yomigaeri* (余身帰). The title, as he explained himself, referred to his return from *yomi*, the land of the dead.

Many later critics interpreted the memoir as an indication of Munehiro's deliverance from worldly attachments and attainment of Buddhist enlightenment, which exaggerated this aspect of his change of heart. In 1877, two months before Munehiro's death, for example, Takahashi Deishū (高橋泥舟), hailed as the greatest spear master of the time and a man of acknowledged integrity, annotated the memoir and characterized it as a record of Munehiro's "having transcended love and hatred, and found equality between friend and foe." Nakamura Masanao (中村正直), in the preface to his translation of Samuel Smiles' *Self-Help* into Japanese, also praised the way Munehiro had risen above the joys and sorrows of life.

From a contemporary perspective, however, *Yomigaeri* is not an account of finding enlightenment. While the memoir is permeated by detached and serene passages, at least the first half of it is full of grieving and despair, revealing a passionate attachment to past glory.

As we will see, it was only after Munehiro—or Jitoku-Ō (自得翁) as he called himself in retirement—was released from exile and, particularly, after he became a student of Ekkei (越渓), a master of Zen Buddhism in Kyoto, that he attained a state of enlightenment. Munehiro was more of a communicator than a seeker after truth. Instead of suppressing his emotions, he was not ashamed of expressing them openly.

Thus, the view of Munehiro as a redeemed figure is an example of portraiture distorted by zeitgeist. This was during a time when a samurai's ability to refrain from expressing his emotions indiscreetly was considered to be a manly virtue. To a person who had reached an age when people started calling him ō (venerable), the epithet "enlightened" was praise. It was not praise at all, on the other hand, for a samurai in those days to be characterized as someone who gave vent to his own feelings.

If Munehiro had been born much earlier, say in the tenth-century Heian period (平安時代, 794–1185) when sophisticated sentimentalism was appreciated, his prose and verse might have been admired as exponents of *mono no aware* (an empathy toward things) and become classics.[*3]

> Upon awakening from a dream
> All that remains is my own shadow
> Where has the person I met there gone?

> I look at the moon
> And feel loneliness
> I wonder if my kin feel the same
> Looking at the moon.

These poems, found in the first half of *Yomigaeri*, express an obvious longing for his homeland and his loved ones. Later, his emotional center of gravity gradually shifted to a more desperate lament, as shown in the following two *waka*:

---

*3 It is impossible to translate his *Man'yō*-style poetry concisely into English. Regrettably, only the rough meaning of Munehiro's poems is presented here.

A boat at the water's edge
Abandoned but not rotted yet
To what does it cling?

When even wind-blown petals are missed
Wind does not carry me away
A person missed by no one.

Here, his state of mind reflects intense self-pity in whatever he sees, be it a wooden punt or flowers. And "On Cherry Blossoms Proudly Shown to Me," his nostalgia for the past is obsessive, with no sign of the transcendence he was supposed to have attained:

Flowers full of memories
I too was once in full bloom
Even the heartless blossom would remember.

The following *chōka* and its *hanka* (accompanying short poem) also entreat the reader's sympathy:

Chōka
Although no cherry blossoms bloom for me
My heart responds to their memory
Although no cherry blossoms float down for me
My heart aches to see them fall.

Oh, sakura, sakura!
How I resemble thee.

Although I had no special gift
My lord allowed my humble self
Time to gather people around me
Like petals clinging to my sleeves and hems.

Then, amidst the happiness of spring
There came a sudden wind and rain
That scattered all the petals

And drove the wagons of my guests away
Where have they gone?

Oh, sakura, sakura!
Is this world a dream, a mirage?
Is it a shadow or an echo?

Like bubbles on the water's surface
Remember that nothing in this world remains.

Hanka
What once was loved when in full flower
Is dust when torn away by winds
So too, alas, is our short life.

In the Meiji period, this kind of *Man'yō*-style pseudo-classical verse was often adapted to modern poetry by people such as Ochiai Naobumi, and some of it became popular when turned into songs for elementary school music classes. As mentioned earlier, the *Man'yōshū* began to be genuinely appreciated around the time of Motoori Norinaga. Since Munehiro was a direct disciple of Norinaga's adopted son, he can be considered one of the forerunners of this brand of modern poetry.

During his exile, Munehiro was haunted by the fate of his children, including the son who described himself as "adrift like a shipwrecked vessel." In a *waka* entitled "On Young Bamboo," Munehiro writes:

I pray
That my children will surpass their parents
Just as young bamboo grows taller than its elders
Unworthy though I am to have this thought.

Another *chōka* is also full of pathos:

My boy who used to whip his stilts
As if to lash a horse
Must now have grown to manhood

My girls who used to have short hair
Must wear it in the upswept way
Not knowing of the changes in the world around them
Are they not waiting for my return, day in, day out?
Do they not miss me, day in, day out?
All hope in this world I have renounced
The world is but a dream I know
But my heart bends like soft bamboo beneath the eaves
When I hear a parent sparrow calling for its chicks
I cannot control my tears.

Even in that manly time in Japanese history, hundreds of years after the Heian period, poets appreciated *mono no aware* and parental sentiment. Some deeply sympathized with the misery the writer was undergoing, while another expressed his reaction to the poem simply in four Chinese characters that read "moved to tears by a true heart."

From Resignation to Buddha's Teachings

In the latter half of *Yomigaeri*, Munehiro recorded how he became immersed in Buddhist scriptures. This part of the memoir traces his development as a philosopher well acquainted with Confucianism, Buddhism, and poetry toward the end of the Tokugawa shogunate.

Munehiro's association with Buddhism began with regular chanting of the Lotus Sutra to pray for the late Lord Shunkyō's soul. He wrote.

Unable to accompany the moon
As it sank behind the western hills
I am left to pray alone
In a world of darkness

And

Seeing the moon go down
Beyond the western hills

Makes me renew my mission
Now to serve Buddha.

The phrase "moon go down beyond the western hills" was a metaphor for Lord Shunkyō, who had died at the Nishihama (Western Beach) palace (西浜御殿). Munehiro's daily devotions were the only way he knew to appease his sorrow and loneliness.

A person with his intellectual curiosity, however, could not remain content with just chanting prayers. He was not the sort of person who could persist in doing something without knowing the meaning behind it. After all, he was once a child who had been averse to reading Confucian texts without any explanation of their meaning.

Thus, he wrote, "Simply chanting the scriptures makes me feel as if I were looking at the back of a mirror." To overcome this sense of frustration, he borrowed various Buddhist texts from a nearby temple and studied them. And in so doing he realized that he knew almost nothing about Buddhism.

Buddhist scripture is the accumulation of a massive amount of writings, more philosophical than religious in nature, compiled by philosophers from Buddha's death in the fifth century B.C. until around the beginning of the Christian era. By the time the scriptures had reached China, Tibet, and Japan, they had become quite turgid, particularly after a series of translations into the vernacular.

The result is that in Japan when monks chant Buddhist prayers during religious ceremonies, there is hardly anyone—layman or learned—who understands their content. This may be comparable with the Catholic Church in medieval Europe, where mass was said in Latin.

From the seventh until the thirteenth century, Japan also saw the introduction of a series of new religious movements. During the Edo period, however, a time when Buddhism was protected by government policy in an effort to suppress Christianity, Buddhism itself was degraded to a mere ritual for funerals and, consequently, respect for the clergy was lost.

The prescribed academic discipline for a samurai in those days was Confucian studies. While *kokugaku* also became quite popular toward the end of the Edo period, Buddhist scripture was never part of the curriculum. Buddhist teachings were simply beyond the samurai's ken—so much so that it was considered appropriate to "abuse those who speak of Buddha and slander those who advocate Buddhism." But Munehiro himself was dismayed at the way this attitude was based on no knowledge of the truth or untruth of Buddhist belief.

Munehiro borrowed the *Issai-kyō* (一切経) a complete compilation of Buddhist scriptures which he found in a temple nearby, and devoted himself to its study for a number of years. Subsequently, he also started reading quotations from the Chinese Zen master Dahui (大恵禅師). Describing the situation he faced, he wrote, "Since I have no learned priest from whom to receive instruction nor a friend with whom to confer, I feel as though I am looking into my own mind, in the confinement of mountains and dark valleys."

Issai-kyō, or *Daizo-kyō* (大蔵経) as the work is also called, is a massive anthology. It is scarcely imaginable that anyone could undertake to study it without the benefit of a basic knowledge of Buddhism, without instructors, or without fellow students. Yet this method of tackling the original text based on the conviction that "repeated reading leads to true understanding" has at least the virtue of making what's learned one's own, independent of others' explanations or annotations.

It is interesting to note that his son went through a similar ordeal of self-teaching during his imprisonment in Sendai late in his life. Mutsu translated Jeremy Bentham's *Introduction to the Principles of Morals and Legislation* (1789), a challenging read even for native English speakers. Bentham himself wrote a modest but humorous note when he presented a copy to a French friend: "Some of my friends declare that what is written in this book is the truth, but all of them declare that nobody but my friends will read it. Perhaps, in all of France, only you and Monsieur Condorcet will be kind enough to read it from cover to cover … if you are confined on a remote island with nothing else to read."

Mutsu read and translated this recondite work with only the help of dictionaries, and revised his translation seventeen times. Of this experience he wrote, "I had no adviser or fellow student to direct my questions to. I had few books I could consult. I had only myself to rely on in translating this book." Through this laborious process, however, he succeeded in internalizing the essence of utilitarianism, one of the pillars of Anglo-Saxon liberal democracy. His ability to read and comprehend English may have been unrivaled among his contemporaries in the Meiji era.

Thus both Munehiro and Munemitsu were two examples of the intellectual energy that some members of their class at the twilight of the Edo period possessed. Two and a half centuries of peace without even a trace of civil war, together with an intensive education system, must also have helped create the intellectual discipline they shared.

Some *waka* in the last half of *Yomigaeri* betrayed a gradual change in Munehiro's frame of mind as his exile lingered on:

> Serenity in solitude is my goal today
> I command you Artemisia
> To cage me in with your leaves.

Here one can detect his wish to leave despondency behind by devoting himself to prayer. Another poem, harking back to a past in which he had let his ambitions and emotions drive him on, reads:

> The horse I once whipped on
> I will tether to Buddha's post.

A later set of *waka* gradually discloses a newfound sense of resignation. In spring, he writes:

> In name I am a mountain guard
> Yet it is the wind, not I
> Who decides when cherry flowers should fall.

In autumn, he writes:

> Nothing is constant in this world
> Yet some rules stay
> The rain never fails to fall
> When autumn turns to winter.

In this, too, one sees an acceptance of the cycle of Nature, an attitude made much more obvious in the following two *waka*:

> Nothing I did today is worth noting
> But a day has passed
> Passed in the sequence
> Of heaven and earth.

> They say the world is full of horrors
> None of which matters
> When one has learned
> Not to think of them.

How many years of despair must it have taken Munehiro to finally attain this frame of mind. It is thought that it was toward the very end of his exile that he was confident he had understood the way of Buddha. A paragraph immediately preceding the section on his release near the end of *Yomigaeri* reads:

> [Although scholars of Chinese studies or *kokugaku* speak ill of Buddhism whenever they can, none of them really know anything about it.] I ventured deep into the mountains of Buddha's teachings to search for the truth. I encountered all kinds of obstructions on the way: rocky paths, high peaks, wolves.... I had no precursor to guide me, nor shelter where I could rest. Although I was afraid, I pressed on, through dark forests and dense valleys. As I went further, however, I realized that the path had become smoother and, looking up, I saw a calm and peaceful sky. Beyond the spring haze, there were flowers in bloom.... I am now determined to reach the distant heights of Buddha's teachings. Now that I know the way, why should I stop short of finding the treasure of the truth?

One can sense his joy at finally mastering the knowledge contained in the many volumes of *Issai-kyō*.

Attaining a State of Enlightenment

Nevertheless, Munehiro's study of Buddhism was not at this point complete. (By the time of his return from exile he called himself Jitoku which, together with Ō, or "an elder" at the end, means roughly a "self-enlightened" elder.) Despite his completion of a massive reading program, it was only when he was hit with the *keisaku*—the "warning stick"—of Zen master Ekkei in Kyoto that he reached another level of understanding.

Once Munehiro arrived in Kyoto, he visited various famous temples to test his knowledge through learned discussions with high priests there. But Munehiro, equipped with ten solitary years' worth of knowledge of *Issai-kyō* and an inherently quick mind, was more than a match for them. Sustained by self-confidence, he decided to approach Ekkei, the great master of Zen Buddhism of the time. The episode is reminiscent of the behavior of his younger, more conceited self.

Although Ekkei must have sized up Munehiro's state of mind at a glance, his attitude toward him was, from the very beginning, amicable, albeit with a touch of the sternness inherent in Zen temples. Approving of his visitor's spiritual accomplishments, Ekkei decided to focus the dialogue on Munehiro's life instead of the technical details of Buddhist scriptures.

Knowing that he was well versed in the study of Chinese classics as well as *waka*, the Zen master invited him to state his position on the Buddhist prohibition on reading anything other than the scriptures. Munehiro immediately started rattling on about how the prohibition should be interpreted or refuted, confident that he was presenting a valid opinion on an issue he knew all too well.

Unsatisfied, Ekkei tried to prod him, saying, "Yours is a good answer for an educated country bumpkin. What I would like to know is the meaning behind the name Jitoku that you have assigned yourself." Munehiro was simply bewildered. Ekkei then followed it up with the classic Zen question, "What lies inside an empty tea cup?" The implication of this was, roughly, "You may talk and quibble, but it's the essentials we should be interested in." And seeing Munehiro unable to respond instantly to this question, Ekkei hit him hard with the *keisaku* before turning him out into the courtyard.

A furious Munehiro ran to fetch his sword from another room, shouting "Even my late lord never touched my head. That monk deserves to die for this." But a deputy to Ekkei who had observed the exchange then told him, "You must be someone of enviable consequence to be struck by the master's *keisaku* at your first meeting. I suggest that you sit in Zen meditation, then decide what to do."

Munehiro took his advice. He sat meditating in a temple room for almost a day and a night, his mood making him indifferent to food or drink. The episode gives some idea of his characteristic reluctance to admit defeat.

After a while, apparently, his expression brightened, as if privately he had made a discovery of some kind. When his request for another interview with Master Ekkei, conveyed by the deputy, was granted, Munehiro asked for paper and an inkstone, with which he composed the lines:

While chrysanthemums come in different colors
The flower has only one distinct scent

Nodding, Ekkei then responded with four Chinese characters, *zui en ji zai*, meaning approximately "perfect freedom in circumscribed conditions" (which gave Munehiro the title of his later anthology of *waka*).

The answer that he had reached was that there is only one truth, whether the way to it is through Confucianism, Buddhism, or poetry. The four-character endorsement that Ekkei gave him in return recognized the fullness that this insight represented, and acknowledged the aptness of *jitoku* in describing Munehiro's spiritual achievement.

Taisei santen-kō

We would be overlooking one important aspect of his intellectual vitality if we did not mention Munehiro's theories on history. Among his written works was *Taisei santen-kō* (大勢三転考, Study of three eras), composed in 1848. This work divided Japanese history into three eras: the first according to *kabane* (family name), the second to *tsukasa* (profession), and the third to *myō* (as in *daimyō* or feudal lord, literally "grand name").

Ancient Japan had a peculiar hereditary system, unknown to any other country, in which a particular clan or *kabane* was assigned to a particular governmental post—for example, members of the Kino and Izumo clans held the post of *omi* (minister), and members of the Mononobe and Ōtomo clans served as *muraji* (general).

The second era of *tsukasa* was the age of bureaucratic domination under a system of centralized government based on the *ritsuryō* law codes imported from Tang dynasty China in the seventh and eighth centuries. The third was the period of samurai government.

In modern times, this sort of historical classification is nothing new, as exemplified by Marxist history. (Incidentally, *Taisei santen-kō* was written in the same year that the *Manifest der kommmunistischen Partei* was published.) But it was a novel approach in Japan, and *Taisei santen-kō* is still well thought of among scholars of Japanese history.

One noteworthy aspect of the book is that it contains what appeared to be a prediction of the demise of the Tokugawa shogunate. Near the end of one chapter is this passage: "While some may find it regrettable that the old indigenous form of government in Japan should become obsolete due to the influence of Tang China, change in the pattern of government may be a natural process, beyond man's wisdom or control. It seems to me that any system is destined to be replaced after five hundred years of dominance. And it should be no surprise at this juncture if some extraordinary development arose to take advantage of the transition."

This was written more than six hundred years after the rise of the Kamakura shogunate (鎌倉幕府, 1185–1333) and, amazingly, more than five years before the arrival of Commodore Perry's fleet. If published, Munehiro would have been punished with a severity surpassing exile in Tanabe. It was, therefore, not until after the Meiji Restoration that the book was publicly circulated. And its structure reflected extra care, as it was only toward the end of the chapter on the transition from the eras of *kabane* to *tsukasa* that mention was made of the five-hundred-year cycle of politico-social trends. Also, the final chapter was full of praise for the extensive period of peace enjoyed under the military rule of the shogun.

It should be remembered, however, that it had already been six years since Qing China had been forced to cede Hong Kong to the

United Kingdom as the result of the First Opium War when Munehiro wrote this book, even though it was still some time before the arrival of the American fleet at Uraga. The Tokugawa government had already been urged by the Dutch king to open the country to the outside world. Domestically, Mizuno Tadakuni's (水野忠邦) Tenpō Reforms, which were a last-ditch effort to tighten official discipline, were a total failure and no map for the future was at hand.

In other words, it would not have been surprising if at that stage someone with a keen sense of history had predicted great change. Still, book reviews in the Meiji era single out *Taisei santen-kō* for its political predictions. Naitō Konan, a historian of the late Meiji and Taishō periods, rated the book among the four greatest works on the history of Japan.

Desertion from the Wakayama *han*

After being released from ten long years of quarantine, Munehiro returned to the Wakayama *han* as a retainer with a minuscule stipend of thirty-five *koku*, a humiliating reduction from the eight hundred that he had previously received. He built a tiny hermitage within the domain and taught *waka* and Buddhism to local students. Meanwhile, he completed preparations to escape to Kyoto. Two days before his flight, Munehiro organized a *waka*-composing party around the theme of "a celebration dedicated to Kyoto." Guests of the party, remembering the uncharacteristic abundance of food and drink, realized in retrospect that it must have been Munehiro's modest gesture of farewell.

Desertion from one's own domain was a new phenomenon seen only in the last decade of the Tokugawa shogunate. Traditionally, the principal role of a samurai was to serve the lord to whom he pledged allegiance and to earn the stipend with which he could support his family and secure the resources for a stable life for his descendants. To become a *rōnin*, or a masterless samurai, automatically meant failure and destitution. Thus during the first two hundred and fifty years of *Pax Tokugawa*, voluntary desertion by a samurai was unthinkable. The sudden fad for desertion in the final ten years must have been an indication of a prevalent sense of uncertainty about the future of the current regime.

Also, there were shelters where deserters could seek refuge. In East Asia, many communities had long had a tradition of offering worthwhile visitors food and accommodation in return for their loyalty to the host. It is believed that Lord Mengchang (孟嘗君) of the State of Qi in China's Warring States period in the third century B.C. took in as many as three thousand such guests. In turbulent times, it made good sense to surround oneself with useful people as a form of self-protection.

It must be because Japan was also going through difficult times that many were willing to accommodate these displaced persons toward the end of the Edo period and the beginning of the next. Mutsu Munemitsu was no exception and, after he became a high-ranking official in the Meiji government, he gave lodging to quite a number of people at his own residence, some of whom had allegedly been such hosts themselves. There were even some who did not know their benefactor's face.

It seems that, in the final years of the Tokugawa government, some feudal lords secretly offered funds to the hosts of these house guests, who in turn functioned as auxiliaries for the sponsoring lords. When signs of impending upheaval became increasingly visible, the popular destination of samurai deserters was Kyoto, the seat of the emperor. Munehiro was warmly welcomed by court nobles and became well respected by the *sonnō-ha*, the advocates of the restoration of imperial rule there. The following two *waka* that he composed in those days in praise of Arashiyama (嵐山), a famous scenic spot in Kyoto, reflect his situation:

> Men from many clans
> Have gathered here
> The power of the emperor is in full bloom
> Like the cherry trees of Arashiyama.

> All Arashiyama is in blossom
> I feel that my lost decades were not wasted.

III

Meiji Restoration

Into the Age of Revolution and Gun Smoke

No Success, No Going Home

After arriving in the shogunate capital at the age of fifteen, Mutsu worked hard studying the Chinese classics under such renowned scholars as Yasui Sokken (安井息軒) and Mizumoto Seibi (水本成美), while earning a meager wage as a scribe or chopping herbs at a Chinese pharmacy.

The later works of Mutsu, particularly those written during his imprisonment, show an exceptionally deep understanding of Chinese literature, comparable with that of top-class scholars. How did he manage to achieve such learning? Considering his stormy life later on, it must have been during a time of intensive education while living with his mother until he turned fifteen and during his subsequent stay in Edo until the age of nineteen.

It was common in those days for an ambitious youth like Mutsu to aim at distinguishing himself in his field of learning. As long as the *Pax Tokugawa* persisted, one of the few ways for a poor youth to get ahead was to become an accomplished Confucian scholar. Examples were Arai Hakuseki (新井白石, 1657–1725), appointed chief adviser to the sixth shogun Ienobu. Also, during the reign of the fifth shogun Tsunayoshi (徳川綱吉), Ogyū Sorai (荻生徂徠, 1666–1728) was a powerful figure under the wing of the shogun's chamberlain, Yanagisawa Yoshiyasu (柳沢吉保, 1658–1714).

The personal background of these two Confucian scholars was similar to Mutsu's. Hakuseki's father, like Mutsu's father, was exiled from his domain. This happened when Hakuseki was twenty-one, and reduced the family to real poverty for fifteen long years. Hakuseki had already been regarded as a prodigy since he was just three years old. During one period of his boyhood, he gave himself the task of transcribing three thousand characters from the Chinese classics daily; when he became too sleepy to continue, he would douse himself with cold well water, even in mid-winter. It is a well-known story that he flatly turned down the offer of a three thousand *ryō* scholarship proposed by business magnate Kawamura Zuiken (河村瑞賢) in exchange for his marriage to Zuiken's granddaughter, saying that he wasn't for sale.

Sorai's family, too, was exiled. Sorai spent the years between the ages of fourteen and twenty-four with his father in the remote countryside of the Kazusa (上総) region. His ordeal continued even after he came to Edo a year later. He staved off hunger by eating the pulp left after the milk is extracted from soybeans to make tofu. A popular story recounts how he surprised the kind tofu maker by paying him back handsomely when he became a top-ranking member of the government.

Opportunities for a samurai to distinguish himself through military feats were lost when Osaka Castle (大阪城) surrendered to the Tokugawa side in the first year of Genna (1615), an event recorded in the popular phrase *Genna enbu* (元和偃武), "the Genna pacification." For two and a half centuries afterwards, there were no wars between feudal lords or any conflict with external enemies. In this unprecedentedly peaceful era, an aspiring youth's only recourse was to achieve success as a scholar. Confucianism is essentially an ethical teaching for the ruling class on how to govern, rather than a universal moral code or, still less, a religion. An accomplished Confucianist meant a person with a superior political education and was considered qualified for a senior administrative post.

A man sets a goal for himself and leaves home
Never to return, even in death
Unless he prospers as a scholar....
His village may have a green mound to be buried in
But there are other green mounds wherever one goes.

This poem by the Buddhist priest and revolutionary Gesshō (月性, 1817–58) echoes the determination of the Spartan youth to whom his mother said, "Return home raising your shield in victory or being carried on it as a corpse." Mutsu must have felt exactly the same way when he left for Edo.

In the history of East Asia, the two hundred years of the Later Han (後漢) dynasty in China between the first and second centuries B.C. and the long span of the Tokugawa period between 1603 and 1868 saw the ascendance of education-oriented rule. The *Sanguozhi* (三国志, Records of the Three Kingdoms) is the most popular Chinese historical tale in Asia. Its brave heroes were also intellectuals. Their words and deeds had depth.

In European history, a parallel might be the era depicted in Thucydides' *History of the Peloponnesian War* (431–404 B.C.). Those who played a crucial role in that war were all highly educated during the heyday of Pericles' reign (443–429 B.C.).

Like these earlier histories, the annals of the Meiji Restoration are a reminder that we are revisiting a period influenced by men who probably possessed a higher level of sophistication than people of our own day.

After the disaster of the Japanese Empire in the Shōwa period (昭和時代, 1926–89), we have become nostalgic about what are felt to be the balmy days of the Meiji era. But we should remember that most of the leaders who shouldered the responsibility for the modernization of Japan, including Itō Hirobumi and Mutsu Munemitsu, were the products of an Edo-period education. Those who led Japan into the disastrous Pacific War were born in the Meiji period and had received the modern education of the Meiji and Taishō periods. The high standard of education in the Edo period, particularly among the elite, deserves to be reevaluated.

From *Pax Tokugawa* to an Era of Heroes

During the ten years of Munehiro's exile, Japan's domestic and external situation underwent drastic change. The very year that his family was dispersed was the year that Perry's fleet arrived in Uraga and demanded that Japan emerge from its seclusion.

The Tokugawa shogunate uncharacteristically sought counsel from many feudal lords on how best to respond, but had no other recourse than to yield to the gunboat diplomacy of the Western powers. It eventually concluded treaties of friendship with the United States, the United Kingdom, and Russia one after another in 1854 and 1855. Foreign pressure forced the country to revise its two-hundred-year-old law on national isolation.

Since very few people knew what was happening outside Japan, particularly the harsh reality of imperialism in the nineteenth century, strong opposition was raised to the decision to change the traditional closed-door policy. In order to appease the opposition and unify public opinion, the shogunate asked for imperial sanction of the treaties of friendship.

As history proves, a revolution can often be triggered by an inadvertent act. The shogunate's first mistake was to have sought the advice of feudal lords for the first time in its reign, awakening them from two centuries of total submission. The second mistake was seeking the approval of the imperial court. Since the latter had been on the sidelines of real political power for close to eight hundred years from the beginning of the Kamakura shogunate, consulting it was a crucial misstep which led the Tokugawa regime to undermine its absolute power. These unintended moves launched it on a decade of steep decline, just as the *États généraux*, held on the eve of the French Revolution after close to two hundred years of neglect, shook up the foundation of the House of Bourbon.

The Tokugawa shogunate took it for granted that imperial approval would be given automatically, as had been the case throughout the Edo period. The court, however, refused to sanction the signing of friendship treaties. Ironically, in seeking its authorization, the shogunate put itself in the position of being blamed for having opened the doors of the country without imperial approval. As a consequence, it became the target of hostile nationalistic and anti-foreign sentiments which were on the rise all over Japan.

The anti-foreign movement was soon armed with the ideology of the legitimacy of the imperial family in Japanese history and developed into a campaign to "revere the emperor and expel the barbarians" (*sonnō jōi*). Eventually, this evolved into a concerted effort to topple the shogunate by the powerful domains in southwestern Japan which had lain low since the Battle of Sekigahara in 1600.

In the hope of suppressing the campaign to restore the emperor to power and expel foreign intruders, the shogunate appointed Ii Naosuke (井伊直弼) to the post of *tairō* (senior minister). However, Ii's excessively harsh measures had the adverse effect of pushing the royalists further toward the anti-shogunate movement.

Only two years after Mutsu's arrival in Edo, Sano Takenosuke (佐野 竹之助, 1815–60) also set out from his home in Mito for the shogunate capital to take part in the assassination of Ii Naosuke. The lines Sano composed on leaving home were quite different from poems written by others embarking on journeys earlier in that period.

> When I made ready to leave
> Resolved to part from them forever
> My brothers and sisters, not knowing
> my intention
> Tugged at my sleeves and asked when I would return.

The days of *Pax Tokugawa*, when youths dreamed of successful homecomings after earning their laurels elsewhere, had given way to turmoil, an era of revolutionaries and heroes.

In his autobiography, Mutsu writes that he, too, decided to drop his plan of becoming an accomplished scholar. He gives a very plain reason for his decision: the end of the shogunate seemed imminent. Instead, he apprenticed himself to some of the leading pro-emperor activists of the time, including Katsura Kogorō[*4] (桂小五郎, 1833–77) of

---

[*4] Katsura Kogorō, later known as Kido Takayoshi, is counted as one of the "three great heroes" of the Meiji Restoration, along with Saigō Takamori and Ōkubo Toshimichi of the Satsuma *han*.

the Chōshū *han* and Inui Taisuke*5 (乾退助, 1837–1919) of the Tosa *han*. These were men whose influence was such that a younger person intent on furthering his career was willing to go to some lengths to make their acquaintance.

It had always been a tradition in East Asia for people to seek out a mentor or a man of character. After hearing a prophesy that he would meet someone of rare good judgment, King Wen (文王, 1152–1056 B.C.) of Zhou (周), when out hunting, encountered the man who eventually became his chief adviser, Taigongwang (太公望). When Liu Bei (劉備, A.D. 161–223, founding emperor of Shu Han during the Three King-doms) heard talk of a wise man named Zhuge Liang (諸葛孔明, A.D. 181–234), he personally visited the hermit three times before finding the right candidate to be his chancellor.

Similarly, militants in the final phase of the Tokugawa shogunate went out of their way to associate themselves with political mentors, however remote their *han*. Mutsu joined their number.

A Quick Escape, Not a Drawn Sword

Mutsu became adept at running away. Allegedly, he used to practice running through crowds in the downtown Asakusa (浅草) area of Edo whenever he had time, getting to the point where he could slip through packed streets like a swallow. Asked why on earth he was doing this, he said, "I am a samurai, so I can expect to have to fight if someone draws his sword. But what's the point of being injured by somebody of no account? So I prefer to run away."

Throughout his life, Mutsu acknowledged only a handful of men as intellectually superior or at least his equals, including Itō Hirobumi*6 and Sakamoto Ryōma (坂本竜馬, 1835–67). To Mutsu, anyone else was an unworthy opponent, and, likewise, common sense made him unwill-ing to put his life at risk against an unworthy assailant. But the other

---

*5 Inui Taisuke, later known as Itagaki Taisuke, became chairman of the Liberal Party and Home Minister of the Ōkuma Shigenobu administration.

*6 Itō Hirobumi, the first prime minister of Japan.

and perhaps more important reason behind his aversion to sword fighting must be the fact that he had never really had proper training as a samurai.

According to the memoirs of Okazaki Kunisuke, the education imposed on children of Kishū *han* samurai in those days was incomparably stricter than today's schooling. Since early childhood, they were given lessons in the Four Books of Confucianism, calligraphy, and such martial arts as kendo swordsmanship, swimming, riding, using a spear, archery, and musket marksmanship. Of these, only the last two were no longer taught to children younger than Kunisuke by two or three years. Rigorous martial arts training began when Kunisuke was ten years old. He remembers that a young sword instructor used to drop by every day at their house on his way to the kendo school, even on the coldest winter mornings, for extra practice. He also remembers walking to the school rubbing his sleepy eyes in a biting wind.

I believe there is scarcely another case in world history where the ruling class maintained such an austere system to instill discipline and morale despite two centuries of peace. Ironically, because of this training, the treatment of former samurai in the new social system became a major issue for the Meiji government, when riots caused by dissatisfied ex-samurai occurred for almost ten years after the Restoration, up to the Satsuma Rebellion of 1877.

Following the Meiji Restoration, the samurai as a social class disappeared, but their ethics were still accepted as the consummate moral standard. Moreover, with the launching of general conscription by the Meiji government, the samurai code returned to center stage as the national moral standard for the military.

Toward the beginning of World War II, excessive emphasis was placed on certain specific values in this code that were considered effective in producing useful soldiers—loyalty, discipline, a combative spirit, and self-sacrifice. As a rebound from this trend, the code ceased to be the main moral standard in postwar Japan. Yet remnants of the tradition can still be found in today's society in a certain sense of honor and shame as well as loyalty.

It should be remembered that young Mutsu was nine years old when the Date family fell on hard times. This circumstance deprived him of the full training of a samurai he would otherwise have received. Samurai in those days were expected to excel both in the literary and military arts. In fact, such leaders of the Meiji Restoration as Katsura Kogorō and Sakamoto Ryōma were also renowned swordsmen. Judging from his appetite for high achievement, Mutsu would have wanted to excel at both skills himself, but it was not to be, however hard he tried to make up for it as a young adult.

Mutsu at the end of the Edo period

In a way, this handicap may have molded Mutsu's future. Starting with the tactic of running away rather than fighting, he broke taboos for samurai one after another. By doing so, he became capable of being a champion of change at every stage of the modernization process. The backdrop to his special role as a pioneer must have been his forced exemption from a conventional education.

Sakamoto Ryōma and Katsu Kaishū

After a while, on the strong recommendation of Sakamoto Ryōma, who saw promise in the young man, Mutsu entered Kobe Naval College (海軍操錬所), an elite school founded and directed by Katsu Kaishū (勝海舟, 1823–99).

Sakamoto and Katsu were the two outstanding personalities to emerge in the turbulent days from the end of the shogunate through the

Restoration. Sakamoto succeeded in building a coalition between two powerful anti-shogunate domains, the Satsuma and the Chōshū *han*; these two archrivals had been bickering like cats and dogs, and their joining forces was a major factor in ensuring progress. Katsu was the chief representative of the shogunate in negotiations with the imperial envoy Saigō Takamori (西郷隆盛, 1828–77), and his efforts led to the bloodless surrender of Edo Castle, thus ensuring a relatively peaceful and orderly transition of power and preventing intervention by foreign powers.

These two men could not have gained prominence in more stable times. They were products of an unruly period. Katsu was from a family of the vassal of the house of Tokugawa (*hatamoto*, 旗本). Despite their status as a family directly serving the shogun, they received a miserable annual stipend of only fourteen *koku*, guaranteeing hardship. Sakamoto came from the lowest-ranking samurai clan in the remote domain of Tosa (土佐).

One thing these two had in common despite their otherwise different backgrounds was their mastery of swordsmanship: both were trained by first-class masters well known in Edo. Katsu's rank of *menkyo kaiden* (full proficiency) was the highest attainable and an indication that there was nothing more his instructor could teach him.

As tradition demanded, both were also well versed in the literary arts. Katsu's hard work was well known: he had made two copies of a three-thousand-page dictionary by hand when he had started studying Dutch learning, and sold one copy to put food on the table. This led to his becoming an instructor at a private school of Dutch learning.

Training in swordsmanship aimed not only at a mastery of technique but at nurturing mental preparedness.

In this connection, it was deemed particularly important to "*tan-ryoku o neru*." Literally meaning "training one's guts," the expression is hard to translate into either modern Japanese or English. Basically, *tanryoku* refers to a state of mind allowing one to maintain one's poise or judgment in a crisis, even when one's own life is in danger. Katsu's own experience is relevant. In his youth, the boy was a boarder at the house of master swordsman Shimada Toranosuke (島田虎之助, 1814–52). Katsu chopped firewood and drew well water for his host between training sessions. As an exercise, Shimada told him one evening to go to the nearby shrine dressed only in his thin training gear, first to sit on a rock to meditate, then practice swinging his wooden sword, and then meditate again on the rock. The purpose of this, according to his teacher, was to discipline his mind. After repeating the set five or six times until dawn, Katsu returned home to start morning practice. Throughout that winter, he did this every night without fail. Occasionally, he was joined by fellow boarders, who would quit after a few days, unable to cope with the cold and lack of sleep. It was due to this night training that he claimed to be able to face any kind of crisis during the disorder that followed the downfall of the shogunate.

Shimada also impressed on his students the importance of Zen. Katsu wrote later:

> During meditation with a group of monks, the high priest used to abruptly hit us with the Zen stick. This usually made people fall over on their back. Even when meditating, the monks often had things like money and food on their mind and were far from concentrating. At first I was also among those who fell backward, but as I got further into it, a blow from the stick ceased to have much effect. I reached a stage where I just looked at the fellow who hit me with half-closed eyes.

> I had four years of intensive training. The combination of Zen meditation and swordsmanship turned out to be extremely useful in later years. I owe my survival to them in dozens of situations before and after the end of the shogunate. Survival was something I put out of my mind when my back was to the wall. Miraculously, I was never killed.

> When you're too anxious to beat your opponent, both your head and your heart will be preoccupied with winning, making you flustered, so you make poor decisions. When you're too eager to escape from danger, your opponent will take advantage of any hesitation. I tried to respond to situations with clear-headedness and unconcern about winning or losing. This habit saved me from difficulties large

and small: I was able to fend off assaults by radicals and other dangers in the lead-up to the Restoration with equanimity.

Judging from Katsu's own experience, *"tanryoku"* might be defined as the self-confidence and composure derived from the completion of self-imposed hard training and an understanding of the essence of Zen; not losing spiritual serenity and detachment even in the most trying circumstances.

True Sympathizer

Katsu had studied Dutch and learned the art of navigation required to captain a Western-built warship that the shogunate had purchased from the Netherlands. When the shogun's envoys charged with the instruments of ratification of the Treaty of Amity and Commerce traveled to the United States on board a U.S. naval vessel, Katsu escorted them as captain of the small three-hundred-ton *Kanrin Maru* (咸臨丸). Only seven years after the arrival of Perry's fleet at Uraga, the Japanese had learned modern Western seamanship to the extent that the *Kanrin Maru* succeeded in safely crossing the rough waters of the North Pacific. The crossing would have been impossible without the determination of the Japanese to modernize the country at any cost—a determination that was clearly shared by members of his crew.

According to Mutsu's autobiography, it was under Katsu's influence that he started paying attention to the world outside Japan, which made him realize the futility of isolationism—an attitude he maintained all his life.

While the movement to restore the emperor to power and expel foreigners was the original force behind the energy for the Restoration, once Japan's isolationist policy was abandoned and people became acquainted with the international situation, it did not take long even for the royalists to realize the inexpedience of Japan's attempt to militarily resist the Western powers. Even Itō Hirobumi, who in 1862 had participated in a raid on the British legation, had his eyes opened to the power of the imperialistic nations when he toured the United Kingdom only one year later. People in leadership positions and intellectuals who had more opportunities to be exposed to international realities were the first to be converted. By the time the shogunate was successfully overturned, there was hardly anyone among the revolutionary leaders who still believed in the "expulsion of the barbarians." Thus, the moment it was accomplished, the Meiji Restoration became almost synonymous with *bunmei kaika* (文明開化, civilization and enlightenment).

Amidst an unstable political environment, Katsu's Kobe Naval College was closed down. Mutsu then joined the *Kaientai* (海援隊), a group founded and directed by Sakamoto Ryōma. Since Sakamoto himself was a deserter from the Tosa *han*, he stipulated that *Kaientai* members had to be deserters themselves. For them, the rigid social system of the Tokugawa shogunate had already collapsed. Mutsu began to identify himself with these people and became an anti-shogunate activist too.

The *Kaientai* was an independent shipping and trading company with its own steamers; it earned its operating funds on its own. Sakamoto's opinion of Mutsu was complimentary. "[Of all the members of the *Kaientai*,]" he once said, "only Mutsu and I can survive without bearing weapons." Nevertheless, Mutsu was not well thought of by his peers. Katsu wrote of him at the naval college in his memoir *Hikawa seiwa* (氷川清話):

> He looked like a smart aleck.... His reputation among fellow students was bad. Most students were from the Satsuma *han*, and were more set on toughness than intelligence. Surrounded by these people, a bumptious character like Mutsu was bound to be given a hard time.

In the social climate of the day, a know-it-all attitude would have been enough of a reason to be ostracized, being seen as a disgrace to the samurai class, thus risking the spilling of blood.

Mutsu faced a similar situation as a member of the *Kaientai*. When one of the company's vessels sank after colliding with the *Myōkō Maru* (明光丸)—the official vessel of the Kishū *han*—other *Kaientai* members arranged to kill Mutsu, ostensibly because he was originally from that

Kaientai leaders. From the right: Shiramine Shunme, Sugano Kakubei, Mutsu Genjirō (Munemitsu), Sakamoto Ryōma, Okamoto Kenzaburō, Nagaoka Kenkichi.

domain. But the fact was, his talk and manner had made him seriously unpopular. His life was only spared at the last minute thanks to the intervention of the young Nakajima Sakutarō (中島作太郎, 1846–99), who went on to marry Mutsu's younger sister and become Speaker of the House of Representatives in the first Imperial Diet, which Mutsu served in as the minister of agriculture and commerce.

Throughout his life, only three men truly understood Mutsu and did all they could to help him make the most of his talents: Sakamoto Ryōma, Itō Hirobumi, and, later, Saionji Kinmochi (西園寺公望, 1849–1940). This is some indication of what an individualistic, difficult person he was. It took people like Sakamoto and Itō who had unshakable confidence in their own abilities or someone like Saionji, the heir of a distinguished court noble with no ambition, to appreciate Mutsu's personality open-mindedly. To all others, he must have left the impression of a disagreeable and aggressive individual.

Of these three supporters, unfortunately, one was murdered on the eve of the Restoration, after his success in facilitating the anti-shogunate coalition between the Satsuma and Chōshū domains. This was Sakamoto. Had he survived, he would certainly have become a key figure in the Meiji government. Sakamoto's death may also have been a major factor in leaving Mutsu with scarcely any friends in Meiji political circles. The loss of Sakamoto was more than a personal problem for Mutsu alone. The Satsuma-Chōshū oligarchy would have been a more subdued presence in the government had a group of innovative and creative talents, such as Sakamoto and Yokoi Shōnan[*7] (横井小楠), joined its nucleus. The subsequent transition to parliamentary democracy could have taken place much earlier.

Battle of Toba-Fushimi

The Battle of Toba-Fushimi (鳥羽伏見の戦い) became the turning point after which the Meiji Restoration raced headlong toward its conclusion. Yet the battle itself was not a large-scale affair, nor was it an engagement for which both sides were well prepared with a long-term strategy.

The Satsuma-Chōshū side made the first move when it seized the guard posts of the Imperial Palace and, subsequently, made tough demands on the shogunate in the name of the emperor. Although the shogunal army outnumbered its opponent, it was afraid of being labeled as an enemy of the emperor if it attacked, prompting it to retreat temporarily to Osaka Castle, where plans were made to settle the issue with compromises. While this plan was being carried out, provocation by the Satsuma *han* in Edo became so fierce that soldiers in Osaka Castle started advancing toward Kyoto.

The shogunate army was fifteen thousand strong, greatly outnumbering the five thousand "imperial guards" from Satsuma and Chōshū. Intimidated by the size of the opposition, some in the imperial court were disinclined to engage head-on with the advancing force, but they were effectively silenced by Satsuma-Chōshū advisers who maintained that any indecision in these circumstances would seriously weaken the authority of the emperor.

Fortunately for the defending side, the shogunal army was driven by a sense of outrage provoked by insults, one of the five dangerous faults in starting a war outlined by Sun Tzu. Neither was it equipped

---

[*7] A statesman-scholar of the Kumamoto *han* who was assassinated for his "republicanism." Sakamoto once recommended that Mutsu work with him.

with a carefully conceived military plan. Since its soldiers marched out of formation on the main road for Kyoto right into the waiting Satsuma-Chōshū lines, which bristled with cannons and muskets, the army was destined to be defeated.

Retaining a sizable military force at Osaka Castle even after the defeat in Kyoto, the shogunate side was capable of a comeback. But the outcome was inevitable. For the fifteenth shogun Tokugawa Yoshinobu (徳川慶喜) had already stepped down two months earlier—a move referred to as the *taisei hōkan* (大政奉還), the return of political power to the emperor.

This was the chief reason for the landslide defection to the emperor's side of domains once loyal to the Tokugawa. After the *taisei hōkan*, the house of Tokugawa was downgraded to the level of other feudal lords. Around the time of the Battle of Toba-Fushimi, heads of domains were confronted with imperial envoys demanding that they clarify which side they were on. No longer obliged to pledge allegiance to the house of Tokugawa, most opted for expedience. If they even faintly hinted at sympathy toward the Tokugawa, their *han* would undoubtedly have been abolished when the imperial court won out, turning their retainers adrift.

Because the Kishū *han* was one of the closest to the shogun among some three hundred estates, it had the toughest time responding to the imperial envoy who arrived when the outcome of the Battle of Toba-Fushimi was still unpredictable. After lengthy consultations, a response was agreed on—that the Kishū *han* would "make endeavors" to support the emperor. This is a traditional rhetorical compromise still used frequently in today's politics.

Since even they took this ambiguous attitude, it was only natural that other domains chose to side with the imperial court in a wave of support. After the Battle of Toba-Fushimi, all the *han* that had pledged allegiance to the imperial court ordered their fighting men to join the military expedition to the east toward Edo. Even the Kishū *han* organized its own anti-shogunate army and had it join the imperial troops.

Politics of Revolution

Why did the shogunate return power to the emperor without resistance in the first place? The development was typical of the dynamics of revolution.

As in any other revolt, the speed at which things evolved and turned around in the Meiji Restoration far exceeded people's predictions. Even one year before the Restoration, the Chōshū *han*, where a radicalized faction had usurped power in a successful coup led by Takasugi Shinsaku (高杉晋作, 1839–67) two years earlier, was the only domain that had firmly determined to oust the shogunate. Anti-Tokugawa forces, including Saigō Takamori of Satsuma and Iwakura Tomomi (岩倉具視, 1825–83) of the imperial court, had yet to control the majority of their own domains. All the other *han* were either supportive of the shogunate or advocates of *kōbu gattai* (公武合体), i.e., collaboration between the imperial court and the shogunate.

Simply put, *kōbu gattai* was a project to promote moderate political reform through mutual compromise. Advocates of this kind of middle course seem to emerge without fail in every revolution, including the French, Russian, and, more recently, the Iranian revolution of 1979, where upholders of a moderate alliance take over, at least temporarily. Since shogun Yoshinobu was intelligent enough to have an accurate grasp of the situation, he decided to return power to the emperor in the hope of promoting *kōbu gattai*.

Once a ruling structure has become shaky, however, any anti-establishment force, encouraged by its advantage, will reinforce its demands for further reform. Although ordinary citizens are generally reluctant to have the stability of their lives upset, history has often shown that they too are driven toward a thorough eradication of the old system once the momentum for reform has started.

In the case of the Meiji Restoration, it was the powerful domains on the southwestern periphery that took the initiative; far removed from the center, these were endowed with sufficient extent and resources. The Satsuma *han* was located at the southern tip of the southern island of Kyushu, and the Chōshū *han* was on the western end of the mainland. The Tosa *han* in the southern part of Shikoku Island also played a unique role as an advocate of *kōbu gattai* at the time of the Restoration and, later, in support of the Freedom and People's Rights Movement.

It was on the advice of the Tosa *han* that the shogunate decided to avoid a military showdown and voluntarily cede power. A congress of lords, an equivalent of the House of Lords in a constitutional monarchy, was scheduled to be convened after the abdication of the shogun, and the shogunate had been assured that the former shogun would automatically become its president. The shogunate reasoned, therefore, that it wouldn't matter much if power was temporarily relinquished. But, as already described, because the Tokugawa side was provoked by the Satsuma *han* and attacked the troops guarding the Imperial Palace, it was stigmatized as the enemy of the emperor. As a result, the other domains gave up on the house of Tokugawa and switched sides.

It was at this point that Mutsu confirmed the accuracy of his judgment. The outcome of the course of events was not obvious to most people at that stage. Because the shogunate still maintained an advantage in terms of military strength, common sense predicted the eruption of widespread hostilities that would divide the country in two. Indeed, even among Mutsu's fellow members of the *Kaientai* there were those who advised hiding in the mountains to prepare for prolonged warfare.

But Mutsu was different. As he said in his memoir, "prompted by my own analysis of the state of affairs," he followed the imperial army's pursuit of the retreating shogunate troops to Osaka, where he requested an interview with Harry Parkes (1828–85), British minister to Japan, via Ernest Satow (1843–1929), who later became Envoy Extraordinary and Minister Plenipotentiary to Japan himself.

After exchanging views with Parkes on the future diplomacy of the new government, Mutsu returned to Kyoto to submit to Iwakura Tomomi his recommendations. Iwakura was a courtier-statesman who played a pivotal role in the Restoration for the imperial court. Mutsu concluded that Japan had no other option than to adopt a progressive line and open up to the world. As a first step, he proposed to notify the envoys of Western powers stationed in Osaka of the restoration of imperial rule and the intention to pursue an open-door policy.

Iwakura wholeheartedly agreed with these conclusions and produced a document dated January 10, 1868, only five days after the Battle of

Toba-Fushimi, to notify the Western powers accordingly. On the very same day, he made a proclamation to the feudal lords, saying, "Compelled by the overall situation, the emperor, after consultation with the court, has decided to sign a treaty of peace and amity."

The genesis of the change of regime had been the shogunate's decision, made under pressure from the gunboat diplomacy of the Western powers, to end seclusion, along with the failure of its desperate attempt to obtain ex post facto approval from the imperial court. This is what triggered the campaign to "revere the emperor and expel the barbarians." Thus, Iwakura's proclamation was an act of betrayal in the eyes of those who had genuinely believed in this doctrine, explaining why he had used the opening words "Compelled by the overall situation." If the shogunate still failed to understand what had brought it down, one can't really blame it: such, after all, are the politics of revolution.

Farseeing Enough to Focus on Diplomacy

On January 11, 1868, Iwakura appointed Mutsu an official in the Secretariat of Foreign Affairs. On the same day, four other talented men from Satsuma and Chōshū were given the same post, including Itō Hirobumi. Among these five, Mutsu was the youngest at twenty-five.

Mutsu writes in his autobiography about this appointment that "it was the first time in my life that I was placed in a position of responsibility, and it was the first step of my official career to serve the country." Mutsu owed the appointment solely to his discernment and action. And this ability to make the right judgment was something the new government urgently needed.

The imperial court had been commonly regarded as advocating the expulsion of foreigners. For this reason, it was imperative for the Meiji government to secure the support of the Western powers now. Particularly worrying was the French reaction, because France had earlier provided the shogunate with naval vessels and funds. In an era of global competition between Britain and France over the expansion of overseas influence, it was obvious that France had hoped to take the lead in Japan by siding with the shogunate; it took Britain to restrain this ambition. In this sense, Mutsu—still only in his twenties—had remarkable foresight in meeting with the British minister immediately after the Battle of Toba-Fushimi, when everyone else was preoccupied with military affairs and possible civil war.

Mutsu's usefulness continued after his appointment to a central position in the new government. He showed considerable adroitness in his handling of the issue of an American-built ironclad warship, for example. The shogunate had ordered the vessel from an American shipyard, but by the time it arrived in Yokohama, the shogunate had been overthrown. Although the Meiji government demanded that the ship be handed over, the U.S. side refused to do so, preferring to remain neutral in the current state of political unrest. Later named *Azuma*, this imported vessel was desperately needed to suppress the continuing resistance by shogunal forces armed with a number of new and powerful warships in northeast Honshu and Hokkaido.

The first step to resolve the situation was diplomatic negotiation. Making the most of his ability to communicate clearly, Mutsu succeeded in convincing the Americans of the legitimacy of the new government, stressing the fact that Kyoto, Osaka, and Edo were already under imperial control. The next problem was to secure the $500,000 required to purchase the ship. Because the government had no funds to spare, Mutsu was obliged to raise the money himself. His initial ploy was to persuade a senior member of the Mitsui trading company to volunteer cooperation. Following Mitsui's example, a number of Osaka businessmen were then pressed into making their own contribution.

Meanwhile, through his connection with the Mitsui executive, Mutsu had found a bride for himself. This was a former geisha, adopted by his Mitsui collaborator. When Mutsu's father, who liked the young woman and approved of the match, expressed some concern about her non-samurai origin, Mutsu told him not to worry: "The difference between samurai and other people isn't going to last long." It was a time of sea change, and other statesmen of the time, starting with Itō Hirobumi, found wives among the demimonde, making no fuss about their lineage. Sadly, Renko (陸奥蓮子), Mutsu's wife, died in 1872 after only five years of marriage, leaving him with an heir, Hirokichi, and a second son, Junkichi (潤吉), who was later adopted by Furukawa Ichibei (古河市兵衛) of the Furukawa *zaibatsu*.

Recommending the Establishment of Prefectures

During such chaotic periods as the years immediately after the Meiji Restoration, while a power vacuum exists before a new regime has completely overhauled a decaying system, the opportunity arises for the recruitment and promotion of talented people from no distinguished background. That was how Mutsu found his way into the heart of the fledgling government. Once the dust settles, however, important official posts are at the disposal of the ascendant faction or group. In the case of the Restoration period, Mutsu's lifelong enemy, the Satsuma-Chōshū clique, was in power. And the latter was soon maneuvering to have Mutsu removed. Not for the only time in his career, he tendered his resignation.

In his letter of resignation, Mutsu attributed the failure of the Kenmu Restoration (1333–36)*8 to the inequity of its personnel policy, which provoked warlords to rebellion and allowed the comeback of a samurai government. This was a precedent that came to many people's mind at the time of the Meiji Restoration, particularly those familiar with the (Chronicle of Great Peace), a record of fourteenth-century events. Mutsu wrote that if, in the present circumstances, talent was not recruited nationwide on the basis of merit, and the current favoritism was allowed to continue, there was every possibility that the new regime would fail. And if corruption persisted, he would be one of the first to leave.

His letter of resignation was never accepted. Instead, Mutsu was appointed governor of Hyōgo in 1869. Being a man of obstinate intellectual energy, Mutsu now turned his attention to the fundamental question

---

*8   The Kenmu Restoration marked the three-year period between the fall of the Kamakura shogunate and the rise of the Ashikaga shogunate (足利幕府), when Emperor Go-Daigo (後醍醐天皇) attempted to reestablish imperial control.

of what shape local administration should take. It was here that, in consultation with Itō Hirobumi, he wrote his recommendation on the abolition of the domain system and the establishment of prefectures.

Although the topic was one of the critical issues of the time and would in fact be implemented two years later, there was no one in the central government who agreed with the recommendation when it was submitted. When Mutsu and Itō went to Tokyo, renamed from Edo in 1868, to outline their views to senior officials, all the leading members of the government including Sanjō Sanetomi (三条実美, 1837–91) and Iwakura Tomomi attended the gathering. As Mutsu and Itō presented their argument, however, people started leaving one after another, until the room was empty. They may have been aware of its importance, but they were constrained from expressing their own opinion. The Satsuma and Chōshū *han* had each just been awarded an increase of a hundred thousand *koku* for their contributions to the Restoration, and the proposal to abolish the domains was considered too radical and dangerous an idea.

The year 1869 witnessed a minor reactionary trend when the frenzy of the transition cooled down. After riding the tide and grabbing control of the new government, Satsuma and Chōshū were confronted with a challenging reality. Feudal lords throughout Japan still held on to their power and were watching carefully for the next move by the government. Satsuma and Chōshū became wary of outsiders, and local officials suspected of harboring dangerous ideas were purged.

The rebuttal that Itō Hirobumi and Mutsu experienced turned out to be the only setback in Itō's life. Being a crown prince of Chōshū, so to speak, it had no lasting effect. In contrast, coming from the Kishū *han*, one of the Three Houses of Tokugawa and the archenemy of the ruling oligarchy, the setback for Mutsu could have been devastating. It was not at all certain that he could ever bounce back again. Against Itō's advice, he left his official position and returned to his hometown in Kishū. In private, a grand scheme, putting the new government in real danger, was evolving in his mind.

$$\text{IV}$$

GIANT WINGS BROKEN

The Rise and Fall of a Prussian-style Military State

War Seems Imminent

In June 1869, the second year of Meiji, the holdout group of Tokugawa loyalists gave up their last stronghold in Hokkaido. This marked the end of the so-called Boshin War (戊辰戦争, 1868–69).

Despite this victory, the newly launched Meiji government was prey to the gravest sense of crisis since the Restoration, as seen in the correspondence exchanged between its leaders. In a letter addressed to Iwakura Tomomi in late April, Ōkubo Toshimichi (大久保利通, 1830–78) wrote:

> Although it might appear that, with the end of the war, peace has arrived, I am most apprehensive about the lords of domains all over the country feeling uncertain about what's coming next and preparing for that eventuality. It's as if a fire has already started under the floor and could burst out above it at any time.

In July, Kido Takayoshi (木戸孝允, 1833–77) wrote to Ōkuma Shigenobu (大隈重信, 1838–1922):

The country will collapse if left unattended. At this point we have only two options: either we formulate a fundamental government policy and bolster the peace and security of the country, or we retreat to our own *han* to quietly build up our military strength in preparation for the coming civil war.

Being the outstanding theoretician among the Meiji Restoration statesmen, Kido's analysis of the situation was accurate. Mutsu certainly shared his assessment.

The rational answer would have been to launch a frontal attack, namely by abolishing the traditional estates and replacing them with a system of provinces and prefectures, and dissolving each *han's* military force for integration into a national army. This, incidentally, was the process that was felt to be essential for countries newly independent after World War II to become modern nation-states. Mutsu had proposed this measure to the central government together with Itō Hirobumi, only to be rejected.

If this fundamental reorganization was not to be undertaken, he reasoned, then future war was unavoidable. This left him, too, no choice but to return to his home domain to help develop its military capability.

When Mutsu went back to Kishū, he had a plan to transform this territory of five hundred fifty thousand *koku* into a modern military state on the Prussian model, making it the mightiest military unit in Japan—unrivaled even by the powerful Satsuma and Chōshū domains. And Mutsu had done enough political groundwork to see his grand design implemented.

Savior of the Kishū *han*

The Kishū *han* found itself in an extremely delicate position in post-Restoration politics. Tokugawa warriors defeated in the Battle of Toba-Fushimi had run to Wakayama to seek refuge in the nearby domain one of the Three Houses of Tokugawa, which lent them support and arranged for them to be sent safely home by boat. This act of sympathy, however, made the imperial court all the more suspicious of its intentions.

In order to prove his allegiance, Lord Kishū went to Kyoto to present himself at court, accompanied by two thousand five hundred soldiers who were to join the eastern expedition of the imperial army. He was among numerous other feudal lords who had gathered in Kyoto from all over Japan for the same purpose. While the latter were eventually allowed to return home, Lord Kishū was detained in Kyoto, as if held hostage. In an attempt to appease the emperor, he offered to donate the one hundred eighty thousand *koku* Ise region of his domain to the court.

Kishū was such a rugged region that, had rebels entrenched themselves in the mountains, it would have been extremely difficult to dislodge them. In fact, the Kamakura shogunate had fallen in the fourteenth century largely because it had failed to subdue the emperor-loyalist Kusunoki Masashige (楠木正成, c. 1294–1336), who had sought shelter in the Kishū mountains. It was, therefore, a strategic decision on the part of the shogunate to assign one of the Three Houses of Tokugawa to govern Kishū. Being such a mountainous area, however, it hadn't a sufficient yield of rice crops to sustain it, which was why the shogun decided to integrate the adjacent Ise region into the Kishū *han*—making it, as a result, a grand domain of five hundred fifty thousand *koku*.

It was this fertile territory that Lord Kishū was offering the imperial court. Receiving no response, however, he and his associates were afraid that, like many of the northeastern domains that had resisted the imperial forces, their *han* might be abolished.

It was Mutsu who saved the domain from this situation. In an attempt to persuade Iwakura Tomomi, Mutsu said:

> Although the court has launched a new government, the country is still far from being governed. People are worried about the future and watching developments closely. The removal of a fief from the Kishū *han* in this unstable situation, when it isn't altogether clear what the *han* is guilty of, would make other domains concerned about being punished themselves. I submit that it would be wiser to encourage the domain to push through political reforms and turn it into a loyal guard of the imperial court, as a model for others to emulate.

After listening to Mutsu's argument, Iwakura immediately declined the Kishū *han*'s offer of the Ise fief. He tapped Mutsu on the shoulder and commented, "There, now you have something to bring back home."

Model of a Modern Nation-State

It is important to note that, prior to his meeting with Iwakura, Mutsu had secured Lord Kishū's approval of proposed changes in *han* politics and administration. Thus it was with this endorsement that Mutsu was able to make a convincing appeal to Iwakura.

Promised reform boiled down to a purge of the conservative pro-Tokugawa element and its replacement with pro-emperor reformists. At a time of crisis, when it was not certain at all that the Satsuma-Chōshū alliance alone could control the entire country, this proposition must have been so attractive to Iwakura that he was prepared to give this young man a chance to "reform" Kishū in his own way.

With Lord Kishū a de facto hostage and with the fate of the Ise region at stake, members of the domain felt obliged to concur. Mutsu was given free rein to implement his ideas under the protective authority of the imperial court and with the full endorsement of the domain lord. Thus the stage was set in Kishū for its conversion into the type of modern nation-state that Mutsu had long envisioned.

The first thing he did after getting the go-ahead was to put Tsuda Izuru (津田出, 1832–1905) in charge of the process. Tsuda was a pioneer of Dutch learning in the Kishū *han*. Having translated a number of Western books on military science, he was considered a leading authority on the subject. Mutsu also appointed a businessman, Hamaguchi Goryō (浜口梧陵) of the soy sauce manufacturer Yamasa, to the post of finance minister (*kanjō bugyō*). This traditionally was the top bureaucratic post among samurai technocrats, and it was unprecedented to assign it to a private merchant—an act that explicitly announced Mutsu's intention to adopt a more egalitarian policy.

Tsuda's most fundamental and radical reform was the slashing of hereditary stipends for samurai households to just one-twentieth of their former level to secure funding for his reforms. In a statement announcing this decision, he proclaimed that the stipends were originally provided for public service and not as personal income. This was tantamount to an actual rejection of feudal privilege.

Pioneer of Military Conscription

Other sweeping reforms included stripping the samurai class of other privileges, applying the penal code equally to all citizens, and permitting freedom of choice in professions. But the innovation with the biggest impact was the adoption of military conscription.

Tsuda decided that Kishū's military system should emulate that of Prussia, and he employed a Prussian officer by the name of Karl Köppen as military adviser. Traditionally, the shogunate had subscribed to the French military system and benefited from assistance provided by Napoleon III. Sons of Kishū samurai studying in Edo in those days, therefore, were also trained in the French method, and these were the young men who formed the basis of Tsuda's military reforms. Vindication of his shift in allegiance came when Napoleon III's army suffered a complete defeat by the Prussian army under the leadership of Helmuth von Moltke only one year later.

Anyone over the age of twenty was liable to conscription regardless of class; only the head of a family or the only son was exempt. The terms of military service were set at eleven years—three years of active duty, four years in the first reserve, and another four years in the secondary reserve.

When its military was disbanded with the abolition of the *han* system and the establishment of prefectures in 1871, it comprised nearly twenty thousand well-trained men. The breakdown was as follows:

Military commander (Tsuda succeeded by Mutsu in 1871)
    2 military supervisors
    179 soldiers attached to the commander and orderlies
    6 infantry regiments (13,230 soldiers)
    About 1,000 foot soldiers permanently stationed at regional
        headquarters

1 cavalry regiment composed of 175 soldiers
2 artillery regiments composed of some 600 soldiers
1 engineers regiment composed of some 500 soldiers
A transport corps composed of some 900 soldiers
250 military cadets
A military hospital manned by 44 staff members
Some 400 snipers
140 soldiers stationed at the armory and infirmary
14,000 rifles and 3 million bullets
20 four-pounder guns

An officer of the Prussian battleship *Hertha* that was visiting Japan around then left a written record of his observations of the Kishū army. He watched four battalions of soldiers exercising on a training field in the Prussian marching style, and noted that they paraded, fanned out in various complicated files, and returned to their original format in perfect order. He also observed that an ammunition factory was producing ten thousand bullets a day for *Zündnadelgewehr* rifles using the same production methods employed in Germany. Soldiers did not have the traditional samurai topknot; they wore leather boots and their lives were generally organized along Prussian lines.

Of incidental interest is the fact, mentioned in the *Nippon kutsu monogatari* (The story of shoes in Japan), that leather footwear manufactured in Wakayama continued to be called "Kishū boots," and was the precursor of the shoe industry in Japan.

These developments created a sensation, and envoys from various countries visited Kishū on inspection tours. Ministers Harry Parkes of Great Britain, Charles DeLong of the United States, and Max von Brandt of Germany were among them. Saigō Tsugumichi (西郷従道, 1843–1902, Takamori's younger brother) and Murata Shinpachi (村田新八, 1836–77) from Satsuma also came to have a look, as did Yamada Ichinojō (山田市之允, 1844–92) from Chōshū.

The main purpose of the visits from other *han* must have been to spy on the situation in Kishū but some visitors seriously wanted to learn from the experience. Tsuda was told that while Saigō Takamori was unable to visit the domain himself he was very interested in the reforms and hoped to discuss them with Tsuda in person.

Developments in Kishū have by now been buried in history and forgotten. At the time, however, they had an undeniable impact on the advancement of the Meiji Restoration as a whole. Had they not been pursued, it is quite possible that fundamental nationwide changes would not have been implemented, including the abolition of the *han* system, termination of the hereditary stipend, or general conscription.

What would have happened if the old system had endured? Japan would probably have seen the eruption of another civil war, centered around the Kishū army this time, and larger in scale by several times than the Satsuma Rebellion of 1877, which would inevitably but violently impose radical changes.

Tsuda's Motto: "Enlightened Rule and Public Welfare"

Tsuda Izuru's autobiography, *Kohi* (壺碑), was published in 1917 by the surviving members of his family. Okazaki Kunisuke contributed the foreword:

> In terms of remarkable human resources, the Meiji Restoration was unique in Japanese history.
>
> Most of those involved, however, merely followed the trend of the times, aiming to become loyal subjects of the emperor after his restoration to power. Only a few were truly devoted to the cause of improving people's lives and reforming society.
>
> Tsuda (Izuru) Shizan-Ō (津田芝山翁) had explored the ideas of Ogyū Sorai, who emphasized the practical merit of enlightened statecraft. Using new developments in Europe as a guideline, he managed to save the Kishū *han* from crisis by revamping its politics and administration and launching military conscription, despite enduring all kinds of resistance and recrimination. More than that, he succeeded in presenting a formula of prefectural government to the entire nation.
>
> Once people saw how successful Shizan-Ō's reforms had been, all the *han* followed suit, relying on his advice and guidance to make their own improvements. Shizan-Ō became a focus of attention.

Nowadays, one often hears people from Satsuma and Chōshū claiming that the reorganization Shizan-Ō was largely responsible for was their own initiative. Had he been originally from their part of the country, his accomplishments and legacies would have been applauded. Even fifty years after the Restoration, the power of the oligarchy is still so pervasive that a man barely capable of running a village of three households is promoted to high office or ennobled merely because he is from Satsuma or Chōshū.

In contrast, Shizan-Ō, who was capable of governing a state, died virtually unnoticed. His descendants also remain unfavored.

Why was heaven so generous in endowing him with talent and so reluctant to reward him? Was this heaven's will, or a turn of fortune's wheel?

Shizan-Ō once said, "While Satsuma-Chōshū men chose to serve the emperor, I chose to serve the people and make their lives better. Our starting point is fundamentally different."

The imperial court rewarded loyal subjects with power, status, and titles. Should we, the citizens of Japan, allow a great statesman who put people's lives first to be buried unacknowledged? In the hope that his accomplishments will be properly recognized, I am happy to make this modest contribution to this publication.

(September 9, 1917)

His foreword itself gives an inkling of a historical orientation that has survived to this day. Our view of the Meiji Restoration is colored by the standpoint of Satsuma and Chōshū. Naitō Konan (内藤湖南, 1866–1934) raised this issue as early as the Taishō era, but it has not been revived until today.

We were all taught in school that the dawning of the Restoration from stagnant feudal rule owed a lot to the pro-emperor revolutionaries of Satsuma and Chōshū, who ushered in an era of civilization and enlightenment that prepared Japan to become a modern nation and eventually spread its wings abroad. Except for a brief interval during the Taishō Democracy, this interpretation has survived as the mainstream view throughout our modern history. And while it may eventually have changed into an "emperor-centered historiography" or a Marxist outlook, any other perspective has been forgotten. Today, it is difficult to find even traces of a different viewpoint.

Objectively speaking, it is fair to say that the ulterior motive of the Satsuma-Chōshū leadership was to gain power by overthrowing the Tokugawa shogunate in the name of "the restoration of imperial rule" rather than for the sake of "enlightened rule and public welfare." While Tsuda's goal was clearly to construct a modern nation-state, it is highly unlikely that the modernization of Japan was the purpose of most members of the oligarchy. It would not be an overstatement to say that their primary concern was to hold on to the power they had snatched from the shogunate.

This becomes obvious when one looks at the Meiji government's personnel policy in the thirty years after the Restoration—namely, whether the criteria for promotion was a person's ability and public-spiritedness, or their compliance with the perpetuation of the oligarchy. And to justify the criteria, priority was always placed on the unassailable cause of reverence for the emperor.

In his memoir, Katsu Kaishū writes:

> Reverence for the emperor won't do any good unless it coincides with reverence for the people.... They say a government is bound to collapse when anybody but the direct sovereign holds the reins of power, but let me point out that the Kamakura shogunate survived for nine reigns from its fourth shogun on without it being a direct line. [Katsu was known to hold the Kamakura shogunate in high regard.] It is like putting the cart before the horse to preach worship of the emperor without consideration for the public at large."

Katsu was clearly implying that if the Kamakura shogunate was acceptable because it was a good reign, the Tokugawa shogunate, too, would have been tolerable if it had ruled well. His point was that the restoration of imperial rule was not enough; it was the people's happiness that mattered. This kind of broad-minded, liberal attitude, as well as the fact that it was once in favor, were completely overshadowed by the Satsuma-Chōshū standpoint and subsequent imperial historiography.

In any case, the Kishū *han* reforms at least demonstrated that the abolition of the clan system or the implementation of military conscription was possible. In that sense, the goal that Mutsu set forth to Iwakura of providing all the *han* with a model of reform was a hundred percent achieved.

Retrogressive Satsuma Philosophy

Undoubtedly those most stunned by the Kishū example must have been the Satsuma and Chōshū domains. Observing the progress the Kishū army was making in training and exercises, Köppen is reported to have boasted that no other soldiers were a match for their troops. Mutsu himself reportedly once declared that neither Satsuma nor Chōshū would pose any threat because Kishū could easily deploy a hundred thousand troops.

Even though both were giant domains of seven hundred seventy thousand and three hundred sixty thousand *koku* respectively, it would have been financially difficult for even them to assemble tens of thousands of soldiers. The cutback of hereditary stipends was possible in Kishū because it had been on the losing side. The *han* was on the verge of extinction as an imperial foe if it didn't handle the situation well. Having witnessed the fate of the northeastern domains and their retainers, Kishū samurai must have convinced themselves that reforms were the least undesirable choice. In the case of Satsuma on the winner's side, however, Kishū-type measures were unthinkable. It isn't hard to imagine that, if another rebellion had erupted at the time, it would have been the Kishū *han* with its large numbers of Prussian-style troops that would be at the center of the fighting.

Of the two domains, Satsuma had a stronger flavor of samurai dominance. Only a member of the samurai class could become a warrior there. Given this background, Saigō Takamori's ideal had always been to build a samurai-led, autocratic, puritanical state. As clearly proven in the Satsuma Rebellion, however, troops composed only of a limited number of men from the samurai class were increasingly at a disadvantage against drafted soldiers with modern training. Members of the former cadre suffered heavy losses in the battle.

Phantom Kingdom

On February 20, 1870, the Ministry of Military Affairs, in an ostensible effort to unify the military system throughout the country, proclaimed that each *han* should limit the scale of its regular forces to one platoon (sixty soldiers) per fixed amount of *koku* and that new recruits should come only from the samurai and nobility. It is obvious that this edict was based on Satsuma military thinking. Although there remains no evidence to prove this, it is more than probable that its authors were acutely aware of the threat that the Kishū *han* represented.

Accordingly, Kishū would be allowed only a little over three thousand soldiers. If recruiting from the non-samurai classes was prohibited, its reforms could not be pursued. The Kishū domain immediately rejected the decree. Its argument was skillful, hinting at the involvement of Mutsu in its drafting. Briefly, it said:

> We wholeheartedly agree with your intention of unifying the nation's military system, and we would eagerly comply with your instructions. We are also confident that the ban on recruiting soldiers from the non-samurai classes must derive from sound reasoning. Currently we in the Kishū *han*, however, are in the midst of reforms based on the principle of social equality, aiming at the elimination of the traditional four-class system. Limiting recruitment to the samurai clan would affect the overall position taken by our new internal administration. Thus, we ask for your understanding in regard to our decision to continue with the current reforms unchanged.

Receiving this deft response, the Ministry of Military Affairs could not really argue back. For a start, trying to preserve a selective enrollment policy was an anachronistic notion that went against the times. It also went against the Charter Oath of 1868 ratified by the new administration.

Moreover, this episode took place before the *han* system was abolished, when each domain was essentially an independent entity. It also formed part of a power play between the domains at a time when the power of Kishū may well have exceeded that of Satsuma or Chōshū. If the ministry mishandled the request from this *han*, it could lead to a major upheaval involving the entire country. So it had no choice but to let Kishū retain its existing troops, thus preserving an independent military capacity that was beyond the control, both in name and substance, of the central government.

Step by step, throughout this process, Mutsu was building his own kingdom. Before he appointed himself as commander of the Kishū army, he had frequently commuted between Wakayama and the Kishū residence in Osaka, actively "headhunting," regardless of people's origins. Some newcomers were Torio Koyata (鳥尾小弥太, 1848–1905), whom Mutsu appointed as deputy military commander; Hayashi Tadasu (林董, 1850–1913), a scholar of international law; Ga Noriyuki (何礼之, 1840–1923); and Hoshi Tōru (星亨, 1850–1901).

Recruiting men of talent and creating the strongest armed force in the country, it seemed that Mutsu had indeed managed to "grow giant wings," the phrase he used in the poem he composed when he left home at the age of fifteen: "But one day I will triumph and grow giant wings / To burst through the clouds / And soar across the heavens."

After firmly establishing his foothold at home, Mutsu took a trip to Europe in March 1870 on his domain's behalf. The official purpose of the visit was to observe the progress of the Franco-Prussian War, but he also planned to invite German instructors in various military fields to Kishū and to procure new and powerful equipment, including guns. If all of Mutsu's plans had been realized, the Kishū *han* would undoubtedly have become a formidable power in Japan.

Disbandment of the Kishū Army

Within two months of his appointment as military commander after he returned from Europe in April 1871, the situation regarding Kishū took a suddenly different course. In July the abolition of the *han* system and the establishment of prefectures, an idea that Mutsu and Itō Hirobumi had proposed earlier without success, was abruptly adopted.

Itō wrote to Mutsu during an official trip to Osaka to suggest that they meet and discuss future proceedings now that their ambition was actually coming true.

Imagining his reaction to this news, Sakazaki Kan (坂崎斌, 1853–1913) wrote in his biography of Mutsu: "How disappointed he must have been! How deeply he must have sighed when this was finally realized, before he rushed back to Wakayama…."

One can only guess what was on Mutsu's mind then. At the time of his death thirty years later, the Satsuma-Chōshū oligarchy was still in place. His position had thus remained delicate, making it difficult for him to disclose his true feelings. But in *Mutsu shōden* (his brief autobiography), in contrast to terse descriptions in other parts, he gave an uncharacteristically detailed account of how difficult his situation was:

© Mutsu Shōko

1871, Mutsu studying abroad in Germany

Since the replacement the *han* with a prefectural system had been a long-standing proposal of mine, I should have been grateful for the imperial decision to implement it…. [However] there was one serious problem involved. For three years, I had devoted myself to the supervision of military affairs in the Kishū *han*, introducing, ahead of other domains, German-style innovations and greatly enhancing our military capability by relying on largely indiscriminate conscription. Then came the order to disband our troops. Although I had a hard time appeasing some of the hot-blooded young officers, who were very vocal in their objections to this decision, I somehow managed to settle the matter peacefully. But I knew there would be tremendous difficulties handling the transition of our particular *han* to prefectural status.

Okamoto Ryūnosuke (岡本柳之助, 1852–1912), who was a regimental commander in the Kishū army, insisted that Mutsu had been misled by Itō and that they should raise the flag of revolt against the central government. It was better to defeat the government in one fell swoop, he argued, than bitterly regret the decision to comply with the order.

It was true that Satsuma and Chōshū must have seen the advantage in depriving Kishū of its military strength. Reduced to a lame beast without teeth or claws, it would have simplified the securing of autocratic rule. History shows that this was exactly what happened.

If, however, Kishū decided to go against the tide and reject the new policy, the refusal would be unjustified. It would identify Kishū as an enemy of the emperor, and its rebellion might end in alienation and failure. Mutsu must have judged that, at that point, it would be wiser instead to wait and watch.

After all, it had been only three years earlier that the very same policy proposed by Itō and him was rejected by the conservatives in power. Now that the same project was about to be put into effect as a Satsuma and Chōshū initiative, Saigō Takamori had decided to go ahead without hesitating, simply saying it would benefit the whole country.

Judging from his decisions and actions before and after the Battle of Toba-Fushimi, Saigō appeared to be a resourceful person. Watching the military developments in Kishū with keen interest and meeting Tsuda for a regular debriefing, he must have realized that the switch to a prefectural system was necessary.

A backdrop to this interaction was one particular encounter between Saigō and Tsuda. Tsuda himself refrained from disclosing the details, as he pointed out in his autobiography: "Talks with Saigō were long.... Even today, after so many years, I cannot reveal what really took place."

Some information on it, however, was given by Okamoto Ryūnosuke, a man who usually was said "never to negate or correct what others said [about him] nor to repeat any secret he happened to learn." This was included in a record he left, *Fū'un kaikoroku* (風雲回顧録, A memoir of troubled times), shortly before his death when none of the concerned parties were still alive and the annexation of Korea, a cause for which he had long fought, had been accomplished.

According to this document, Tsuda went to Tokyo at Saigō's request in February 1871 and received Saigō himself at his lodging. The latter was apparently deferential, asking for advice on matters of statecraft. Tsuda impressed upon him the need for reorganizing the *han* system and for issuing an ordinance on conscription. He also stressed the importance of appointing someone of real ability as prime minister to push through the reforms, suggesting that Saigō himself should serve in that role. When Saigō declined, saying he was not up to the task, Tsuda volunteered his own services. Saigō then told him: "I will do everything in my capacity to make this happen. I beg you not to back out if you are asked to assume the post. And I personally will do my very best to follow your leadership."

Tsuda's appointment, however, never materialized. Saigō campaigned in his favor, but met with resistance. Later, he dispatched his younger brother Tsugumichi to apologize to Tsuda for having made him an empty promise.

Judging from what is known of the personalities involved,, I am inclined to believe this account. It also helps explain the speed with which Saigō agreed to undertake the reforms Tsuda had advised, among them the resulting Imperial Edict on Nationwide Conscription promulgated in November 1872. The cabinet directive accompanying it reads:

> In the distant past, in an emergency the emperor became our commander-in-chief and the people his soldiers. More recently, we have seen some of his subjects take up arms themselves. As so-called samurai, armed with two swords, they have done untold harm by their arrogant and violent behavior.

The directive upheld the principle of equality among the four classes and emphasized the public's role in defending national security, marking the beginning of a general conscription system.

But despite the ordinance and Saigō's personal commitment to it, Satsuma remained an independent power centered on the samurai. It was not until five years after its promulgation that a new government army of conscripted soldiers succeeded in defeating the clan in the Satsuma Rebellion.

Back to Officialdom Again

Meanwhile, the Ministry of Taxation was abolished in July 1872, to be replaced by a Ministry of Finance, a powerful institution that was to oversee a wide range of civilian affairs. Inside this ministry were gathered a cast of competent officials including not only Satsuma-Chōshū men such as Inoue Kaoru (井上馨, 1836–1915), Itō Hirobumi, and Matsukata Masayoshi (松方正義, 1835–1924), but also Tsuda Izuru and Hamaguchi Goryō from Kishū. At the same time, Torio Koyata and Okamoto Ryūnosuke, also from Kishū, were named high-ranking officers in the government army.

Here was one indication that Kishū's accomplishments as a forerunner in the process of modernization had been recognized. These personnel choices also meant that, at least temporarily, Kishū, with twenty thousand crack troops, was treated as an equal.

Mutsu's handling of matters at the time appears to foreshadow his later involvement in the Tripartite Intervention (三国干渉) of 1895. Under the terms of the Treaty of Shimonoseki (下関条約), which ended the First Sino-Japanese War (1894–95), Japan was awarded the Liaodong Peninsula (遼東半島), allowing it to believe it now had under its control a vital gateway to the Chinese continent. Russia, Germany, and France intervened, expressing their concern about Japanese acquisition of the territory. Relinquishing it was bound to be painful, but given the unfavorable prospects it faced, Japan was disposed to quickly avert a crisis and ascertain how to be adequately compensated for acquiescing. If it attempted resistance and was unsuccessful, there would be no compensation. The best solution was to capitalize on a fait accompli and withdraw from the situation promptly.

The episode was a good example of the pragmatism that had made Mutsu practice running away from trouble as a young man in Asakusa.

Back in time, Mutsu was able to secure important government posts for Tsuda and Hamaguchi, and position himself for a return to the center of Japanese politics as the prefectural governor of Kanagawa. But he no longer had the backing of an independent region or large numbers of troops at his disposal. From now on Mutsu was to endure the trials of a lone bureaucrat in a government dominated by Satsuma and Chōshū.

His predicament found an echo in a poem his father gave him in 1873:

Until spring winds blow away
The snow confining you
Like a bush warbler in the valley
Keep silent all winter long.

V

A Bush Warbler
in Winter

Involved in Tosa's Adventure

Resentment against the Personnel Policy

Despite repeated frustrations, Mutsu's intellectual energy was unaffected. In fact, he had already started working on a reform of the tax system, a major adjustment that was indispensable for the modernizing of Japan, now that initiatives for changing the *han* system and military conscription had been taken.

The Japanese economy in those days was heavily dependent on agriculture, which occupied a high percentage of the nation's GDP. Consequently, government revenue was almost solely dependent on the tax levied on rice farming.

Traditionally, the amount of tax on rice had been determined by "prior estimates." Local officials were dispatched by the domain lord before the harvest to estimate the season's yield; based on this assessment, the amount of tax was decided by multiplying a fixed rate. The revenue calculated in this way was liable to fluctuate, however, depending on the actual yield, which made prior fiscal planning difficult. The situation was further aggravated by dishonest officials and peasants who frequently manipulated harvest estimates.

In place of this traditional method, Mutsu proposed the introduction of liberalistic economics. He reasoned that the market mechanism would automatically determine the land price depending on its fertility once the restriction on land trading (basic to feudalism) was removed. Subsequently, the amount of tax should be determined by the land price multiplied by a fixed percentage (three percent in the beginning). The rate was later reduced to 2.5 percent, in response to disquieting public sentiment on the eve of the Satsuma Rebellion.

Mutsu's proposal was immediately adopted by the government. In June 1872 he himself was appointed head of the tax collecting agency.

A mountain of work awaited him. To begin with, land certificates had to be issued to all landowners. The clerical work for this task was so onerous that he had to set up a Secretariat for Land Tax Reform within the Ministry of Finance, which he presided over.

Simultaneously, Mutsu and his team were confronted with the task of forming the government's first new budget. As the administration's modernization policies advanced, every ministry started demanding more schools, more railroads, more post offices, and so on, resulting in endless requests for funding. A budget based on the prospect of accurate revenue was needed to control these demands.

With its underdeveloped bureaucracy, the Meiji government seemed to rely on Mutsu for practically everything. One can only admire his willingness to accept and cope with this workload while lesser officials were promoted for doing less.

Saigō Takamori and Itagaki Taisuke (板垣退助, 1837–1919) resigned from their cabinet posts in protest following the *Seikanron* (征韓論), the 1873 debate on whether to invade Korea.*9 But the likes of Itō Hirobumi,

---

*9 This was a major political dispute in which. Saigō Takamori and his supporters insisted that Japan should confront Korea due to the latter's refusal to recognize the legitimacy of the Meiji Restoration. The proponents of war also saw the issue as an opportunity to find useful employment for thousands of out-of-work samurai, who posed a threat to the government. In contrast, other Japanese leaders strongly opposed these plans, setting a priority on Japan's domestic modernization. It was finally decided that no action was to

Ōkuma Shigenobu, and Terashima Munenori (寺島宗則, 1832–93), who had once been Mutsu's colleagues at the Secretariat for Foreign Affairs, were all given cabinet posts, while Mutsu alone remained with the lower rank of acting director-general.

Mutsu's patience finally ran out. In exasperation, he drafted what became a historic treatise entitled *Nippon-jin* (日本人, The Japanese), furiously condemning the monopolizing of government positions by the *hanbatsu* (a group composed of politicians and bureaucrats from Satsuma, Chōshū, Tosa, and Hizen). He urged people to recall the Restoration's ideal of liberating society from the autocracy of the Tokugawa shogunate and building a modern nation-state. Inevitably, when the treatise was circulated, it enflamed the hatred that many Satsuma partisans already felt for him.

Unbreakable *Hanbatsu*

With the publication of *Nippon-jin*, Mutsu resigned from his post, though it was not long that he remained unemployed.

In 1874–75, the Meiji government was facing a crisis. As a result of the *Seikanron* debate, it had lost such prominent figures as Saigō and Itagaki, who retired to Satsuma and Tosa respectively. Kido Takayoshi also resigned in protest at the Taiwan Expedition of 1874 and retreated to Chōshū.[*10] Consequently, only Ōkubo Toshimichi and young Itō Hirobumi remained to steer the ship.

Alarmed, the remaining Meiji oligarchs called a meeting in Osaka in an attempt to reconcile differences and persuade Itagaki and Kido to return to the administration in exchange for a commitment to move gradually toward representative democracy. As another concession, it

---

be taken against Korea, and many of those in favor of war, including Saigō and Itagaki, resigned.

*10 The Taiwan Expedition was a punitive expedition by Japanese military forces following the murder of fifty-four crewmembers of a wrecked Ryukyuan merchant vessel by aborigines on Taiwan in December 1871. The expedition marked the first overseas deployment of the Imperial Japanese Army and Navy.

was agreed that a Council of Elders (元老院, *Genrōin*) should be established as a step toward a constitutional government. The decisions reached at the Osaka conference were officially sanctioned by an Imperial Proclamation in April 1875, and Mutsu was among those who were appointed as members of the Council.

The *Genrōin* was, initially, a legislative body established as a guarantor of the separation of powers, endowed with the right to propose bills. Serving in it, Mutsu made strenuous efforts to consolidate and expand its authority in the hope that it could function as a legitimate "checks and balances" organ vis-à-vis *hanbatsu*-dominated government (藩閥政府).

The *Genrōin*, however, was doomed from the start. For one thing, Iwakura was a staunch believer in the restoration of an absolute monarchy and, as such, was reluctant to hand over any of the power that had been laboriously wrested from the shogunate to an unfamiliar institution with a "parliamentary function."

When he asked Ōkubo about it, he was told "It can be something for Kido to take care of," making Iwakura further inclined to be uncooperative. And with Kido and Itagaki's return to the central government, the authority of the *Genrōin* was gradually watered down. By 1875 its jurisdiction was limited to technical deliberation on bills.

Even with this setback, however, Mutsu was opening yet another door to the country's development—the revision of its laws. At Mutsu's request, his comrades Ga Noriyuki, Hayashi Tadasu, and Shimada Saburō (島田三郎, 1852–1923) translated Jeremy Bentham's works on legislation, civil law, and criminal law. These translations were being published consecutively in 1878, when Mutsu was arrested and imprisoned. Had he not been arrested, the reforming of Japan's legal system could have advanced much faster and possibly even been completed before the negotiations for revision of the treaties with foreign powers, as will be discussed in Chapter XI.

Mutsu, however, was on the verge of committing what he himself later called the most disastrous mistake of his life. The circumstances that drove him to make this mistake were, in practice, quite understandable.

No matter how hard he had tried to break down the walls of the *han-batsu*, they were unshakable. No matter how many letters of resignation he tendered or how widely his written protest was read, he could hardly make a scratch on these walls. The Prussian-style stronghold that he had built in Kishū had been neutralized. His attempt to restrict the supremacy of the executive branch by securing the independence of a legislative branch was also nullified before long.

Then the Satsuma Rebellion started. And it was understandable that Mutsu should decide to use this incident as a heaven-sent chance to topple the *hanbatsu*-dominated administration.

A Man Called Saigō Takamori

To understand the Meiji Restoration, it is essential to understand Saigō Takamori. Indeed, more than that, it matters if one is to gain a true understanding of the Japanese, and Asian values too. The fact that there have been a significant number of Saigō admirers among modern Chinese is no accident.

Simply put, Saigō Takamori was by nature a profound humanist, a philosopher who rose above the petty things in life, a virtuous and austere practitioner of morals based on Zen and the Confucian philosophy of Wang Yangming (陽明学, 1472–1529). At the same time, he was a statesman-cum-revolutionary who helped bring about the Meiji Restoration.

Saigō took his own life by ritual disembowelment in his native Satsuma following the failed 1877 Satsuma Rebellion. Many writers have lamented his fate, but none have ever expressed dislike or contempt for him. This was true even during the rebellion itself, as eloquently revealed in one of the war songs sung by the government troops dispatched to suppress it:

> The enemy general is a hero
> And his soldiers will fight to the death
> But we must put these brave men down
> For they stand against the emperor.

Similarly, the lyrics of *Tabaru-zaka* (田原坂), which is also known as *Gōketsu-bushi* (Song of a hero), a latter-day folk song composed in memory of the Satsuma Rebellion, are:

> Saigō Takamori
> A man you can trust
> When he says it's for your country
> Trust him with your life.

This exhortation was addressed not to the rebel troops but to soldiers of the Meiji government, setting them an example.

One would expect there to be an endless lineup of folk tales about a person like Saigō, but the fact is that there are none. Every word and deed of his was well documented, leaving no room for legend. The image people have of him today is based on reality, not myth or fiction. He also left behind some outstanding written works and pieces of calligraphy. One of his well-known poems written in the Chinese style reads:

> Both public acclaim and slander
> Have as little weight as dust
> And no one knows what's true or false
> But I loved my island exile
> Where I could commune
> Not with men of the present
> But men of the past.

Before the Meiji Restoration, many people who eventually emerged as its heroes were persecuted by the shogunal authorities and only narrowly escaped death. Saigō, too, was exiled to the remote southern island of Tokunoshima, where he was detained under harsh conditions. His cell was like a kennel, with a lattice wall that exposed him to the elements. But there he sat, as if in meditation. Although a local official, out of sympathy, gave him a pair of clappers so that he could call for something he needed, he never used them, and his health quickly deteriorated.

Looking back, however, Saigō referred to his "island exile" with deep nostalgia. Freed from "public acclaim and slander," his contact with the outside world was limited to the classics and the discourse of ancient sages. He was a truly extraordinary person.

None appreciated his qualities more than Katsu Kaishū. Katsu once said, "I have met only two men who terrified me. One was Yokoi Shōnan, and the other was Saigō Nanshū[11] (西郷南州)."

Yokoi Shōnan, who was assassinated in 1869 for alleged republicanism, was a prodigious scholar and a champion of the enlightenment philosophy in Japan on the eve of the shogunate's downfall. When Mutsu had been picked on by traditionalist students at the Kobe Naval College, Katsu had once tried to put him in Yokoi's care. If that plan had actually come about and Yokoi had survived the Restoration to let Mutsu work with him, the subsequent development of Japanese political thought and, indeed, Japanese politics itself might have been quite different.

Katsu even predicted that the Tokugawa shogunate would be doomed if Saigō undertook to carry out Yokoi's ideas. The shogunate laughed off his prediction, badly underestimating the influence of these two men. But history shows that the shogunate was indeed brought down by Saigō.

Katsu's admiration for Saigō led Sakamoto Ryōma to pay Saigō a visit in Satsuma. Katsu provided a letter of introduction. Sakamoto's comment on his return was, "Yes, Saigō is a remarkable man. He's like a great temple bell. Strike it lightly and it rings. Strike it hard and it resounds." By this he meant that while Saigō willingly paid attention to detail, he also had a good grasp of the big picture and could address any issue thoughtfully. This assessment made Katsu conclude that Sakamoto himself was a shrewd judge of character.

Only a few years later, direct negotiations between Katsu and Saigō led to the bloodless handover of Edo Castle. Although they knew that these talks could determine the fate of Japan, the two negotiators were surprisingly relaxed each having full confidence in the other. Knowing that the imperial court had already decided to stamp out the other side entirely, Katsu made a number of direct proposals to protect the Tokugawa clan and the livelihood of its retainers. Saigō, taking what

---

[11] Nanshū was one of numerous pseudonyms Saigō used while in exile in 1862.

Katsu said at face value, assured him, "There may be some serious disagreements, but you have my word for it—we will do as you say."

This historic encounter saved the city of Edo from the flames of war and allowed the Tokugawa clan, once an imperial foe, to survive as an ordinary feudal fief of seven hundred thousand *koku*, sparing the lives and livelihoods of its followers. Most importantly, the negotiations succeeded in preventing a full-scale civil war between the British-backed imperial court and the French-supported shogunate, allowing Japan to overcome a life-threatening crisis in the age of imperialism.

Rising in Revolt against the Meiji Government

It was this same Saigō Takamori who later raised the standard of revolt, ordering his Satsuma troops to advance northward. When the rebellion erupted, Meiji Japan was riddled with dissatisfaction,, ranging from a longing for the return of samurai glory to demands for more thoroughgoing democratic reforms. Minor insurgencies broke out everywhere. Against this background, the news of Saigō's revolt electrified the nation.

It should be recognized, however, that the whole incident was started not by Saigō himself but impulsively by his subordinates. Saigō initially reacted with surprise and dismay but subsequently submitted calmly to the will of his followers, acting as a symbol of the rebellion without giving a single battle command in person. His death was a gesture of chivalry toward the men who had remained loyal to him since the beginning of the Restoration movement.

Katsu's reference to Saigō's death in his memoir *Hikawa seiwa* is a penetrating comment:

> One is better off without any supporters. Look at Saigō. He had to die for what they did.... I am probably unique in having no hangers-on. It's why I am free to do whatever I feel like doing....
>
> What a loss it is that nothing could have been done to save such a great man from dying for others' sake. If I had as many followers

as Saigō, I suppose even I would feel obliged to do something on their behalf. I wouldn't have the heart just to ignore them. But I couldn't die for them. I would probably look for some other way.

The truth is, it would take someone of his own distinction to appreciate a man like Saigō. He was far beyond the scope of ordinary people. He wasn't a politician or an administrator. He was a man of transcendent virtue. . . .

It is clear from the above that Katsu himself was someone of rare generosity, able to praise Saigō open-heartedly in comparison with his own more rational attitude.

There can be no doubt, though, that Saigō had long felt disillusioned with the new government and recognized that his own political life was over.

The degeneration that set in quite soon after the success of the Restoration made Saigō wonder what the revolution had been for. In despair, he considered retiring from politics. Although their ideals differed, Mutsu shared his outrage at the abuse of power on the part of the Satsuma-Chōshū oligarchy. While Mutsu clearly believed in modern parliamentary democracy, Saigō's ideal polity, if any, tended toward a government of integrity based on the way of the samurai—something akin to the puritan government that Oliver Cromwell initially had in mind. But Saigō was also well aware that his was an impossible ideal.

It was this despair that led him to advocate the dispatch of troops to take over Korea in 1873. One is reminded of the remark of Charles de Gaulle that only a major enterprise (*une vaste entreprise*) could save France from corruption and banality. Of course, from the Korean point of view, this objective was outrageous, but it was proposed in a period of active imperialism. According to *Jiyūtō-shi* (自由党史, History of the Liberal Party)*12 compiled by Itagaki Taisuke, he and Saigō attributed the decline of the Meiji government to the failure to press on hard after the first gains of the Restoration; it would take another national crisis to pull the country together.

---

*12 Itagaki Taisuke, compiled. Uda Tomoi (宇田友猪) and Wada Saburō (和田三郎), eds. *Jiyūtō-shi* (History of the Liberal Party). Tokyo: Iwanami Shoten, 1910.

When the idea of dispatching troops to Korea was defeated by those who gave priority to domestic issues, Saigō retreated to his home province, to hunt rabbits. He may have considered that he was no longer any use to his country. This would account for his submission, after initial dismay, to the event precipitated by his subordinates.

Tosa Temperament

Saigō's co-advocate of the conquest of Korea, Itagaki Taisuke from Tosa, also left the imperial court. Itagaki then established the Risshisha (立志社, Self-Help Society) in Tosa to promote the Freedom and People's Rights Movement, the first genuine program for democracy in Japan.

Tosa's position and role in Meiji history were rather unusual. Along with Satsuma and Chōshū, Tosa was a leading force in the overthrow of the Tokugawa shogunate. One only has to remember that it was Sakamoto Ryōma from that area who was instrumental in forging the Satsuma-Chōshū alliance. However, despite having produced this distinguished figure, the region remained without representation in the inner circle of the Meiji government.

The main reason for this seems to have been a matter of temperament. Its people are known for their independent disposition. Their inability to band together to form a Tosa faction to protect their interests—as the Satsuma and Chōshū clans had done—was a serious setback.

On top of that, Tosa people are idealistic and willing to sacrifice personal gain for political conviction. In this sense, Itagaki was typical, alight with idealism throughout his life but short of money. It must have been this temperament that made him indifferent to promotion despite his immense contribution to the Restoration. Instead, he initiated an essentially anti-government movement that came to play a special role in the political history of Japan.

When the news of Saigō's revolt reached Tosa, all its leaders were sympathizers. Believing in Saigō's victory, Itagaki made plans to raise an army in support of his advance across Kyushu into the mainland.

Mutsu, having maintained close relations with Tosa leaders ever since his *Kaientai* days, conspired to take advantage of the revolt to cut down Satsuma's strength and, ultimately, overthrow the *hanbatsu*-controlled administration in cooperation with such Tosa radicals as Hayashi Yūzō (林有造, 1842–1921) and Ōe Taku (大江卓, 1847–1921). Aside from Tosa taking up arms, Mutsu's plot involved the assassination of dignitaries allegedly including not only Ōkubo Toshimichi but such long-term friends as Itō Hirobumi and Torio Koyata.

In his communications with Tosa, Mutsu employed the code that was used in the *Genrōin*, which later became undeniable evidence of his involvement.

On January 30, 1877, the rebel army began heading toward Tokyo only to face unexpectedly strong resistance from Kumamoto Castle, making it impossible to move fast through the southern island. When, in April, government reinforcements succeeded in breaking the blockade and connecting with the castle defenders, the rebellion came to grief. Saigō escaped to Kagoshima, only to take his own life at Shiroyama (城山) in September.

Meanwhile, Mutsu silently attended to his clerical work at the *Genrōin*, to camouflage his sedition. It became increasingly obvious, however, that his arrest was inevitable. Tosa members of the government, feeling he was bound to be found guilty since there already seemed to be solid evidence against him, made Mutsu a scapegoat in order to distract the prosecution from impeaching Itagaki.

In retrospect, it appears that, throughout Mutsu's life, good luck and bad alternated like the strands of a rope because of his association with Tosa. At the time of the Satsuma Rebellion, he became entangled in Tosa's brave but unrealistic schemes; he was even imprisoned to divert attention from Itagaki. But Tosa people never forgot the debt they owed him. It was indeed his close connection with Tosa's Liberal Party that later made Mutsu an indispensable figure in Japan's parliamentary politics.

Mutsu Arrested

When Mutsu knew that he faced imminent arrest, he paid a visit to Torio Koyata and confided in him. Originally from Chōshū, Torio was a rough-edged individual unpopular with most people, but Mutsu had made him a staff officer in the Kishū army, and the two had been close friends ever since. Torio now advised him to turn himself in, assuring him that he would personally look after the family Mutsu left behind. Torio had once been on his hit list.

In times of turmoil, those involved in national affairs are likely to put their political convictions ahead of personal feelings. Not uncommonly back then, a marked man might find himself in affable conversation with his would-be killer. As it happens, Sakamoto Ryōma first met Katsu when he was set on bumping Katsu off for his pro-Western views, but was so impressed by him in conversation that they became, in due course, good friends. What mattered was whether one was doing it for one's country or not. Differences in political views were tolerated between friends no matter how hotly they were debated. Thus Torio, too, could willingly offer to look after Mutsu's family.

Despite Torio's advice, Mutsu was arrested on June 10 before he had a chance to surrender. During the subsequent trial, he began, in his eloquent way, by refusing to give in an inch. But he was gradually cornered into partially admitting his guilt, although he consistently maintained that his intention had always been to promote the reform of the Meiji administration, not to subvert it, using the unrest as a lever. He argued that the conspiracy of the Risshisha in Tosa was "a stimulant dangerous only in appearance."

This wasn't far off the truth. But it was equally true that he would not have hesitated to choose a more radical alternative had the first option been found to be unviable.

In the end, he made the following statement:

As I look back, when the initial scheme for the reform of our present polity fell short, what remained was the simple fact that I had knowingly approved of and remained silent about a rebellious plot, for which I am guilty, and I am deeply ashamed of it. Although my heart was filled with good patriotic intentions, I was foolish enough to rely only on my ingenuity, and for this I am rightly accused. I now regret what I have done. Indeed, I already regretted it when I returned to Tokyo last year, and have been too ashamed to mention it to anyone since.

Later in his life, whenever he was asked about this episode, Mutsu would wave his hand and say, "No more of that. That was the worst mistake I ever made. It was so absurd that I don't even want to think about it."

Among twenty other affiliates of the Risshisha who were convicted, Hayashi Yuzo, Ōe Taku, and Iwakami Noboru (岩神昴, 1841–1926) were sentenced to ten years of imprisonment, a harsher punishment than Mutsu's five. All three had been in close contact with Mutsu.

Iwakami in particular was distraught when he learned of Mutsu's prison term. To a puzzled fellow prisoner who asked why, he replied, "We've harmed a person we're deeply indebted to."

Iwakami was not the only member of the Risshisha who felt this way. Mutsu's rational nature might have dismissed this kind of sentiment, but for Tosa people he was a confederate who had undergone the same experience, in both hope and despair, and a comrade who had effectively blocked the judicial authorities' investigations of Gotō Shōjirō (後藤象二郎, 1838–97) and Itagaki Taisuke. Future events showed that this relationship became an invaluable political asset for Mutsu.

1877: The Fateful Year

What unlucky fate was it that made 1877 such a disastrous year for him? It proved to be the year of this misadventure; the year he lost Kido Takayoshi, his only sympathizer among the oligarchs; and the year his father, Munehiro, passed away. One consolation was that Munehiro died before the arrest, allowing his son to arrange a dignified funeral corresponding to his father's official position and court rank of the time.

The next to last letter Munehiro addressed to him, presumably written in 1876, included the following advice:

> A clever, thoughtful person with high ideals is bound to get tired, and prone to illness. He may have drive and ambition, yet fail ever to relax. He may feel energetic in a heated argument, but become depressed when things are quiet. The cleverer you are, the more liable you are to this kind of mood. To keep well, try not to be distracted by passionate ideas that make you either love something or hate it.

As a parent, Munehiro must have known how his son's character made him careless and prone to excess; how his aversion to *hanbatsu*-dominated politics could blind his judgment and put his life at risk.

Munehiro must also have been familiar with the *Yijing*. The "Book of Changes" is the oldest and most authentic Chinese writing on divination. The *Yijing* oracle is determined by a combination of six bars of either *yang* (—) or *ying* (- -). *Yang* symbolizes "day," "heaven," or "masculine," and *ying* stands for "night," "earth," or "feminine." Altogether, there are sixty-four possible combinations, each yielding a philosophical commentary, many of which are thought to have been formulated by Confucius. The *Yijing* is usually studied in the final stage of Confucian learning.

In his 1873 letter to Mutsu, Munehiro wrote that since he had acquired the forecast ☷, he should bide his time and refrain from provoking controversy.

The forecast represents a pinnacle of *ying*. In a simplistic reading, it symbolizes the last leaves of autumn, on the verge of falling from the top of a tree. There would seem to be no favorable prospects implied by it.

In Oriental philosophy, however, where everything is thought to metamorphose and nothing is constant, that isn't the end of the story. According to the *Yijing*, Mutsu's forecast also indicated a return to life in the form of a bud on the ground; that after a certain time, *yang* would return. Till then, one was advised to wait, stay quiet—like a bush warbler waiting for spring.

But Mutsu, ignoring this advice, had published his indictment in *Nippon-jin* and resigned his post. As a result, he had provoked the enmity of the dominant factions, leading to his arraignment in the late 1870s.

In retrospect, there was no need to plot the assassination of Ōkubo since he was to be killed by a pro-Saigō former samurai in 1878. Kido died in the middle of the Satsuma Rebellion, murmuring, "Saigō, haven't you done enough?" His death marked a shift of authority in the Chōshū clan to Itō Hirobumi. After the rebellion was quelled, anti-government activities converged on the promotion of parliamentary democracy. In the midst of this, Mutsu could have been an important conduit between the administration and the Tosa people as well as an advocate of parliamentary democracy. It is conceivable that the Itō-Mutsu era might have arrived ten years early.

Ironically, hindsight shows that Mutsu's best course of action would have been to do nothing. Yet we also know that for a person of his inclination this was precisely what he could never do.

VI

Burning the Midnight Oil Again

Study during Imprisonment

Preparation for a Great Leap

Mutsu was imprisoned for treason between 1878 and 1883. He used his time in confinement for reading and thinking. Released in 1883, he spent the subsequent three years traveling to observe political systems in the United States, the United Kingdom, and other European countries. These eight years were the last occasion where Mutsu could concentrate on intensive study, away from practical matters, and prepare for active involvement in state affairs during the last decade of his life.

In the early days of his imprisonment, he composed quite a number of poems. Poetry tends to be most moving when induced by suffering. This is true of some of Mutsu's work as he looked back at his life.

> I am fond of pleasure, but loathe money
> I have courage, and speak well
> I have left my footprints on five continents
> And read all the books worth reading

> But I wonder at how small Guan Zhong is
> And how incomplete is Mencius.

Although a little exaggerated, this self-portrait is not inaccurate. Mutsu could be eloquent, and wasn't easily cowed. It took eloquence to persuade Iwakura to endorse the great reforms of the Kishū domain which Mutsu carried out with courage. Nobody else could have done it. It is also true that he enjoyed banquets and parties, but was always strict about money.

Unusually for a Japanese in those days, he had traveled abroad. And he was astonishingly well read.

Guan Zhong had long been considered a paragon of the statesman in China. But Confucius (孔子), while praising him as a statesman in vol. 14 of the *Lunyu* (the *Analects of Confucius*), also referred to him in vol. 3 as a man of "small caliber." Mutsu clearly knew the Chinese philosophers well.

Remorse

After boasting about his first thirty-some years, his poetry turned remorseful.

> Looking back
> I can see
> How proud and reckless
> Was my bid for fame.

And again:

> There is no substance to our world
> When a statesman in the morning
> By night can be an exile
> Borne in a cage to a barren place
> Where mountains and rivers all are bleak.

The theme of power being suddenly eclipsed like this was already a feature of the Chinese classics, notably in Han Yu's (韓愈) poetry of the Tang dynasty. He wrote of giving the emperor a memorial in the morning, and being banished eight thousand *ri* away in the evening.

Another poem of Mutsu's said:

I write in the air
Fantasies
Skills I once had
Enough to slay dragons
Now are wasted
In this dark cell
Where I sit meditating.

Mutsu poured out a chain of poems—wishing he had taken his father's advice; about his longing for his family; and a good piece hoping that his children flourish. But after a while he suddenly stopped. The last poem of his days in prison was prefaced with the words, "People have wondered why I should stop writing. The following is my answer":

I cannot groan when I am not sick
I cannot write and rewrite verse
If, as the Muse knows well
The Muse is silent.

Without inspiration, he is saying, there is no point in polishing poetry. Why fake suffering when one isn't ill? It was typical of Mutsu to say out loud what he was determined to do or not to do and to stick to his word.

This marked the end of the first half of a life in which he went his own way, driven by his convictions. It was also the end of his self-criticism. From this point on until his death, he devoted his life to study and, then, to state affairs. He also completely abstained from worldly pleasures. Although he has the image of someone who loved entertainment, his son, Hirokichi, testifies that as far as he could remember Mutsu never indulged in this sort of thing again after his release from prison.

Formation of Mutsu's Thought

During his first two years of imprisonment, Mutsu finished drafting three treatises—*Menpeki dokugo* (面壁独語, Monologue facing a prison wall), *Fukudō dokugo* (福堂独語, Mutsu's monologue), and *Shiji seiri-dan* (資治性理談, The principles of governance)—which were a compilation of his ideas and insights. Three years later, and after numerous revisions, he finished translating one of Jeremy Bentham's books, *The Principles of Morals and Legislation*. He also produced *Sashi jirei ippan* (左氏辞令一斑), which referred to sophisticated examples of diplomacy in ancient China.

Mutsu's thoughts expressed in these books are worth introducing here, not only for a better understanding of his intellectual development but as an example of the formation of ideas among Japanese intellectuals after the end of national isolation.

First, *Shiji seiri-dan*. This outlined his own political philosophy. In its preface, he writes that he decided to explore certain truths that he had not found in the Confucian philosophy of the Song and Ming dynasties, which he had studied since childhood, or the Western theories which he had been exposed to later in life. In order to explain what he meant, we need to touch briefly on the Confucianism that had provided the intellectual foundation of the Japanese for two hundred and fifty years under the Tokugawa shogunate.

In the early Tokugawa period, Zen Buddhist priests in the Kyoto and Kamakura Five Mountain monasteries served as Confucian scholars, following the tradition of the Muromachi period (室町時代, 1336–1573). In 1688, the Confucian temple Yushima Seidō (湯島聖堂) was built under the aegis of the fifth shogun Tokugawa Tsunayoshi. Since then the teachings of Zhu Xi (朱子学) had become the orthodox Confucianism endorsed by the shogunate.

Although Mutsu had also studied Zhu Xi since early childhood, he kept Ogyū Sorai's *Bendō* (弁道, Distinguishing the way) and *Benmei* (弁名, Distinguishing names) close by throughout his life.

An explanation on the difference between Zhu Xi's and Sorai's doctrines would be helpful here.

The principle of Neo-Confucianism is to follow the interpretations of the extensive commentaries written by Zhu Xi (1130–1200) on the *Four Books* of Confucianism. Zhu Xi was a philosophical giant. His book *Song mingchen yanxing-lu* (宋名臣言行録, Words and deeds of illustrious statesmen of the Song dynasty), a work comparable with Plutarch's *Parallel Lives*, is still regarded as the supreme textbook of politics. Emperor Meiji regularly read the book aloud with a group of his subjects at court.

Zhu Xi's teachings are not mere commentaries. They are tantamount to a new interpretation of Confucianism, weaving the thinking of Confucius, Mencius, and others into a coherent philosophical system. This subsequently became the Confucian orthodoxy of the governments of Ming China (明) and Korea's Yi dynasty (李朝), and was officially endorsed in Tokugawa Japan.

What follows is a very simplified summary of Zhu Xi's theories. First and foremost, there is a "way" (Chinese *dao*) of heaven that, from the beginning of time, is unchangeable. This is the *li* (principle) that every person is endowed with, and is expressed in human behavior in the form of *ren* (benevolence), *yi* (righteousness), *li* (courtesy), *zhi* (wisdom), and *xin* (sincerity).

Although Confucianism was not a religion in the beginning, its teachings became and have remained at the heart of the ethics of Chinese civilization since the time of its founder (552 B.C.–479 B.C.). It differs from Christianity or Islam where ethics is something presumably given to man by God through prophets like Moses and Muhammad. In the case of Confucianism there is no God. When preaching the virtue of good deeds, Christians can support their argument by saying, "God is everywhere, watching you." There is nothing in Confucianism that presides over man's behavior. No one is watching him.

Still, some kind of theoretical coherence was necessary in order to defend the moral principles upheld for close to two thousand years. Here was how the concept of the "way of heaven" was called into service—the idea that there is a constant, unchanging, and eternal conscience that everyone is provided with.

In origin, this "way of heaven" was not an invention of Zhu Xi's but a reflection of a traditional Chinese belief in a higher kingdom, and came to be accepted by the Chinese universally.

The Confucian classic *Daxue* (大学, The great learning) says, "Their persons being cultivated, their families were well ordered. Their families being well ordered, their states were well governed. Their states being well governed, the whole world was made peaceful and happy." Zhu Xi's doctrines drew on this tenet that social and political stability depended on the fulfillment of our *li*, our human nature, thus uniting an ancient ethos with a political guideline. By cultivating virtue one was cultivating peace.

Shiji Seiri-dan

In contrast, Tokugawa Japan saw the emergence of the Kogaku (古学, classic study) school of Confucianism, a unique phenomenon made possible only by the sophisticated academic environment of the Edo period. The Kogaku school amounted to a new approach in an Oriental world where, for centuries, Neo-Confucianism had monopolized the center of orthodox thought, dismissing all other doctrines as heresy. The evolution of an unorthodox doctrine in the stable circumstances of Edo society was no threat to the political regime. It can in fact be seen as an indication of the degree of freedom of thought that people enjoyed at the time.

Although new, the Kogaku school was not eccentric; it emerged naturally as scholars explored the writings of Confucius and Mencius with characteristic seriousness.

The depth of study of the Chinese classics during the two and a half centuries of the Edo period was unprecedented. The only comparable erudition was focused on the Greek and Latin classics in Europe, particularly by scholars associated with Oxford University. But there was a difference, shown in the degree to which a foreign language was absorbed into the vernacular. What makes it more surprising is that Japanese and Chinese belong to entirely different branches of linguistic trees, while English shares the same Indo-European roots as Greek and Latin. Every work of the Chinese classics was, during this period, translated into fluent and comprehensible Japanese with detailed commentary. Even today, Japan remains the best place for scholars to obtain texts that are faithful to the original yet include full references to different versions from various eras. Works that are available only in libraries in China are readily available in bookstores in Japan, and it isn't rare for Chinese scholars to have their first chance to read some texts when they visit.

Ogyū Sorai was a master in terms of his knowledge of the Chinese classics. According to Sorai, neither Confucius nor Mencius had ever said some of the things Zhu Xi claimed in his annotations. While the two sages might have mentioned the "way", they were actually referring to the "way of earlier kings," i.e., the manner in which legendary kings such as Yao and Shun had ruled—the specific techniques of governance applied in their kingdoms. Sorai even declared explicitly that the "way" is actually a "technique." Although followers of Zhu Xi were averse to the term, he proved that this interpretation had once been current.

According to Zhu Xi, as long as rulers adhered to a righteous path, people would follow them, guided by the *li* with which everyone was born. Sorai argued that the notion of righteousness of body and soul leading automatically to a peaceful society was an interpretation borrowed from Buddhism or Daoist thought (老壮思想). While virtuous behavior was necessary, since it was human nature to despise and distrust a corrupt leader, Sorai realistically observed that such behavior was only one of a range of political "techniques."

In return, a Zhu Xi scholar, Muro Kyūsō (室鳩巣, 1658–1734) said:

> There is an outrageous theory that the "way" is something that ancient kings practiced rather than a gift of heaven. It also claims that, among human virtues, affection between men and women is the only thing that is innate. Everything else, such as reverence for a ruler or respect for one's parents, can be attributed to a historical cause rather than something inherent in our nature. While numerous heretical doctrines have surfaced over the centuries, I have never encountered anything else so contrary to the essence of Confucianism.

The logical conclusion of Sorai's argument is that, if we accept that everything is essentially a technique for interpersonal relations, in the final analysis the only factor that derives from human nature is love and lust. Mutsu, however, made a more daring observation.

Mutsu was a child of a new era. From the very beginning of his *Shiji seiri-dan*, he declared that there is no such thing as a virtuous or vicious instinct in human nature; there is only expedience.

Since man in primitive times was constantly exposed to natural threats and assault by enemies, he was driven to seek refuge in religion and authority. In the beginning of mankind, there can't have been a clear demarcation between the ruler and the ruled. No one would willingly sacrifice his own welfare for someone else's benefit. But this sacrifice could buy him the protection of someone stronger. As this tradeoff continued, however, the weaker party was liable to lose everything to the greed of those stronger than him unless he willingly gave up some of his own needs in deference to authority. This, Mutsu argues, was how the role of "loyalty" emerged from the conditions governing the survival of the fittest.

Throughout the Edo, Meiji, Taishō, and Shōwa periods until Japan's defeat in World War II, loyalty to the ruler was a dominant moral value. Confucianism endorsed the virtue of loyalty as the apotheosis of heaven's way. Against this background, Mutsu's iconoclastic outlook, attributing the root of loyalty to expedience, was startling.

His stimulus for this must have come from within himself, but he would also have been influenced by the rising tide of intellectual energy elsewhere during the age of enlightenment—or the age of reason—in the eighteenth and nineteenth centuries.

Bentham's Influence

It was an age when everything had to be traced back to its origin and rationally explained. Charles Darwin came up with the theory of evolution in the quest for a fundamental, rational explanation for the presence of multiple species. Jean-Jacques Rousseau set out on his own intellectual inquiries by wondering how property rights were invented and the lines that define a man's holdings were drawn up, leading him to take a negative view of many of the rules that human society has instituted. Karl Marx searched for an answer to the fundamental question of where profit comes from and to whom it should belong.

It is interesting to note that Mutsu was critical of communism. In *Shiji seiri-dan*, he divided human nature into primary and secondary levels. Man's primary objective was the fulfillment of his desires, while the other, including the virtue of loyalty as discussed above, was a derivative. Such values as fairness and equality were only second nature, deriving from our desire to live happily.

In Mutsu's view, communism was "an erroneous doctrine based on the fallacy of regarding the secondary human impulse toward fairness and equality as primary in nature. Originally, the aim of a just society is to promote people's wellbeing. If the imposition of a just society ends up, conversely, harming people's wellbeing, the original purpose cannot be achieved." Forty years before the Russian Revolution and more than a century before the collapse of communism, Mutsu accurately analyzed the defects of communism—and predicted its future, too.

Besides Ogyū Sorai, Mutsu's thinking was also heavily influenced by Jeremy Bentham.

Bentham, too, was a man of the age of reason. Being of an unusually gentle and sweet-tempered nature, he found it hard to adjust to social norms. Hunting, for instance, was an essential communal activity for the English upper class, but Bentham couldn't stand the brutality that hunting entailed.

In England at that time, punishment could be severe and cruel. The notion of one man punishing another was an odious one, even if it was for the good of society as a whole. That being so, it was Bentham's idea that punishment should accord with the wellbeing of people at large, including the offender. Here was Bentham's principle of the greatest happiness of the greatest number. Immediately after Mutsu was imprisoned, he wrote, "Nothing visible, since my setback, has been any consolation. But Bentham's ideas about the pleasures of memory and the imagination, the eleventh and twelfth items in his table of pleasures, have helped raise my spirits. The great man has never disappointed me."

While Bentham divided pleasure and pain into twenty-six types, Mutsu combined everything in the single factor of desire—a human trait traditionally condemned in Oriental ethics. Within this spectrum were, for example, both the desire for pleasure and the desire to avert pain. But though his and Bentham's theories differed, they were both permeated with the spirit of an age that sought fundamental explanations. In Mutsu's case, they give us a glimpse of a modern mind uninhibited by the moral codes of the past.

Merits and Defects of Wang Yangming

One of the reasons why Mutsu failed to get along with members of the Satsuma-Chōshū clique may have been the difference in the Confucian orientation between them.

Starting with Saigō Takamori, most heroes of the Meiji Restoration were deeply influenced by the teachings of Wang Yangming. As a doctrine, they remained within the established body of Neo-Confucianism, but they laid emphasis on actual observance of the teachings based on the principle of the inseparability of knowledge and practice. Toward the end of the shogunate, this emphasis had a strong appeal to high-minded samurai intent on carrying out reform and revolution. It was under the influence of Wang Yangming, for example, that young Itō Hirobumi joined the raid on the British legation, driven by a sense that it wasn't enough merely to talk of expelling foreigners.

"The man doesn't measure up" was one of the accusations frequently leveled at Mutsu. Most activists in the Restoration, including Saigō and Yoshida Shōin (吉田松陰, 1830–59), Chōshū's philosophical leader who had died young in prison during the harsh suppression of *Tairō* Ii Naosuke, were convinced they could only transform the state and its people if they transformed their own character. To these "ideal individuals," a person like Mutsu, who proselytized without doing much to change himself, would not have "measured up."

Sorai would have argued, however, that raising the moral character of a country's leaders alone wouldn't save the world; to do that, good governance suited to the time and occasion was required. Mutsu had made an attempt to reform Japan's military, tax, and legal systems. He must have been confident that these reforms were what Japan needed to modernize and, ultimately, the only way to protect its people in an age of strategic expansion.

Saigō may have been an exemplar, but his highly questionable proposal to take over Korea was scarcely exemplary, and his untimely suicide after being dragged into the rebellion by his followers was a waste. Were we to compare Saigō and Mutsu on a strictly personal basis, it would perhaps be correct to say that the former was a generous character in the full sense, while Mutsu was insignificant. When asked, however, which of the two made more of a contribution to their country, it would not be totally amiss to choose Mutsu. Certainly, Sorai would have given Mutsu a higher score.

The failure of traditionally educated people like Saigō, to adapt to Western rationalism may be attributed to Wang Yangming. His teachings were the culmination of Confucian thinking. Once you are convinced that perfecting your character would benefit society as a whole, there is no uncertainty in your day-to-day life, no need to be bothered by material poverty or praise or censure. Even if you fail in everything, you are still confident that you have walked the way of heaven It would be a waste of time trying to preach the virtue of modern thought to a "perfected person" whose mind is already made up.

Reviewing the process of the Meiji Restoration, it seems undeniable that the Wang Yangming message stressing the importance of action was a goad. Ōshio Heihachirō (大塩平八郎, 1793–1837), who in 1837 led what turned out to be the only revolutionary endeavor during the Tokugawa shogunate, was an authority on Wang Yangming's precepts. Yoshida Shōin's role in fostering Chōshū dissidence should not be overlooked, either. But it is also a fact that, in the post-Restoration years, followers of this doctrine had a tendency to stand in the way of modernization, including Shinagawa Yajirō (品川弥二郎, 1843–1900), who clamped down on the attempt at parliamentary democracy. Useful as they may have been during the revolution, Wang Yangming's teachings seemed to be incompatible with progress.

Basics of Politics

Through his research, Mutsu came to a good understanding of Anglo-Saxon utilitarianism. Evidence shows that he also grasped the essence of economic liberalism:

> In the feudal era, the government instituted a strict program where people were constrained by detailed regulations on everything from food, clothing, and shelter to daily activities. Denouncing an ornamental hairpin maker as a useless provider of luxury goods, and forcing him to work on the land, merely resulted in a starving family.

It should be recalled that the economic policy pursued by Munehiro, Mutsu's father, which was mentioned in an earlier chapter, was the very antithesis of this traditional austerity policy, for which Munehiro was first promoted but later demoted. Mutsu's liberal approach is summarized in his personal reflection, "The best way of increasing the wealth of a nation is to promote the industries that are judged to be most profitable, whatever they might be, and for the government to protect them from interference."

This conviction was reflected in his decisions when he was later appointed as minister of agriculture and commerce. Mutsu's grasp of liberalism, moreover, was not confined to economics. He stated that, since social wellbeing was nothing but the sum of the happiness of a society's individual members, the ideal would be for each individual to make the utmost effort to satisfy his or her desires and for the government to avoid obstructing these efforts.

At this point, Mutsu seemed well acquainted with the main points of Anglo-Saxon social thought exemplified by people like Adam Smith, John Stewart Mill, and Jeremy Bentham.

Beyond that, however, his thinking about democracy had not taken a fixed shape yet. Or rather, the notion of democracy had yet to take firm shape elsewhere in the world.

Today, most people have no doubt that democracy is a good thing. There are, admittedly, countries that are not yet democratized, but the general assumption is that they will catch up sooner or later. Nobody in Japan questions the benefits of democracy. People vaguely assume or have been taught that they are happier today than in the past when freedom was limited. The Japanese in post–World War II days have ceased to ask such fundamental questions as, were people in the past really less content? What are the criteria for happiness and unhappiness? Was it the absence of democracy that made them less favored? And was democracy really absent back then?

In contrast, the Japanese of the Meiji era were much more serious about democracy, being more speculative in general. They asked such basic political questions as, what is freedom? What are people's rights? What is good politics? And what constitutes people's happiness?

In *Menpeki dokugo*, Mutsu notes:

> While Europe was freed from the constraints of the feudal system, people in China lost the taste for freedom they had had during the Spring and Autumn through the Warring States periods (770 B.C.–221 B.C.), after centralization under the Qin (秦) and Han (漢) dynasties. Everything, it seems, depends on time and place.

The word *hoken* in *hoken-shugi* (feudalism) originally referred to the policy of the ruler of the Zhou dynasty (1027 B.C.–771 B.C.) to award his relatives and meritorious retainers with domains and subjects as hereditary property. The term *hoken-shugi* has come to be used particularly by socialist thinkers to refer to all pre-modern systems of government. It should be remembered, however, that initially it referred to the existence of semi independent feudal lords within a state in contrast to a central absolute monarchy.

Feudal lords in the Zhou dynasty subsequently became independent dukes during the Spring and Autumn periods (春秋時代) and, eventually, heads of independent states during the Warring States (戦国時代) period. And it was during these centuries that Chinese civilization blossomed, giving birth to liberal and broad-minded politics and philosophy. This latitude was lost, however, under the centralization of the succeeding Qin dynasty and the Confucian empire of the Han dynasty. Chinese history in the intervening two thousand years proves that the feudal system was a better protector of the freedom of thought.

Mutsu also recognized the positive aspect of autocracy, arguing that, "Depending on the time and situation, it can be more effective for the protection of peace and prosperity for the majority of people to have the power of a state concentrated in the hands of one ruler."

Mutsu's objective was not solely the establishment of democracy—which, to him, was only a secondary condition. The ultimate goal was the pursuit of the maximum happiness for the maximum number of people. It is a relevant fact that, for many of the newly independent countries after World War II, "developmental dictatorship" was, at least for a limited period of time, the more effective system for facilitating modernization.

People have espoused a number of theories on the ideal political system, from the sacred rule of Yao and Shun in China, the philosopher-king advocated by Plato, to contemporary parliamentary democracy. It was Mutsu's idea that each of these hypotheses should be evaluated according to the measure of public well-being.

Do people automatically become happier if power is equally distributed among them? While contemporary Japanese would never doubt the validity of this proposition, it remains universally a challenging question.

Mutsu was also aware that the equal distribution of power was closely linked to the current of the times and the direction that a society sought to take.

> When it comes to choosing a political regime, people today are single-mindedly in favor of a constitutional polity and believe that freedom can never be attained in its absence. That may be so. But I have never supported the idea that it should be hastily adopted regardless of time, place, or level of civilization.

Looking back at his achievements, this statement appears to be true. After all, it was Mutsu who pioneered the abolition of the feudal stipend and the establishment of a prefectural system, as well as military and taxation reforms. And it was not democratic power but his direct persuasion of those at the heart of state authority that made it possible for him to implement these reforms. One might wonder whether he could have seen them through if, instead, power had been more evenly distributed.

Fukuzawa Yukichi's View on Civilization

We need to tackle the concept of the "level of civilization." Western imperialism at the time was in its heyday. Populations were stratified and those on lower strata were discriminated against. Let me quote Fukuzawa Yukichi (福沢諭吉, 1835–1901), founder of Keio University (慶應義塾大学):

> Looking around the world, it is simply common sense nowadays to regard Europe and the United States as the most civilized regions in existence; such Asian nations as Turkey, China, and Japan as half-developed; and other areas such as Africa as undeveloped. It is not only Westerners, in self-approval, but also those from less advanced states, who agree that this is the case.
>
> Intelligent citizens in these countries must surely recognize how advanced the West is and, consequently, condemn their own backwardness, becoming either determined to catch up with it or to resist it. This has become a pressing concern, particularly in Asia.

Born in a small domain in Kyushu, Fukuzawa, a great proponent of enlightenment in Meiji Japan, had studied the Chinese classics, Dutch learning, and English since early childhood. After the Restoration, he chose to remain outside the government, to criticize retrogressive thinking and advocate the modernization of Japan from an unofficial stance.

It might already be beyond the imagination of contemporary Japanese, but the goal not only of intellectuals but everyone in Japan was once to catch up with the West and to put an end to the international discrimination Japan had endured since Commodore Perry's arrival in Uraga.

When I went to Cambridge in the mid-1950s as the first Japanese to attend the university after the Second World War, it was noticeable how focused students from Asia and Africa were on the need to modernize their own countries. That had been true for Japan as well since the Meiji period until very recently.

The urgency of modernization was particularly acute during the era of colonial expansion in the nineteenth century. Once a country was labeled as "primitive" to any degree, it became a target for colonization. In a race for colonies among civilized nations, there was no room for sympathy for the underdog. The unsympathetic attitude of the United States as Korea's last hope against Japanese annexation in 1910 was clear evidence of this fact. It was a time when everyone had to look out for themselves. Even if a half-developed country was lucky enough to avoid colonization, it was likely to be prey to unequal treaties.

Thus, Fukuzawa says, "The ultimate aim is to maintain independence. Civilization is the means to achieve it." This finds an echo in Mutsu's monologue in *Fukudō dokugo*, written around the same time:

> In the past twenty years, Japan has been strong-armed by Western nations to the extent that it is even doubtful whether we can keep up the appearance of an independent country. Every sensible man in Japan feels we have to remedy this situation. This calls for resolve: to do our utmost to develop the country, and to have the courage to even the score.

The repeal of unequal treaties was a priority then for every "sensible man in Japan," including Fukuzawa and Mutsu. And it was to be accomplished, finally, with the help of Mutsu himself, as described in Chapter XI.

With all the time at his disposal during his imprisonment, Mutsu compiled *Sashi jirei ippan*, annotated excerpts from the Chinese classic, *Chunqiu Zuo zhuan* (The Commentary of Zuo on the Spring and Autumn Annals), a collection of ancient historical narratives. Few Japanese or even Chinese nowadays have read it; even those interested in the classics are content to stop at the *Shiji*, the "Records of the Grand Historian" compiled in the second century B.C. But it seems to have been quite popular reading in the Edo period.

Fukuzawa once boasted, "While most students won't get beyond volumes three and four of the *Chunqiu Zuo zhuan*, I have read the entire fifteen volumes about eleven times. I have even memorized some of the most interesting parts." He added, "I challenge any scholar of the Chinese classics in Japan to have a better knowledge of the subject than me." This was from someone who went on to promote Western education at the university he founded.

In *Sashi jirei ippan*, Mutsu often referred to the diplomatic ordeal of a tiny state, Zheng (鄭), which, during the Spring and Autumn period, was sandwiched between Jin (晋), a traditional powerhouse in the region, and Chu (楚), an emerging power on the southern periphery. Around the time Mutsu was imprisoned, Japan found itself sandwiched between the Anglo-American nations on the one hand and Russia on the other. Japan had been under constant threat of invasion from Russia, but there was no guarantee that England or America would come to its rescue in time. There was indeed a parallel with Zheng, repeatedly invaded by Chu yet unable always to depend on Jin's help despite a long-standing connection with it. Twenty years after writing *Sashi jirei ippan*, during the Tripartite Intervention in 1895, when the suggestion was made to ask Britain for help, Mutsu pointed out: "Britain is not Don Quixote—identifying with others' suffering."

Admiration for America

The exception to Mutsu's cynicism was the United States, in which he placed a special trust, as revealed in his attitude to the country during his tenure as minister of foreign affairs. His confidence in it grew while he served as minister over there, so much so that he once seriously considered permanent residency.

In practice, his trust in the United States had already found expression during his imprisonment, in a poem written after reading about world history:

Peace and war on six continents, at home and abroad
The rise and fall of countries in three thousand years

A dog-eat-dog world, a slaughterhouse
Where no one died for a good cause
This is the history of mankind
Thus, like fresh air on tired eyes is it to read
The Declaration of Independence.

In fact, his trust in the United States seems to have been shared widely by the Japanese in those days. Let me quote again something that Fukuzawa wrote, in 1897. After pointing out that U.S. diplomacy toward Japan had been, since the end of the shogunate, remarkably fair-minded in contrast to other Western powers, he went on to emphasize that, as a result, the Japanese government had great confidence in its American counterpart. And, he concluded, "I guarantee that everything will go well during a trip if the traveler claims to be an American. His nationality functions like a passport for good treatment here."

Although the United States also became a late member of the colonizing powers toward the end of the nineteenth century, annexing Hawaii and suppressing the independence of the Philippines, the Japanese had hitherto looked up to it with a sort of adulation, as a country quite different from the imperialistic powers.

VII

Burning the Midnight Oil a Third Time

Is a Prussian-style Constitution Appropriate?

Release from Prison

In January 1883, Mutsu was released from prison eight months early under a special amnesty.

On returning to his hometown of Wakayama, he received a frenzied welcome, like the triumphant return of a war hero. People rushed to the reception from Osaka as well as the Kumano area, the southern tip of the mountainous part of Kishū. It became an event of unheard-of scale in the prefecture. Tokyo newspapers compared it to Lord Kishū's homecoming in olden days and commented that it was an obvious indication of Mutsu's popularity locally.

Political prisoners back then were often admired in Japan. They had done what ordinary people would not have dared. If someone of Mutsu's educational background and social standing was prepared to lose his position and risk his own life for his country, he deserved to be admired. That was how people had traditionally felt.

His release was also welcomed by the Jiyūtō (Liberal Party), which faced a crisis at the time. It had difficulty controlling its radical elements, which had made protests against governmental oppression. It also lost an objective after the issuance of the 1881 imperial edict promising the establishment of a national assembly in 1890. Furthermore, its leader Itagaki Taisuke took off on a research trip to Europe in spite of objections within the party. And in fact the Jiyūtō was finally forced to dissolve in the following year. Its members thus put their last hopes in Mutsu's backing for the party's revival.

Mutsu rejected their overtures. He had been firmly determined to get into the center of Japan's power structure, in order to achieve his own political aims. Besides, before being released, he must somehow have been given a message from Itō Hirobumi, who was abroad studying constitutional affairs, urging him not to take any steps until his return.

Concerned about Mutsu's health, Itō had made arrangements for him to be transferred from the prison in Yamagata to one in Sendai. He was also behind Mutsu's early release. He clearly was unwilling to leave Mutsu out on a limb at a time when the Freedom and People's Rights Movement needed help.

Itō's Friendship

Mutsu met Itō several times after the latter returned to Japan in August 1883. The nature of these meetings can be gathered from Mutsu's letters addressed to Hamaguchi Goryō, who acted as his patron.

These letters reveal that Mutsu did not intend to be heavily reliant on Itō. Close friends though they had once been, it was five years since they had last contacted each other. And five years earlier, while Itō was playing a central role in support of the government, Mutsu took part in the conspiracy to bring it down. Besides, Mutsu had made plans for the assassination of Ōkubo and Itō, albeit inconclusively. Could he still count on the friendship of an old friend?

Mutsu was not sure of Itō's political convictions, either. He had not been well informed about Itō's thinking or his course of action during the political turmoil of 1880–81. He was in the dark concerning Itō's attitude toward constitutional democracy. To begin with, it was not certain if Itō was really serious about the establishment of a national assembly. Mutsu must have wondered if he could still share the same passion for state affairs with this man—a passion that the trio of Itō, Nakajima Nobuyuki, and himself had demonstrated in their youth in front of senior members of the Meiji Restoration government for the abolition of the domains.

The two seem to have discussed national affairs and the world situation from a broad perspective, particularly issues such as the transition from the incumbent autocratic regime to constitutional democracy; the roles to be played by non-governmental parties, including the Freedom and People's Rights Movement; the amendment of unequal treaties with foreign powers; and the progress needed to allow Japan to join the ranks of the advanced countries.

Through these discussions they appear to have reconfirmed their mutual trust and cooperation, which lasted until Mutsu's death fifteen years later. The very fact that Itō met Mutsu several times during the busy month immediately after his return from overseas testifies to respect and ease they felt in each other's company. Ito must have realized anew that there was nobody else with whom he could share what he had learned during his seventeen months in Europe, exchange views and insights, and put his own ideas in order. In return, Mutsu would have argued the value of the Anglo-Saxon pragmatism that he had learned about during his imprisonment. After a vacuum of ten years, they may even have laughed together about how little they had changed.

Studying Abroad

Mutsu was encouraged to go abroad for further study, not only by Itō but also by leaders of political and business circles. Some even offered to pay his travel expenses.

Aside from a genuine wish to let a promising person have a chance to see the outside world, there was an ulterior motive. With Itagaki Taisuke overseas, it was feared that Mutsu would become an antagonistic leader of the Jiyūtō in Itagaki's absence. Government leaders knew it wasn't wise to leave him to his own devices and yet they couldn't find room for him in a government dominated by Satsuma and Chōshū. From their standpoint, therefore, Mutsu had best be sent abroad, whatever the pretext for his travels might be.

Mutsu himself had been eager to go, but was too busy putting his house in order in 1884. When Itō approached him again in early 1885 to encourage an overseas trip, Mutsu gladly accepted the suggestion. As he sailed away from Yokohama on board the French steamship *Océanique* on April 26, it was the start of a journey to a new life.

1884–86, Mutsu traveling abroad in Paris

If Mutsu's aptitude was legendary, so was Itō's.

Yoshino Sakuzō (吉野作造, 1878–1933), a typical intellectual of the Taishō Democracy period, wrote, "Although in later years he posed as a great statesman, Itō in those days was quite modest and studious—in fact, as if he really was a student."

While in Europe, Itō went to lectures given by Drs. Rudolf von Gneist and Albert Mosse in Berlin, but was put off by the German precision and rigidness with which layer upon layer of logic were infused. Then a lecture by Lorenz von Stein (1815–90) in Vienna struck a chord, as is shown in a letter he sent to Iwakura Tomomi:

> There is an ominous trend in Japan to blindly accommodate the arguments of progressive liberals in Britain, the United States, and France as if they were a sort of golden rule. I am glad to inform you that I have found a theory and measures with which to counter this tendency and steer the nation in the right direction. I believe I have obtained a formidable resource at the very moment that I can best serve the country. I look forward to facing the days to come with a sense of having found where I want to die.

That last phrase has long since gone out of use, but in pre–World War II Japan it wasn't uncommon. Depending on the context, it could literally mean where one expected one's life to end. What Itō really meant here was that he had acquired a political conviction to which he could devote the rest of his life. He didn't care if he had to fight and die for it, but it gave him hope, and allowed him to "look forward to facing the days to come."

The Anglo-Saxon vs. the Prussian System

Lorenz von Stein was a professor at Vienna University, a major academic center in pre–World War I Europe. He was recognized for the unparalleled range and quality of his writings in the fields of sociology, political studies, public administration, legal systems, public finance, economics, and national defense. He had been given numerous awards not only in his own country but elsewhere in Europe.

Stein attracted students from all over the world with the intellectual energy he brought to a comprehensive analysis of human society, and is thought to have had a perhaps decisive influence on the drafting of the Meiji constitution.

Mutsu himself became one of those students.

While Itō headed for Berlin and Vienna from the start of his trip, Mutsu, in contrast, first visited Washington, D.C., to study the American parliamentary system firsthand; moved on to Chicago, where he observed party conventions to nominate presidential candidates; and spent nine months in the United Kingdom, before going to Vienna.

His experiences in America and Britain made him one of few people in his own country who had an understanding of the workings of Anglo-American democracy. Every other government leader around the time of the drafting of the Meiji constitution was inclined to adopt the Prussian model.

His itinerary was chosen deliberately, one feels. He must have been aware of the administration's bias toward an Austro-German form of government. He also knew that his friend Itō wanted his cooperation in the promotion of a Prussian-style constitution, and that cooperating with him would perhaps be the fastest way to realize his own ideals.

Nevertheless, there were a couple of questions he wanted to explore in more depth first.

Mutsu had already participated in the drafting of a constitution during the *Genrōin* days. Also, having translated Bentham's *The Principles of Morals and Legislation,* he had become something of an authority on Anglo-Saxon liberal democracy.

In many ways, Great Britain at that time was a world leader both culturally and politically. There was a lot to be said for Japan's copying the legislative system of this advanced country. Would it really be unfeasible to do so? Would introducing the Prussian system, which appeared to be a compromise between autocracy and democracy, have greater benefits? Only after these questions were satisfactorily answered could he work hand in hand with someone who had "found where he wanted to die."

Mutsu's application can be gauged from seven notebooks now in the possession of the Kanagawa Prefectural Kanazawa-Bunko Museum. All of them, with the thickest one being three hundred and fifty pages long, were filled from cover to cover with fine print-like handwriting. Judging from their content as well as the neatness of the writing, the notebooks were clean copies made from scribbled notes, quite a task in itself. When asked by his family for descriptions of some interesting episodes in his stay in Europe, Mutsu replied in a letter, "I devote about ten hours every day to my studies, so I haven't got anything much to report."

Skepticism on the Prussian Constitution

During a visit to Cambridge, Mutsu put a direct question to Professor Wallaker. "Am I right in thinking that the essence of constitutional government lies in the fact that the cabinet can maintain its power as long as it is supported by the majority of the lower house?"

Here was the fundamental difference between the British and Prussian political systems. Simply put, under the British system, the party elected by a majority chooses the prime minister, while under the Prussian equivalent the monarch appoints the prime minister regardless of parliamentary preference.

The Meiji constitution was promulgated on February 11, 1889. Only one day after the promulgation, Prime Minister Kuroda Kiyotaka (黒田清隆, 1840–1900) made a speech in which he said, "It is inevitable that we are going to get a variety of political parties. But the government will have to chart a constant direction throughout and should remain aloof from party politics, placing itself at a higher level of impartiality."

In the earlier days of the Meiji constitution, the government called itself a "transcendental cabinet" (chōzen naikaku).

Mutsu was well aware that Itō had already decided to adopt the Prussian system. But he wanted to ascertain once again with his own eyes whether this would really be appropriate. "Looking around Europe," he said, "Great Britain seems to be the only country that's well managed. While France might appear to be close behind, it is still too new, and beset by power struggles between splinter groups."

Generally speaking, people's opinion then of French politics tended to be low. Ever since the French Revolution, their political system had bounced from monarchy to republic, to an empire, to a republic again, and to an empire once more. Besides, the Japanese were disinclined to emulate a country that suffered a crushing defeat by Prussia in 1871, only a few years after the Meiji Restoration. In retrospect, the Third Republic, created in the wake of the Franco-Prussian War, proved to be successful in maintaining democracy there over a century that included two world wars. But when Mutsu made the above observation, the republic had just been born and nobody could predict what the future held for this young regime. Besides, as Mutsu rightly noted, power struggles between splinter groups have remained a characteristic feature of French politics.

Against this background, Mutsu raised a hypothetical question about Japan:

> Let's extrapolate. Take a country that intends to adopt a parliamentary system instead of an absolute monarchy, but only twenty years ago was divided into numerous independent provinces with their own rulers. Subsequently, the country is controlled by a central government, showing great progress in terms of national integration. And yet differences in regional interests from feudal days still remain and a parochial sentiment lingers in former domains. If a

parliamentary system is introduced in this kind of situation, the risk is that it will fragment into small rival groups. The question is whether a country like this can effectively adopt such a system at this time.

Here Mutsu was presenting Professor Wallaker with the direct concern that conservatives such as Iwakura and Itō felt. In fact, Iwakura had already raised this issue in his Iwakura Brief of 1881, in which he stated:

In the case of Japan, numerous small parties are likely to emerge, making it difficult to form a united front. They may be united temporarily in attacking the government and they may even be able to overturn it. But when one of them tries to form a cabinet, other parties will challenge it, making the political situation very unstable. Consequently, political leaders will be unable to attend to such fundamental matters as what policies they should implement and, even more basically, what issues are of national importance. This is the major difference between the United Kingdom and Japan.

Mutsu followed this up by asking, "If a parliamentary system can't be introduced in Japan, what would adopting a constitutional government entail?" In response, Wallaker told him:

It is highly unlikely that a country like Japan can immediately introduce a parliamentary system. After all, it took the United Kingdom two centuries to adopt it.... But I believe it would still be beneficial to have a constitutional government even if cabinet members were not given all the same responsibilities in the British system.

Foresight

Wallaker's persuasive suggestion notwithstanding, Mutsu had not retreated at all from his position that a parliamentary system should be their ultimate goal. It might not be accomplished quickly, but it was something that had to be attained someday. In his judgment, the only way to prevent rule by a clique was to formally introduce democracy. And the future showed that, after Mutsu's death, the shift made by his direct successor, Hara Takashi (原敬, 1856–1921), marked the beginning of Taishō Democracy.

Mutsu's thinking further revealed itself in his dialogue with Professor Wallaker. Wallaker explained:

> In the United Kingdom, cabinet members hold responsibility on behalf of both the monarch and parliament. In practice, though, the cabinet must implement policies that are supported by the Commons, not by the person who officially sanctioned their leader's appointment.

In response, Mutsu said:

> Yes. Otherwise, it would not be a "constitutional" government. What's more, I'm sure that scaling down the monarch's power is an effective way of protecting and prolonging the monarchy. Adopting a constitutional system should be seen as an act of loyalty to the monarch.

This view of "constitutional monarchy" was shared by Mutsu's lifelong friend Itagaki Taisuke, who in 1882 stated in his "The Monarchism of the Jiyūtō," criticizing the reactionaries:

> … They don't understand why Great Britain is a flourishing society. They don't understand that it derives from the freedom from tyranny and repression that the monarchy and its subjects enjoy under a liberal system.
>
> In countries like China, Russia, and Turkey, however, the monarchy looks down on its subjects—who look up to their kings with awe and resentment.... We in the Jiyūtō revere the imperial family … but the reactionaries, in their blind defense of the supremacy of the emperor and their resistance to preparations for a constitutional government, are actually endangering the imperial family....

It is a sound argument. But it was also a defensive argument vis-à-vis those who treated the advocates of political change as "scum" for their disloyalty to the emperor.

Mutsu's position was more forward-looking. In later days, even after a parliament had been established, he maintained publicly that, no matter how many times parliament was dissolved, as long as a sufficient number of opposition parties had seats in the lower house, the prospect of an oligarchy could be kept at bay.

Itō Chiyū (伊藤痴遊, 1867–1938), a popular storyteller/politician, once commented, "Although Itō Hirobumi originally believed in a 'transcendental cabinet,' not only did he gradually depart from this view to draw closer to party politics, but he ended up implementing policies in cooperation with the political parties. It was Mutsu who was responsible for this."

Mutsu's later decision to join the cabinet without opposing Itō's endorsement of a Prussian-style constitutional government was a calculated, anticipatory move. His vision of a political future, combined with Itō's realism and flexibility, paved the way for the type of democracy established in the Taishō era.

Stein's Political Philosophy

After sorting out his views on Anglo-Saxon political thought during a nine-month stay in the United Kingdom, Mutsu moved to Continental Europe to see Professor Stein.

Mutsu seems already to have been convinced of the usefulness of the Prussian constitution, since he concentrated on learning about its substance and theoretical background without debating the subject with Stein.

The essence of Stein's belief was a sharp distinction between the legislative and executive branches of government, with the monarchy standing above, but supported by, both.

Stein's conviction mainly derived from his knowledge of the grand historical experiments and their lessons during the period of unprecedented turbulence in political thinking from the French Revolution through the Franco-Prussian War. This coincided exactly with the last hundred years of Japan's self-imposed seclusion, during which it had been left behind by these cataclysmic changes. Stein's historical view can be summarized as follows:

> Before his execution by guillotine to the cry of "Vive la République," Louis XVI's attempt to represent a constitutional monarchy after the revolution was blocked by the National Convention. The question was whether the legislative branch could single-handedly govern the country. A Committee of General Security was established as if to address this question, but soon became the de facto government under the oppressive control of Maximilien Robespierre. This episode provides the historical lesson that, if the legislative branch itself becomes the government, it will inevitably become autocratic. Subsequently, an Executive Directory was set up, separate from the legislative branch, but since this body was not accountable to the legislative branch, it also became dictatorial, paving the way for the emergence of Napoleon Bonaparte....
>
> Today's France is a republic with an American-style president as head of state, whose term is four years. The term was limited to this in the belief that it would be too short for a president to maneuver government for his own benefit, yet would provide voters with a long enough time to observe the quality of his leadership. In reality, a four-year term is too short for the person to implement any long-term national policy. Instead of attending to national policies, therefore, the appointment of his protégés to important positions is about the only thing a French president does during his tenure.
>
> Seen from this angle, no political system is superior to a constitutional monarchy. Since the monarch's position is hereditary, he can take a long view of the national interest. It is, however, also true that the monarch is inevitably overthrown if he decides to rule himself....

From this viewpoint, Stein drew the conclusion that a monarchy with independent legislative and executive branches was a sound polity. He said, "Bureaucrats are not a king's courtiers or his servants. Once appointed, even a king cannot dismiss them at will. They must remain members of an independent organization."

Stein also recommended necessary qualifications for bureaucrats. These should include not only professional competence but, more importantly, some knowledge and insight into history and ideas, together with a well-formed view on what their role should be and what power was all about. In order to make them feel responsible, he argued, they had to be given a certain authority and discretion. Bureaucrats must be armed with the conviction that they are serving the country and their fellow citizens.

The Wisdom of Meiji People

These arguments would have been readily acceptable to Japanese people with a history-based outlook such as Itō and Mutsu. In fact, Stein's proposition was made more acceptable because it demanded exactly the same qualifications of bureaucrats in China's state examination system which recruited the best-educated people with a high level of integrity. Almost all the better Chinese poets, philosophers, and statesmen since the Tang and Song dynasties were products of this system.

In Japan, this examination system was never adopted owing to the monopoly of power held by the Fujiwara line during the Heian period, and politics in subsequent eras was dominated by the samurai. Seen from China and Korea, this was evidence of Japan's backwardness. Intellectuals in Japan, too, understood and admired this system. Even among the ruling samurai class, though recruitment and promotion were done on the basis of lineage, its literary education aimed to accomplish exactly what Stein advocated.

Although Mutsu was an adherent of Anglo-Saxon political thought, he agreed with much of what Stein had to say about the bureaucracy, as revealed in his notebooks. And it was Mutsu who, as minister of foreign affairs, reformed the Foreign Ministry's recruitment system and started its entrance exam in later years.

While American-style democracy was widely introduced in post–World War II Japan, the system of recruitment by examination for public servants remained Germanic rather than American until recently, favoring the best and the brightest.

What, then, are the advantages and disadvantages provided by the introduction of the constitution chosen by our forerunners in the Meiji era?

The Japanese after World War II have been cut off from their history. Junior and senior high school teachers may lecture that "prewar Japan failed because it had a German constitution, but postwar Japan has prospered because it adopted an American one." But the rest is dismissed.

The actual flow of history, of course, isn't that simple. One might wonder what would have happened if Japan had immediately opted for the Anglo-Saxon system instead. On their independence, many Latin American, Asian, and African countries did so. Yet most or even all those countries failed at least once to retain the system and experienced some form of military or police dictatorship.

It is not uncommon for a newly independent country to be governed by a duly elected president without a major setback until it faces the next presidential election. Since, typically, the country has never experienced a peaceful transition of power before, the outgoing president and his supporters tend to have misgivings about their future after he steps down, leading to an attempt at a constitutional amendment or a seizure of power to prolong their tenure.

Democracy can also fail in a country that aspires to modernize even where a less selfish motive is involved. In the case of Turkey, Kemal Atatürk made two attempts at free elections, believing the time was ripe for democratization, only to restore a dictatorship both times because elected parliamentarians representing the interests of the old regime actually obstructed the process. This finds a parallel in many developing countries that obtained independence after World War II. A period of "developmental dictatorship" became prevalent.

In Japan, even though a "transcendental cabinet" was successfully maintained under the new constitution, government authority was so rattled by the rise of opposition parties after the second Imperial Diet that it started interfering in elections and, at one point, even spoke of abolishing the constitution. Had the British parliamentary system been adopted from the outset, the predictable result would have been a reactionary administration suspending the constitution when seriously challenged by the opposition, and restoring an absolute monarchy, with no intention of relinquishing power. Thus, the parliamentarianism that managed to survive even during the militarism of the 1940s, when it had died out in Germany, Italy, and Spain, would already have been rejected at this point.

If that were the case, the founding of a parliamentary system would have had to start again from scratch. Once a constitution is suspended, however, it is liable to happen again and again. And if that had occurred, a representative system might never have been firmly set up in Japan.

But in reality, Meiji leaders had opted for a compromise solution in order to mitigate the uneasiness associated with an abrupt change of regime. This, by the time of Taishō Democracy, had shifted to a de facto two-party system. Seen from this angle, what Iwakura and Itō advocated under the name of "gradualism" was not just a euphemism to conceal conservatism. It was a real intermediary.

Thus, the "transcendental cabinet" under the Meiji constitution was transformed into the genuine democracy of the Taishō era. In politics, reality takes precedence over what the law stipulates. It took a degree of Japanese wisdom to get this far. Regrettably, though, this young democracy was not given enough time to become firmly embedded. In retrospect, the effects of international isolation as the result of the annulment of the Anglo-Japanese Alliance and the Great Recession of 1929 came too early. Japanese democracy was not able to withstand the current of the times.

One could justifiably argue that it was unfortunate that this was Japan's first experience of democracy. To successfully pursue this course, one needs to be armed with the lessons provided by preceding events and a sort of resigned acceptance such as that expressed in Winston Churchill's comment, "Democracy is the worst form of government except for all those other forms that have been tried from time to time." After all, it took the United Kingdom five centuries of trial and error to learn enough to find democracy. American democracy, new as it may seem, directly inherited Britain's experience.

Japan, on the other hand, failed to keep to a democratic bearing when, faced with domestic and external crises, it entrusted politics to a stronger leadership, the military, which ended in catastrophe.

From the present perspective, Japan's democracy is now one of the most robust institutions in the world. Its people have learned the hard way that a military takeover can never be a solution, no matter how deadlocked democratic politics becomes.

Carving Out a Future for Himself

While in Vienna, as his notebooks show, Mutsu worked hard. Let me quote from a letter Stein sent him:

> I wish to acknowledge that I have received your lecture notes. It gave me great pleasure to read them. It must have been a challenging task to produce hundreds of pages within only a few months, and I am deeply impressed.
>
> When one is as old as I am, one often ends up giving up midway even on something one set out with a firm determination to complete. Seeing how thorough your lecture notes are with my own eyes, I can only applaud.... I have always known that the Japanese were not only intellectually but morally impressive.... I look forward to hearing of your success after you return to your country....

It was not merely Stein who was impressed. The then Japanese minister to Vienna, Saionji, reported to Itō on two occasions how seriously Mutsu took his study: "Although he used to follow the English example, it appears he has stepped up to another level since arriving on the continent. His willingness to learn is simply astonishing."

He also wrote:

> You will find him a new man when you see him again. In my opinion, it would be a loss, not only for Mr. Mutsu himself but for our government, to let a person of his ability go to waste in the private sector. I hope he will be promptly given an official role. (I should quickly add that I am not trying to do him a favor.)

Nobody ever doubted Mutsu's talent. He also had lasting encouragement from a few people at the center of power. Nevertheless, this letter from Saionji must have reinforced Itō's trust in Mutsu and his determination to protect him.

If Mutsu had indulged in composing sentimental poems during his imprisonment, then joined other Japanese dignitaries in Europe doing little but say, "I'm too old to learn," he would not have made much of an impression in later life. Mutsu always carved out his own future with his own hand.

A great Confucian toward the end of the Tokugawa shogunate, Satō Issai (佐藤一斎, 1772–1859), wrote:

> Study hard in your youth, and you will flourish in maturity,
> Study in your maturity, and you won't fade in old age,
> Study in your old age, and you won't wither in death.

THE ORIGINS OF
JAPANESE DEMOCRACY

Building a Modern Nation-State

Consensus—a Japanese Tradition

Where should we look for the sources of Japanese democracy?

In tracing the origins of modern Anglo-Saxon democracy, scholars frequently cite a passage in Tacitus's *Germania* describing how the forest dwellers in ancient Germanic tribes sorted out their affairs; how matters of little significance were dealt with by the chief, while things of greater consequence were taken care of by the entire community.

This is very different from the decision-making process in certain parts of the East. Confucius, for instance, said, "It is easy to make people follow, but it is difficult to make them understand."

Interestingly, the final article of Prince Shōtoku's (聖徳太子, A.D. 574–622) Seventeen-Article Constitution*13 reads: "Decisions should not be made by one person alone. Although minor matters may not

---

*13 *Jūshichi-jō kenpō* (十七条憲法) is a document attributed to Prince Regent Shōtoku in 602. It was adopted in the reign of Empress Suiko.

require consultation, in general they should be deliberated by many people to arrive at an appropriate conclusion." A philosopher-king well respected in Japan, Shōtoku drew on a wide range of literature, from Buddhist texts to almost all the key Chinese classics, as sources for the wording of his document.

In contrast, many Chinese reference works, it should be pointed out, regarded "peremptory decision-making" as a virtue in a ruler. The *Guanzi*[14] to which Prince Shōtoku made reference, notes, "A wise ruler makes his own decisions by fiat after listening to the views of others." Beyond sharing the prince's opinion on the merit of listening to what others had to say, the text claimed that a good administrator should make decisions alone. And the *Han Feizi*[15] simply asserts that a propensity to make peremptory judgments is a trait befitting a national leader. In this sense, Prince Shōtoku's counsel against arbitrary rule is a distinctly original contribution to the history of Eastern thought.

Similarities between Feudal Japan and Europe

The merits of decisions made alone in answer to some crisis are illustrated throughout Chinese history in the words and deeds of heroes and kings. The same can also be said of notable figures during Japan's own Warring States period in the sixteenth century. In terms of a historical pattern, however, this period was a rather brief, exceptional interlude; throughout the rest of history Japan was more often than not managed by consensus among a group of leaders. Even today, its politics remain consensus-oriented, a fact to which a lack of strong political leadership is often attributed. Henry Kissinger after his retirement admitted that he had failed to realize that consensus was the dynamic of Japanese politics, and how rare this characteristic was.

---

*14 A compilation of Chinese philosophical materials named after the seventh-century B.C. philosopher/statesman Guan Zhong, prime minister to Duke Huan of Qi.

*15 A work written by Han Feizi at the end of the Warring States period in China, detailing his political philosophy. It is valuable for its abundance of anecdotes about politics in pre-Qin times.

Among about a hundred generations of Japanese emperors after Prince Shōtoku's time, there was no equivalent to "King Somebody the Great" in the West. Even Meiji, the hundred-and-twenty-second emperor, was quite different from his contemporary kaiser in Prussia or the Russian tsars. Emperor Meiji governed the nation based solely on the consensus reached by his ministers, and neither his personality nor his opinions directly influenced the politics of his reign.

The history of Japanese politics has always been separate from that of continental Asia. While, admittedly, the imperial court of the Nara period (奈良時代, 710–794) tried to import the political institutions of the Tang dynasty, subsequent courts followed an independent path from the Chinese model, not adopting, for instance, the examination process that was at the heart of the administrative system not only in China but in the Korean Peninsula and Vietnam. Instead, ownership of "manors" (shōen) spread in local areas, which, after the twelfth century, developed into a feudal system that was more akin to that in medieval Europe than to the centrally governed Asian state.

Edwin Reischauer, a scholar of East Asian history and former U.S. ambassador to Japan, characterized Japan as the only non-Western country that developed feudalism. He saw it as the key to the country's success in rapidly modernizing.

Compared to an autocratic monarchy where power is concentrated in the hands of one individual, the feudal system can be defined as an arrangement where power, and therefore responsibility, is more widely dispersed among feudal lords, if not among ordinary people.

Another common feature Japan shares with Europe is the historical fact that both areas narrowly escaped Mongolian conquest, thanks to two typhoons (kamikaze, or "divine wind") in the case of Japan and to the sudden death of a Mongolian leader in the case of Europe. Mongols treated the conquered more like livestock than human beings. Once a people undergoes a demoralizing experience like that, they can lack the will to resist a tyrannical ruler for generations.

Checks and Balances

In the history of Japan, one era that has long been admired as a paragon of samurai rule is the Kamakura (or Hōjō) period. Here, there existed a kind of "checks and balances" correlation between the imperial court and the shogunate, in a sense a forerunner of democracy. After all, the British parliamentary system was created to provide a form of "checks and balances" vis-à-vis the king.

Ever since its power was usurped by the samurai in the late twelfth century, the imperial court had remained alert to the slightest sign of misrule on the part of the Kamakura shogunate and of people's disillusionment with its government, giving it a chance to issue an imperial decree proscribing samurai rule. As soon as Hōjō Takatoki (北条高時, 1303–33) became regent to the shogun, though neither tyrannical nor corrupt but merely mediocre, the shogunate was overthrown. This showed how an embryonic samurai government—not long after taking power from an imperial line stretching back to the dawn of history—stood on a precarious stance, maintained only by providing good government.

Here a system of "checks and balances" worked in reverse to the British example, but with not dissimilar results.

The British historian George Macaulay Trevelyan wrote in the prologue to his *History of England* that the sources of parliamentarism and common law unique to England should be sought in the Middle Ages. *Goseibai shikimoku*, established in 1232, was a formulary of fifty-one articles based on the unwritten laws followed by samurai households at the time, when the *ritsuryō* system[16] imported from Tang China became increasingly removed from reality in areas outside Kyoto. The relations between the *Goseibai shikimoku* and the *ritsuryō* system were similar to that of common law to Roman Law. The *Goseibai shikimoku* has long remained the epitome of good government by the Hōjō shogunate. Matsuo Bashō (松尾芭蕉), the seventeenth-century haiku master, praised it with the words: "Its creation was like the rise of a bright moon."

A Council of State consisting of thirteen members was required to

---

[16] The legal system based on Chinese Legalism which was practiced between the seventh and tenth centuries.

take written vows not to be swayed by personal sentiment or to cower before authority, and to abide by the final verdict even when individually in disagreement. It was also decreed that members of the Council must vacate their seats when they themselves or their relatives were involved in the case to be discussed. This may well be behind the traditional incorruptibility and fairness of the Japanese judiciary during ensuing periods of history.

The political philosophy of Prince Shōtoku and the administrative system during the Hōjō shogunate have been passed on to generations of Japanese as the best system of government in their history. Korean philosopher and statesman Yu Ji Noh once said, "While patriotism takes different forms in different countries, the uniqueness of Japanese patriotism is attributable to people's trust in and identity with the government." Compared to other countries, Japan has been characterized by a stronger confidence in government and a more law-abiding spirit among its citizenry. Behind it is the collective memory of a good precedent, which provided a foundation for the stability of Japanese society, whether during Meiji absolutism, Taishō Democracy, or today's post World War II democracy.

After the Kamakura period, however, politics in Japan underwent a transformation quite different from the pattern of British development. Two and a half centuries of civil wars ensued, when the rule of law was necessarily weakened, until toward the end of the sixteenth century the country was unified and peace was restored. It was at this juncture that Japan encountered the West, which had already left feudalism behind. Feudalism in Japan, however, was artificially preserved for another two and a half centuries by the Tokugawa shogunate's policies. The legal system, meanwhile, continued to be developed, and during the reign of the eighth shogun Tokugawa Yoshimune the *Osadamegaki hyakkajō*, (Hundred-Article Book of Rules) was compiled. As Katsu Kaishū rightly pointed out later, this Edo document was underpinned by the *Goseibai shikimoku*.

Yet a structure of "checks and balances" did not develop during the Edo period. Under the Tokugawa shogunate, the power of the imperial court was so attenuated that until the rise of the campaign to restore the emperor toward the end of shogunate, it could not function as a counterbalance.

Feudal lords during the shogunate were divided among themselves. Aside from the Three Houses of Tokugawa, there were the *fudai daimyō*—families that had served the Tokugawa clan since before its rise to national primacy and had been promoted to feudal lords in recognition of their services—and the *tozama daimyō*, families that submitted to the Tokugawa shogunate after the Battle of Sekigahara in 1600. Given such potential adversaries as the Shimazu and Mōri clans, which had been on the losing side in that battle, the shogunate judged it would be too risky to adopt a consultative mechanism representing the entire samurai class. And as things turned out, no sooner had it sought the counsel of the feudal lords on the arrival of Perry's black ships than the stability of the regime gave way.

Thus, the feudal system during the Tokugawa era followed a unique path of development, ensuring that Japan was almost totally lacking in the rudiments of democracy when it faced the Meiji Restoration, apart from a long tradition of the rule of law and policy-making by consensus, together with a comparatively strong underlying trust between the government and the people.

What Was the Meiji Restoration All About?

Japan's political system had largely to start afresh. Which makes one wonder what the Restoration really meant.

Seen from the historical perspective of the imperial court, the Meiji Restoration was a second attempt at what the Kenmu Restoration had aimed to achieve in the early thirteenth century. In the earlier days of Meiji, when there was little historical precedence to refer to, the Kenmu Restoration was the first thing that came to mind. Mutsu, for example, in the letter of resignation he wrote in April 1868, the very first year of Meiji, referred to the Kenmu Restoration and the inequity of giving rewards to favored parties.

In his early critique of the British political system, Iwakura said, "Real administrative power there is in the hands of political parties in parliament, not the king. This is no different from Japan's experience after the Kamakura period when political power belonged to the samurai." In his view, the Meiji Restoration was essentially about the removal of power from the samurai clans—a rehash of the Kenmu Restoration.

From the perspective of Satsuma-Chōshū, on the other hand, the Restoration was an opportunity to avenge the humiliation they had suffered at the Battle of Sekigahara, which led to their being subjugated by a Tokugawa autocracy for several centuries. Some even attributed the modernization of the country to the oligarchy's break with a feudalistic system. Kabayama Sukenori, naval minister in the Matsukata cabinet, caused a stir in a speech of 1891 by saying, "Today's Japan owes its existence to Satsuma-Chōshū management."

In his 1874 treatise, *Nippon-jin*, Mutsu described the process of the Restoration as follows:

> Toward the end of the shogunate, the arrival of Commodore Perry's fleet highlighted the threat to our national security. But although this called for the entire nation's cooperation, the government instead oppressed those who dissented with it and even murdered many of them. Voices raised in good conscience cannot be silenced by tyranny. It only magnified criticism of the shogunate, leading eventually to the return of political power to the emperor.

Mutsu was obviously harking back to the French Revolution when he referred to "tyranny." He went on to argue that, to begin with, the Restoration had aimed at the elimination of cliques, whose predominance had plagued Japan from the time of the Fujiwara clan all the way down to the Tokugawa shogunate and beyond.

Addressing the same theme, Itagaki Taisuke was even more uninhibited. Like Mutsu, he criticized the long history of autocracy and defined the Meiji Restoration as a movement to "destroy the politics of rule by cliques which had for almost a thousand years encroached on the imperial court's authority, enchained people's civil rights, and brought everything to a standstill."

But he further claimed that the Restoration was "the result of an explosion of pent-up resentment at three hundred years of Tokugawa self-interest which had stifled the promotion of genuine ability. Foreign pressure only happened to add fuel to this explosion. While the pretext for the Meiji Restoration might have been reverence for the emperor or the expelling of foreigners, its true purpose was to bring down an autocratic government, wipe out a poisonous factionalism, and release the public from intense frustration. Its aim, in other words, was both to restore the authority of the emperor and to expand the power of the people."

Itagaki went on to observe that the majority of Restoration activists were from the lesser samurai clans which "didn't even have an underfed horse in their stable or enough low-grade rice to fill their stomachs." The Restoration, he concluded, was not accomplished by a handful of courtiers and landowners but as the result of public awareness and the spirit of the times.

It is a historical fact that the core of the Restoration force was made up of samurai of lower status from Satsuma and Chōshū who, under normal conditions, would not even have been permitted to discuss politics.

Under their influence, Itagaki asserted, the government had decided to adopt policies more in line with public opinion. The reforms that had resulted, however, were abandoned midway. Bureaucrats closed their ears to public sentiment. This, according to Itagaki, was what the Freedom and People's Rights Movement was up against.

Political Thought in the Twilight of One Era and the Dawn of Another

Ordinary Japanese in the Edo period had absolutely no knowledge of the political systems in the West. Although "Dutch learning" was permitted, it was confined to the study of science, technology, and medicine, while books and documents on politics or religion were strictly banned.

It was after the news reached Japan of Qing China's miserable defeat by the British in the First Opium War that people began to pay attention to politics in the West. Whereas concern for national defense had made military science and technology the main focus of attention, a succession of books introducing Western political thought began to be published after Perry's arrival.

From 1855 on, only one year after Japan opened up to the outside world, books written by British or American authors were being translated. After a while, original works by Japanese writers also began to be published. The most influential of these was *Seiyo jijō* (Things Western, published in 1867, 1868, and 1870), written by Fukuzawa Yukichi. Volume one gave an outline of politics in the West, with a clear distinction between monarchy, republic, and autocracy; volumes two and three provided detailed accounts of the political situation, particularly their governmental institutions, in the United States and the Netherlands (volume two) and the United Kingdom (volume three).

The trilogy was a smash hit, selling about one hundred and fifty thousand copies in Edo alone and another hundred thousand in the Osaka area. Considering that the entire number of samurai came to about three hundred thousand, and that in those days it was customary for friends to share books, it can be said that virtually all Japan's intelligentsia acquired a fairly accurate grasp of political systems in Europe and the United States through Fukuzawa's trilogy.

Thus, by the eve of the Restoration, the educated public had already been presented with political options from which, in the period of revolutionary change to come, they could select the one most appropriate for their country.

The knowledge thus gained was quickly reflected in the process of the Meiji Restoration.

What triggered immediate change was the return of political power to the emperor by the then shogun Tokugawa Yoshinobu. This had been promoted by Yamauchi Yōdō (山内容堂, former lord of the Tosa *han*, who advocated the union of the court and the shogunate, which in turn was advanced by Gotō Shōjirō and Sakamoto Ryōma.

Sakomoto drafted *Senchū hassaku* (Eight Proposals Made in a Boat) in 1867 on his way to Edo from Tosa by ship. After the first proposal, calling for a return to imperial power, the second urged the establishment of a bicameral parliament where every policy should be deliberated and decided by parliamentarians. It would be needless to point out that the idea behind this was derived from the bicameral system of European and American assemblies. Tokugawa Yoshinobu followed this advice, with the shortsighted intention and results already mentioned earlier in this book.

Leaders of the Meiji Restoration were at first highly idealistic. This was made obvious in the Charter Oath of March 1868 and the *Seitaisho* of April 1868 (Document on the Government System of 1868, which British diplomat Ernest Satow translated as "Constitution"), both of which were based on the concept of the equality of all classes and the handling of all national affairs by parliament.

In the very early days of the Restoration, a form of democracy was actually promoted. Each *han* and prefecture selected certain people to participate in the Kōgisho (public conference), the equivalent of a parliament. But while the participants included some who later actively contributed to progress, the majority were advocates of conservative or even reactionary thought obstructive to reform, such as the expulsion of Christians and opposition to a ban on carrying swords.

This phenomenon often appears in the process of democratization. In Turkey, for instance, Kemal Atatürk's attempts to introduce multi-party democracy were stymied by Islamic conservatives. Another example might be the Russian Duma immediately after the collapse of the Soviet Union, where the influence of the Communist Party remained prominent. Under these circumstances, as in the case of Atatürk, it made sense to go back to a dictatorship to ease the transition—a so-called "developmental dictatorship."

For the same reason, the Kōgisho did not function as expected. Though it was renamed the House of Representatives, its actual function was limited to responding to inquiries made by government members; and eventually it became inactive. The original ideal of the separation of three branches of government and implementation of parliamentary politics failed to be realized. Instead, a bureaucratic oligarchy came to the fore in the first few years after the Restoration. It was not that nobody tried to resist this trend. As we have seen, Mutsu tendered his resignation in protest. But the Satsuma-Chōshū hold on power remained unbreakable.

Japan's pursuit of democracy in subsequent years continued to be a history of attempts to establish a genuine parliament to counter the *hanbatsu*. Unlike the French or Russian Revolution, this process was not accompanied by an insurrection or war. The situation in Japan was a rare case where democratization occurred through a relatively peaceful movement led by enlightened thinkers.

Drafting the Meiji Constitution

Briefly, it is worth tracing the process from the initial hindrance to political reform in the first year of Meiji to the actual promulgation of the Meiji constitution.

It was their tour of Europe and the United States by such Meiji leaders as Iwakura Tomomi, Ōkubo Toshimichi, and Kido Takayoshi from November 1871 through September 1873 that opened their eyes to the advances made by Western civilization. Itō Hirobumi accompanied the tour as an associate delegate.

By the time of the delegation's visit, Europe and America had experienced a complete metamorphosis in the space of a hundred years, including independence, the French Revolution, and the Industrial Revolution in Britain, France, and Germany. In the early 1870s when the Japanese visitors landed, the economies of European countries had made great strides forward in the aftermath of the Franco-Prussian War, the last war in nineteenth-century Europe. Members of the delegation were bowled over by their energy.

Had it been the Europe of the sixteenth or seventeenth centuries, the one Japan had known before it went into hibernation, the delegates would not particularly have felt any inferiority or discomfort, though they might still have found the customs and lifestyle quite different from their own. For the Portuguese vessel that landed on the coast of a tiny Japanese island in 1543 brought to Japan the gun, a weapon previously unknown there. While gunpowder and firearms had been Chinese inventions, they were remodeled into modern weapons by Europeans and imported back, so to speak, to East Asia. And by the end of the sixteenth century, Japan had already become the world's largest manufacturer of small arms, indicating that there was not much of a gap in manufacturing capacity between Japan and pre–Industrial Revolution Europe. But to the eyes of the nineteenth-century Japanese, technology in post–Industrial Revolution Europe represented something that must be, and could be, caught up with sooner or later.

Yet it was the European and American political systems, rather than their technological advancement, that impressed Kido and Ōkubo more deeply, according to their own memoirs. What they saw for themselves was far removed from the political situation that had existed in seventeenth-century Europe. (In fact, the Netherlands had already developed a fairly modern political system in those days, but it went unnoticed by the Japanese.) As a consequence, the delegation concluded that the countries they inspected were prosperous and energetic because both their rulers and the ruled enjoyed inherent rights and freedoms, the citizens were given opportunities to make the most of their ability, and members of society cooperated as a whole in shoring up the foundations of their nations. Particularly, Kido was so impressed that, on his return to Japan, he immediately gave orders that an annotation of the American constitution and a translation of Charles-Louis de Montesquieu's works be produced. He even ordered the preparation of a draft constitution.

The first concrete step toward establishing a parliamentary system in Japan was taken in 1874–75.

In 1874 Itagaki submitted a written petition in favor of a popularly elected (not appointed) parliament and established the Risshisha (Self-Help Society), a political organization that later became the core of the Freedom and People's Rights Movement. As described earlier, the Meiji government set up the *Genrōin* in 1875 to bring Itagaki and Kido, who had withdrawn to his hometown Chōshū, back into the government. Mutsu also joined the *Genrōin*.

But from the outset, Itagaki's radical demand for a prompt launching of a national assembly collided head-on with Kido's gradualism. Their disagreement was reflected in a heated debate between the daily *Hōchi Shimbun*, which supported Itagaki's argument, and the pro-government *Nichinichi Shimbun*.

The government had absolutely no intention of following Itagaki's urgent demand. A growing sense of crisis prompted it instead to enact a Libel Law in 1875 to restrict freedom of speech, resulting in the imprisonment of many intellectuals. Earlier, when Saionji Kinmochi was asked during his stay in Paris if Japan had any laws impeding freedom of speech, he was able to say no, to his French friends' surprised approval. Thus the latitude of the immediate post-Restoration days had already become a thing of the past. And as a consequence, Itagaki became increasingly isolated, and eventually tendered his resignation to retire to private life.

It was from amidst these developments that support for an elected parliament gradually gained momentum. On the part of the government, Iwakura himself admitted that a constitution would be inevitable before long, and in 1876 an imperial edict was issued to start on a draft of it.

The *Genrōin* began what turned out to be speedy preparations for a constitution modeled after those in European countries and America; but their efforts were soon stalled by the social and political instability that led to the Satsuma Rebellion. Mutsu, too, was imprisoned during this period.

Then the movement for the establishment of a national assembly lost one of its prime sympathizers, Kido, who died during the rebellion. Also, after the successful suppression of the revolt, the government felt it no longer needed to make any compromise to the movement.

The draft constitution was thus rejected, with Iwakura saying he found it "unfit for Japan's national polity."

The Political Crisis of 1881

In the wake of the Satsuma Rebellion, the anti-government sentiments that had arisen like a great wave everywhere in the country began to be channeled into a more peaceful course directed at the establishment of a parliament, instead of another armed struggle. The years that followed saw the founding of political parties and the private drafting of a series of constitutions.

In 1881, however, public opinion reached boiling point again regarding the government's scandalous disposal of property held by the Hokkaido Development Office, which triggered not only a chorus of criticism by various private entities including newspapers but also a rift within the government itself. Among those consulted on how to handle the growing desire for constitutional government, Ōkuma Shigenobu argued for the immediate adoption of a British-style parliament. Since Ōkuma was not known for his political convictions, the memorandum he submitted was interpreted as a free ride on the wave of public feeling, probably with the help of the likes of Fukuzawa Yukichi. Itō and others violently opposed him.

Throughout this crisis, it was Itō who most accurately grasped the course of events, presented the most realistic solutions, and actually guided government policies.

Itō Hirobumi

Itō was born into a family belonging to a minor samurai clan. In fact, his father originally had been a peasant who was adopted by the Itō clan, making Hirobumi a son of the lowest of the lower samurai. He was fortunate, however, in serving under a well-meaning superior who helped him enter the Shōka Sonjuku, a private academy run by Yoshida Shōin, allowing him to associate with first-class people in the Chōshū *han*.

From the beginning, Itō was more of a man of action than a theorist, and Yoshida, his mentor, once described him as "a promising broker."

Itō was the type of person who would have been promoted for his usefulness under any circumstances in any period of time. He was so robust that he once made Emperor Meiji say in admiration, "Itō's healthiness is almost unhealthy." Apparently he needed very little sleep or rest. Yet he was always a good-humored and patient worker who put himself out for those around him.

In the period between the Korea debate (*Seikanron*) of 1873 and the Satsuma Rebellion of 1877, it was only Ōkubo Toshimichi from Satsuma and Itō from Chōshū, then in his mid-thirties, who supported the young Meiji government under Iwakura Tomomi. Ōkubo said about Itō, "I can't even think of another person who is as loyal, as sharp-witted, as wise, as active, or as meticulous as Itō, who can be an excellent deputy, chief secretary, and personal aide all at once."

But Itō was more than that. It often happens that a person of his application and self-confidence demands similar qualities in his subordinates and is intolerant if he doesn't find them. Itō, however, was open-minded, willing to associate with someone like Mutsu, who was constantly at odds with those around him, and, later, eager to welcome Hoshi Tōru, the most independent and uncontrollable anti-government hardliner, to his camp. He rather liked mavericks. While diligence is often incompatible with deep insight, Itō went to the trouble of studying different constitutions and took it upon himself to prepare a draft of one.

In a memorandum he wrote in 1880, he analyzed the current situation as follows: first, the rise of anti-government sentiment was largely attributable to widespread dissatisfaction among former members of the samurai class. These people were used to having an annual stipend, which freed their family of worry about living expenses and basic education. They also had the pride of men bearing official responsibility, a disposition that persisted after the regime change. The Meiji Restoration deprived hundreds of thousands of former samurai of wages and property, making them resent the new government and hanker after the recent past. Since ordinary people tended to follow their example, unrest among the newly dispossessed built up into a national crisis.

Seen even from today's perspective, Itō's analysis appears to be accurate. It was only natural for public sentiment to be unstable when a large number of the educated elite had become dissidents. In a pre-Marxist, pre-democratic society, the common people followed those better informed than themselves rather than cultivate their own views.

Peasant uprisings, even during the feudal days, had certainly taken place, but they were a different phenomenon from the campaign for the establishment of a parliament—although postwar Marxist thinkers tend to connect the two. In fact, activists in the Freedom and People's Rights

Movement, the bulk of whom came from the ex-samurai class, preferred not to identify with a grassroots movement.

Given this analysis, the government's best policy was obviously to redirect the attitude of the intellectuals among the former samurai toward a more supportive role. This was achieved twenty years later when the Jiyūtō, the largest opposition party of the time, became the core of the Rikken Seiyūkai (Friends of Constitutional Government Association), which took over the government under the presidency of Itō.

Itō was of the opinion that the Freedom and People's Rights Movement was well in line with trends in the rest of the world:

> … No nation has been immune to the influence of the French Revolution a century ago. It seems inevitable for any country to dismantle an oligarchy and start sharing political power with the people. In Japan, too, political unrest has become widespread among members of the former ruling class, and its intensity seems unstoppable. Some have conflated them with irresponsible arguments and rash, blind actions, but they should be understood in the context of a broader, global trend, like grass growing after a shower.

Anyone armed with an assessment as accurate as that is not going to hesitate about what to do next. When Itō had to persuade Iwakura, by far the most conservative person in the government, he always resorted to the justifiable reasoning, "We have no other choice, given the circumstances." When some of the activists in the Freedom and People's Rights Movement took wild, irresponsible action, his attitude prevented their hasty suppression, encouraging a certain composure in the way the government operated.

Itō was assassinated in later years by Korean patriot Ahn Jung-geun (安重根, 1879–1910). Ahn's defense counsel opposed the death sentence, quoting Itō's tolerance toward a Japanese radical who had attempted to assassinate him earlier: "Had Lord Itō survived, he might have sympathized with Ahn and would never have dreamed of imposing the death penalty on him."

In these qualities, Itō Hirobumi showed a certain greatness. He may have seemed a very different personality from Saigō Takamori, but they actually shared some traits: both believed in seeing the big picture instead of making a fuss about detail. The philosophy of "Revere heaven, love man" in the case of Saigō took the form of a tolerance that was almost nonchalant in Itō.

Itō ended his 1880 memorandum by saying, "How can we inspire confidence among people when the direction of national politics is so uncertain? What is required is an imperial edict announcing a gradual shift toward constitutional government." In 1881, he drafted the edict himself and wrote about it in as letter addressed to Iwakura: "We have no other choice, given the circumstances. Unless an early settlement is made on the issue of a national assembly, the difficulties our government faces will reach far into the future. I would say that the formation of a national assembly by 1890—give or take a year or two—should be our target."

It was on October 12, 1881, four days after this letter, that the imperial edict was issued, promising the enactment of a constitution in 1889 and the opening of a national assembly in 1890, as Ito had suggested. He also received a separate imperial request that he leave for Europe in March 1882 for a study tour on other constitutions.

Itagaki Taisuke

Aside from Itō, there is one other person who should not be overlooked in reviewing the process toward parliamentary democracy in Meiji Japan: Itagaki Taisuke, who has already been mentioned often here.

Among other notable figures of the time, Itagaki was highly unusual. As a statesman, his character has been unanimously judged to be "naïve." In fact, it would be hard to find anyone else whose innocence enabled him to truly appreciate the nature of human rights.

Itagaki had been grounded in the arts of war since his youth. During the Restoration wars, he led three thousand men in the Tosa army in an attack on the same number of samurai in Aizu, one of the last strongholds of the pro-Tokugawa forces. At the end of a desperate battle, virtually all the Aizu troops had perished, sharing the fate of their home domain.

Itagaki's personal reflections after this experience distinguished him from ordinary people. As a professional soldier, he gave serious thought to why battles were won or lost. In his judgment, if the townspeople and peasants of the Aizu *han* had joined forces with their samurai warriors against his army, he would undoubtedly have lost. But, in actuality, the civilian population fled from their domain. Itagaki attributed this development to the failure of the samurai class to build up a rapport with ordinary people during the feudal days. Since they refused to share their pleasures with the hoi polloi, the latter in turn refused to share the suffering of their superiors.

The world itself was in the grip of imperialism, when a moment's inattention might cost a nation its independence. Itagaki therefore believed that Japan must defend itself by attaining equality among its disparate classes, where both pleasure and hardship were shared among all, so that the country no longer had to depend on one class to defend itself. This pragmatic view, remarkably, was one he maintained all his life.

Itagaki attributed his own character to his samurai education. "We were taught that the ideal samurai should unconditionally despise money, not seeing, hearing, or speaking of monetary profit. Instead, he should concentrate on mastering the military arts, becoming a man of honor, and keeping his integrity."

This was a variation on the Confucian idea of the complete man—a man who, in terms of gain, thinks of virtue and who, in terms of danger, is prepared to give up his life.

Since early childhood, Itagaki had an obsession with cleanliness, so much so that "he required a full pail of water to wash his hands in and, when traveling, always brought his own rice bowl with him lest he had to use one that didn't belong to him." This obsession extended to money, inducing him to put up with poverty in an age when material wealth was rapidly developing and his former colleagues and peers were increasingly well off. All of Itagaki's comments and proposals came straight from his convictions; none came from self-interest.

In later years when he went abroad for research, some suspected that the trip was financed by an element in government that wanted, in his absence, to suppress the movement he had founded. Such accusations developed into a major crisis in his camp. Judging from testimony that was disclosed later, it seems almost certain that the funds for his tour did actually come from the government without his knowledge. But whatever the truth of it, nobody dreamed of doubting Itagaki's own honesty.

The Freedom and People's Rights Movement

Ever since Itagaki had submitted a written petition for the introduction of a popularly elected parliament in 1874, he had remained a central figure in the Freedom and People's Rights Movement of the Meiji era. As this demand gained momentum from around 1880, the desire for a national political party with a liberal focus resulted in the Jiyūtō being founded in 1881. Itagaki then became head of this party, carrying the full weight of people's expectations on his shoulders.

The Jiyūtō was the first full-fledged political party in Japan, and it has maintained a central position in the parliamentary politics of Japan until this day, giving rise to such successors as the Rikken Seiyūkai (1900–40); the Jiyūtō (1950–55); and the Jiyū-Minshutō (Liberal Democratic Party, 1955–).

When it was first formed, however, it found itself embattled, and in the brief period until its dissolution three years later, it faced a series of serious impediments.

The optimism it raised initially among the general public was considerable. Itagaki wrote in his *Jiyūtō-shi* that "the term 'jiyū' (freedom) became such a vogue word that we saw the emergence of the jiyū public bath, jiyū candy, jiyū medicine, the jiyū dance, the jiyū hat, and so on. It was an indication of people's high hopes at the time."

In April 1882, another political party, the Rikken Kaishintō (Constitutional Reform Party), was formed under the presidency of Ōkuma Shigenobu. In contrast to the radical stance of the Jiyūtō, the Rikken Kaishintō advocated gradual change and moderation. The actual difference between the two parties was confined to their style or image— rowdy Jiyūtō members vs. gentlemanly Rikken Kaishintō. In terms of policy platforms, they both pursued British-style democracy as an ultimate objective. The Rikken Kaishintō network formed another mainstream in modern Japanese politics, along with the Seiyūkai, starting with the Rikken Minseitō (Constitutional Democratic Party)—a rival party to the Rikken Seiyūkai during the Taishō Democracy—up to the Minshutō (Democratic Party) in post–World War II days.

When the leftist, anti-establishment movement was at its apex in the late 1960s—concurrently with the anti-Vietnam War movement in the United States and the generation of 1968 in Europe—people tended, erroneously, to locate the source of anti-establishment thought in Japan in the philosophy of the Jiyūtō during the Meiji era, seeing this party as supporting French-style republican politics as opposed to the Kaishintō's pursuit of British constitutional government. Admittedly, it was true that some advocates of freedom and people's rights did refer to the French Revolution and praise Jean-Jacques Rousseau. As far as their fundamental policies were concerned, however, the entire lineup of the movement's intellectual leaders, from Itagaki all the way to Nakae Chōmin (中江兆民, 1847–1901), who was later labeled as the "Oriental Rousseau" by postwar leftists, held joint government by the monarch and the people (constitutional monarchy) as the ideal polity, and none of them advocated French republicanism.

By the time the above-mentioned two parties were formed and the Freedom and People's Rights Movement had become a nationwide, political front, the government had already begun taking countermeasures against these developments.

First, it announced that it would establish a national assembly nine years later, which deprived the Freedom and People's Rights Movement of its central goal, exactly as Itō had calculated.

Secondly, the government itself began serious preparations for the formulation of a written constitution. As a first step, it sent Itō Hirobumi on an overseas study tour, allowing the one and only talent the government had to be out of the country for almost a year and a half.

Thirdly, it also encouraged such leading anti-government figures as Itagaki, Gotō, and, later, Mutsu to go abroad to observe the reality of the constitutional systems in the West. This was partly a posture, emphasizing that the times called for research instead of popular movements, but also an attempt to separate these leaders from their campaigns.

Fourthly, along with the issuing of an imperial edict on the establishment of a national assembly, it reinforced the oligarchic regime by suspending the scandal-ridden sale of government property and dismissing Ōkuma Shigenobu. This move effectively expelled a potential snake from the bosom of the government in the decade to come.

Finally, it carried out various maneuvers to weaken solidarity among the political parties and, at the same time, battened down on party activities. These measures proved to be quite effective. After they were taken, the Freedom and People's Rights Movement rapidly lost steam, the Jiyūtō was forced to dissolve in 1884, and the Kaishintō began to unravel.

A situation where an autocratic government seems likely to persist indefinitely might justify diehard radicals in risking their lives to bring it down. Even these people, though, would hardly feel the same way if their actions served merely to shorten the time in which the government promised to set up a national assembly. The same thing could also be said about their financial sponsors, which resulted in the Jiyūtō suffering from a shortage of funds. Consequently, moderates in the party decided to temporarily suspend some of their political activities, while isolated radical elements became increasingly militant.

Because these elements were, as Itō had correctly spelled out, discontented former samurai who lived to express their frustration through political action, the promise of eventually establishing a national assembly would certainly not have appeased them. Moreover, when the restrictions imposed by government officials were clearly unjustifiable in their severity, they were not going to knuckle under. Consequently, a series of bloody clashes between Jiyūtō radicals and police authorities erupted in various regions, uncontrolled by the party leadership.

The drama surrounding these violent events ensured that they were passed down from generation to generation. The left-wing historical view after World War II even made them central to the whole Freedom and People's Rights Movement. This, however, is a distorted view. The fighting was the result of rogue behavior by certain partisans against the will of the Jiyūtō mainstream, including Itagaki.

From Civil to Sovereign Rights

The mid-1880s also saw a major transition from a public concern for civil rights to sovereign rights. In 1884, the Kapsin Political Coup erupted on the Korean Peninsula. This was an attempted coup d'etat by Korea's Gaehwapa (Enlightenment Party), which urged rapid Westernization after the Japanese model in expectation of Japanese assistance, but was put down by Chinese garrison forces. Japan had no choice but to back out in the face of China's military superiority. This humiliation gave rise to widespread nationalism in Japan for the first time since the Meiji Restoration. As discussed later in detail, when the Beiyang fleet of Qing China made a port call in Nagasaki in August 1886 the memory of the earlier showdown was still fresh. The arrival of the *Dingyuan* (定遠) and the *Zhenyuan* (鎮遠), the world's most advanced battleships, was taken as an act of intimidation, adding fuel to the popular sense of outrage.

Government criticism was reinforced by two other factors: former members of the dissolved Jiyūtō and Kaishintō joined forces under the slogan a "Great Coalition" (*Daidō danketsu*); and nationalistic sentiment was further aroused by the process of remedying the unequal treaties with the Western powers, as we will see in Chapter XI.

The prevailing current was moving from civil rights to the sovereign rights of the nation.

IX

THE DAWN OF
CONSTITUTIONAL
GOVERNMENT

A Samurai Democracy to Be Proud of

Legacy of the Meiji Constitution

The Freedom and People's Rights Movement fulfilled its mission in 1881: that year, the government was forced to make a public commitment to forming a national assembly within nine years. This was a critical outcome for a movement with that explicit aim.

For its part, the Meiji government adhered to its pledge. It had no intention of sabotaging or delaying it. Remarkably, advocates of the movement, including Itagaki Taisuke, never doubted that it would keep its promise despite periodic acts of repression—an example, rare in political history, of mutual trust.

It should be emphasized that during those nine years, the Meiji government had done its own groundwork.

In August 1883, immediately after his fact-finding trip to Europe, Itō embarked on reforming government institutions. In 1885, he established a cabinet system by abolishing the traditional Grand Council of State, and became the first prime minister. From 1886 to 1887, he focused on drafting the constitution. On resigning as prime minister in 1888, he set up and headed a Privy Council with the constitution its chief agenda. After a series of deliberations in the presence of Emperor Meiji, the council adopted the final draft of the Meiji constitution in January 1889. This was formally promulgated on February 21. Itō was forty-nine.

During a three-month summer retreat on Natsushima Island in 1887, Itō, though he was prime minister at the time, conferred with his colleagues like a fellow student. Itō Miyoji (伊東巳代治) described his stay as follows:

> We debated even during meals, and didn't stop talking until eleven or twelve o'clock at night unless we were writing something. It was the most peculiar three months we ever had. When Inoue Kowashi (井上毅, 1844–95) and I challenged something that Lord Itō put forward, he did his best to defend his argument until we had him cornered. When he started yelling "You crafty bastard!" at me and "You rotten Confucian!" at Inoue, we knew we'd won. The morning after this sort of exchange, he'd come to us and say, "About the thing we discussed last night, I've decided to let you rotten Confucians have your way."

While he was at Yoshida Shōin's private school, Itō was known for reading popular historical tales rather than some academic work, so it was surprising that, later in life, he could devote so much attention to the study of constitutional matters. Not only did he edit what others had drafted, but he also wrote his own material. His brilliance lay in his flexibility and versatility, as well as his determination to take his country forward. While people nowadays would probably say that legal matters are better left to legal experts, Meiji leaders had a sense of responsibility and the self-confidence to do whatever was necessary themselves, as there were no such experts around.

Itō's book *Kenpō gikai* (憲法義解, Commentary on the constitution) is still considered a work of unparalleled authority on the subject. And during the deliberations of the Privy Council, he repeatedly had to provide a rational defense of his thinking against criticism from conservatives.

Unfortunately, Japan's present constitution did not emerge in the same process. If its wording were a true reflection of the people it represented, it would be a great legacy, based on the long quest for liberal democracy. But the Japanese public has never been able to regard it as more than a translation of an English document hastily written by the Occupation forces.

Applause for the New Constitution

The Meiji constitution, essentially Prussian in nature, was welcomed by all parties including the opposing Jiyūtō and Kaishintō, which had originally wanted an Anglo-Saxon system. On its publication, all political prisoners were released in a general amnesty. According to Itagaki's *Jiyūtō-shi*, "the entire country was in a happy, triumphant mood, as if a war had been won. It was the culmination of a long-term dream and celebrated as though the strife of yesterday was forgotten in one night." And "people who had been risking their lives for these goals until just yesterday were now at peace and linked in friendship." This was endorsed by all the major newspapers' editorials.

Some history books written after World War II referred to a number of opponents of the Meiji constitution, and mentioned among them Nakae Chōmin's snide disapproval on his first acquaintance with it. But they exaggerated, under the influence of postwar recalcitrance. The actual mood of the overwhelming majority of people then, including intellectuals, was one of acclaim.

First General Election

The first general election of the House of Representatives was held on July 1, 1890, a month and a half after Mutsu took the post of minister of agriculture and commerce.

It was the first election ever to be held by a Japanese constitutional government. All references to this election acknowledge that it was free of intervention or corruption.

To quote Itō Chiyū:

> When you compare today's elections with those of the past, it is striking how different they have become.
>
> While there might have been some votes influenced by personal considerations, there was absolutely no vote buying. All candidates, including unimportant ones, were leading people in their respective communities, and most were figures of national renown. Regardless of the outcome, voters held them in respect.

"Votes influenced by personal considerations" refers to those affected by canvassing by relatives or acquaintances on behalf of a particular candidate—a common enough event nowadays, but regarded then as contrary to the spirit of a free election.

Okazaki Kunisuke, Mutsu's younger cousin and confidant, left the following observations in *Kensei kaikoroku* (憲政回顧録, Memoir on parliamentary government), published in 1935:

> From my experience, the only elections that have been carried out as they should be were the first and second general elections. Since there was already a hint of corruption in the second one due to government intervention, however, probably the only election in the past forty years that genuinely deserves to be called fair and square was the first, in 1890. This was held at a time when people's knowledge was still relatively low and the level of civilization behindhand, yet it was admirably done. In contrast, today's elections are regarded as corrupt despite higher levels of civilization and education. It makes one wonder what civilization and education are all about....
>
> The first election was ideal for two reasons: first, people had great expectations and an enthusiasm for a parliamentary government; and second, the Japanese are not by nature dishonest. An election smeared with dishonesty was simply unthinkable for people at the time.

Having seen the last of feudalist rule, the public felt inspired to improve themselves. People were convinced of their ability to loosen the heavy hand of the Satsuma-Chōshū clique and its bureaucracy, and began to view themselves as a driving force in the nation's future. Reflecting the general mood, the first election was a competition among local communities all over Japan to select representatives who could be entrusted with state affairs in place of the oligarchs.

The type of ambitious person who dared to run for election on his own was likely to be viewed with disfavor. Men of character without necessarily a desire to run for office were voted into Diet seats, sometimes against their will. Some were even elected without knowing they had been selected as candidates....

Any chance of vote buying was forestalled by the nature of campaign fundraising at the time: campaigns were fully financed by voters, including a few wealthy volunteers, without any financial burden on the candidates. For this reason, expenses for an election campaign remained small despite the absence of restrictions. All this made for the one and only election that deserves to be called a model of its kind both in name and substance.

Being a prominent figure in Wakayama prefecture, Mutsu had overwhelming support from the local population. Even during his tenure at the Japanese embassy in the United States, voters in his district nominated him as their candidate and voted him in.

This at least applied to the Wakayama 1st District. Things were different in the 2nd District. Okazaki writes:

After a strenuous search, voters in the 2nd District decided to nominate as their candidate, without his consent, a certain Mr. Matsumoto, a former governor of Wakayama prefecture with a good record who had retired from public life.... All campaign expenses, starting with those for public appearances and well-wishers' gatherings, were borne by volunteer supporters.... Matsumoto offered to repay them out of his annual allowance as a Diet member, but his supporters refused, saying it was only natural for them to finance his campaign because they had asked him to represent them.

The problem was solved by both sides agreeing to offer Matsumoto's donation to a different organization.

Similar phenomena were reported elsewhere. For instance, Ōe Taku, who had been imprisoned with Mutsu in 1877, ran for the 5th District of Iwate prefecture, the very location of his prison, and won. To quote some paragraphs from Ōe Tenya den (大江天也伝, A biography of Ōe Tenya):

Mutsu around 1890 (middle). Photo taken upon returning home to Wakayama.

> In those days, political prisoners were rarely seen as criminals and, in fact, were often regarded as honorable men. Some of the local people, realizing that Ōe Taku and Hayashi Yūzō had been locked up in the prison there, even declared that it was an honor to have them in their prefecture.
>
> When the general election was announced, volunteers from Iwate went straight to Tokyo to persuade Ōe to run for a seat. At first he was unwilling, saying, "I'm not interested, politics is a rotten business." But he was eventually persuaded, warning them that "I may be useless in politics. I'm penniless. If you still insist on making me a representative, I may become a waster, doing it just for the fun of it."

After a successful first term as chairman of the House Budget Committee, Ōe was again "forced" to run in the second general election. But this time, his persistent refusal to visit his constituency cost him his reelection, stoked by heavy government prejudice. After his defeat, he received a letter from his Iwate supporters apologizing for not running a more successful campaign, and thanking him for making it a much better constituency.

Bitterness

Had Japan's politics succeeded in retaining the fairness shown in the first general election, the country might have become the world's most effective "samurai democracy."

What, then, changed this almost ideal process to a more worldly one in a short space of time? Okazaki Kunisuke claims that it was governmental interference:

> The second election in 1892 was disrupted by the administration putting pressure on the parties standing against it. This notorious "intervention" marked the beginning of electoral corruption, the derailing of constitutional politics, and the numbing of the public's conscience.

At a glance, his *Kensei kaikoroku* would seem to be philosophical and detached, but the bitterness it conveys is apparent.

When the book was published in 1935, a militaristic mood prevailed in the country. Frustrated by party politics, the public and the press alike appeared to favor a new regime led by military officers and reformist bureaucrats. The system established in the Meiji era seemed to have come to an end.

Only three months after its publication, the February 26 Incident occurred, a prelude to military despotism. During this attempted coup, Okazaki, aged eighty-four, went around snowbound Tokyo trying to salvage what remained of the Seiyūkai. The effort cost him his health, and he died the following summer.

As Mutsu's successor, Okazaki devoted his entire life to the cause of party politics. A member of the House of Peers, a witness to the prosperity of Taishō Democracy, he must have found these threatening events heartbreaking.

A paragraph toward the end of the book reads:

> It took thirty-five hard years to achieve what only lasted eight: between the formation of the Katō three-faction cabinet of 1924 and the fall of the Inukai cabinet in 1932. Party politics may not lie

buried forever, but it will take intense analysis of what went wrong and a firm desire to change for the better to resurrect it.

By the mid-1930s, a disillusioned public looked for a remedy from clean, upright military officers, with reformist bureaucrats, centered on the Home Ministry, leading the chorus demanding more disciplined elections. But Okazaki, early in his book, pointed out that it was precisely bureaucratic intervention that had poisoned past elections. No bureaucracy, he argued, could reform or replace the role of a free, representative electoral system.

Treachery of the Tosa Faction

During the first general election of 1890, one hundred and thirty Rikken Jiyūtō candidates and forty-one Rikken Kaishintō candidates were elected, winning an absolute majority for the anti-*hanbatsu* parties out of the three hundred parliamentary seats available.

These immediately proposed a ten percent cut in the eighty million yen government budget. They insisted on removing all unnecessary government expenditure from the budget, which had never been screened by the Diet. They also asserted that an overburdened public deserved the benefit of a ten percent tax cut.

In an attempt to reach a compromise with the opposition parties, the administration offered to trim the budget by some six million yen, while preserving military-related funding. During these negotiations, twenty-six Tosa members of the Jiyūtō defected from the party and supported the government proposal. This was what is known as the "treachery of the Tosa faction."

Mutsu, who had joined the cabinet in 1890 as minister of agriculture and commerce and maintained close relations with Tosa, was also behind the compromise. Having closely observed parliamentary management in the United States as the Japanese minister to Washington, he was convinced that compromise, as well as confrontation, was necessary in a democracy.

As will be discussed in more detail in Chapter XI, the greatest diplomatic issue for the Japanese government since the Meiji Restoration was the revision of unequal treaties with the Western powers. In order to accomplish this, it was felt to be essential for Japan to show the world that it was a civilized nation on an equal footing with its counterparts. This applied also to its ability to handle a democratic political system.

The people of the Tosa faction shared this conviction. Ōe Taku, who was chairman of the House Budget Committee, left the following description in his memoir:

> There were differences of points of view between myself and the parties opposed to oligarchic rule. The latter were completely against whatever the government proposed, taking pride in their opposition. Understandably, they could not be expected to study the content of the budget in detail and to comment on each and every item. But I personally was more mindful of the overall management of parliamentary politics than just the budget itself. In those days, it was a common enough belief abroad that a constitutional system wouldn't work yet in East Asia, and that it was premature for Japan to adopt one. Given this outlook, I felt our priority should be to demonstrate that we were capable of engaging in parliamentary politics by debating the budget in the Diet, issue by issue, and reaching compromises between the government and parliament.... My refusal to cut even a penny from the army and navy budgets was surely justified by their impressive record in the Sino-Japanese War, which erupted within three years of the budget controversy.

It was again Itagaki Taisuke who played a leading role in the budgetary process, insisting on letting the budget pass by trimming six million off it. *Kensei kaikoroku* commented:

> Young Diet members who had experienced bloodshed and imprisonment for the cause of the Freedom and People's Rights Movement were unwilling to listen to him. In response, he declared that,

as the head of the Rikken Jiyūtō, he would have no other choice but to leave the party, taking like-minded members with him if the hardliners prevailed.

The author added: "I feel like taking my hat off to him even today. His convictions were as solid as a mountain. His top priority was always serving the country."

As promised, when the majority of the party sided with the extremists' argument, Itagaki led moderate members out of the party he had headed.

Compromise in the First Imperial Diet

In the background of this episode was the process through which the Meiji constitution was drafted. Interestingly, it was advisors from Prussia, the experts concerning the constitution, who constantly put forward more conservative and undemocratic ideas than the Japanese drafters.

Itō had the following to report on Rudolf von Gneist, under whom he had studied while in Europe: "[Prof. Gneist judged that] parliament might raise radically obstructive arguments if it were given a say on the budget. In the present circumstances, it would be prudent to allow them at this early stage only very limited authority."

And it was Albert Mosse, one of Gneist's disciples and a legal advisor on the Meiji constitution, who clashed with Inoue Kowashi on giving the Diet the right to approve the budget.

In the end it was decided, contrary to the advice of the Germans, that under the Meiji constitution any increase in government expenditure required the approval of the Imperial Diet.

Parliament thus had a controlling hand in budget matters at a time of rapid economic growth and military buildup. Party politics was in fact introduced in Japan earlier than in Germany, where no government representing a majority in parliament existed until 1919.

What would have happened if the budget proposal had been rejected, failing to secure the support of the Tosa faction? The government would have been obliged to dissolve parliament, with no guarantee that its party could win a majority again, however often parliament was dissolved in the future. Rejection might even have precipitated the abolishing of the constitution, sending the country back to the drawing board. It was rumored, incidentally, that Emperor Meiji himself had confided to an aide that establishing an Imperial Diet may have been premature.

Had the constitution been scrapped and autocratic government restored, the country would have retained the ability to wage the First Sino-Japanese War, but would have lost whatever international reputation it had gained, making the revision of international treaties all the more difficult. Most importantly, it isn't certain that genuine democracy would have been attained, albeit briefly, in the subsequent Taishō era— the genesis of today's democracy in Japan. In fact, when Japan lost the Pacific War, Edwin Reischauer, who later became the U.S. ambassador, advised that Japan should resurrect its Taishō Democracy, the value of which was readily accepted by the public at large.

The first Imperial Diet ended its term so successfully that Chairman of the House of Peers Itō stated in the closing statement, "This year's session has been our first attempt to apply the new constitution. Nowhere else in the world has been able to do this in as fair and orderly fashion at its initial stage. I wish to express my gratitude to all my fellow Diet members for their efforts."

A Promising Start

The process had indeed been unique. All of Europe experienced democratic revolutions after the Napoleonic Wars, though Russia, the only country that France had failed to subjugate, stayed put. In contrast, Japan underwent a largely bloodless revolution under the pressure of a nationwide campaign by intellectual leaders in a quest for freedom and people's rights. If there were foreign influences at all, they remained about as indirect and cerebral as, for example, the effect of French enlightenment thought on British parliamentarianism.

Britain, the United States, France, and the Netherlands shared with Japan the fact that their revolutions were carried out without any foreign assistance. But four of them took place in the abnormal circumstances of a war or through bloodshed. The 1581 Declaration of Human Rights in the Netherlands was issued in the midst of a war of independence with Spain. Britain's 1689 Bill of Rights was declared immediately after the invasion by William of Orange. The 1776 Declaration of Independence of the United States was, of course, the product of its war of independence. And, needless to say, a lot of blood was shed during the French Revolution in 1789.

Japan was the only one, belatedly, to bring into being a peaceful parliamentary government, though like other Asian independent states in the nineteenth century—China, Korea, Siam, Persia, Turkey, and Egypt—it had experienced its own kind of "expelling foreigners" movement.

What happened in Japan was a natural course of events. Crucial was the vigor and yearning for reform maintained not only by anti-oligarchy libertarians like Mutsu but central figures of the Restoration such as Saigō Takamori and Itagaki Taisuke, who contributed to regime change in pursuit of ideals frustrated by the subsequent corruption of power. It is no surprise that the Freedom and People's Rights Movement became the centerpiece of the spiritual and political activities of disaffected members of a once dominant class for whom the Korean issue and the Satsuma Rebellion gave no relief.

Political change was an indication of a high cultural standard. Few other countries fostered such a wide stratum of highly politicized, educated individuals in the mid-nineteenth century intent on the emergence of a new social order.

The Jiyūtō's success in developing such a wide support base had a prolonged influence in subsequent years, and spawned a variety of political offshoots. The ensuing Taishō Democracy laid down foundations that survived practically intact through even the militaristic period. And it was only natural that in the immediate postwar turmoil, the Japanese people, still nostalgic for the 1920s, should want to return to a reign of parliamentary politics.

As a curious piece of incidental information: the Glorious Revolution was launched in 1689 in Britain; the French Revolution took place in 1789; the Meiji constitution was announced in 1889; and in 1989 the Berlin Wall fell as change swept through Eastern Europe. Sheer coincidence, but great celebratory democratic events seems to have occurred every hundred years in different corners of the world.

X

First Setback for the Parliamentary Democracy

Bloody Intervention in the Election

The Matsukata Cabinet and Its Diet Relations

The first Imperial Diet made an impressive start. Its significance, however, was fully understood by only a few pioneers, such as Itō, Mutsu, and Itagaki.

The compromise involved in passing the budget did not satisfy either side. The concession was merely linked to the "treachery of the Tosa faction" by anti-*hanbatsu* hardliners, while it represented a humiliation for the majority of the Satsuma-Chōshū oligarchs, whose political goals for the next election were now to interfere with and weaken the power of those in opposition. Japanese democracy was again hard-pressed.

The Yamagata cabinet steered the first session of the Imperial Diet to a successful end, but Yamagata Aritomo (山県有朋, 1838–1922), whose health had suffered in the unfamiliar job of managing parliamentary politics, then resigned as prime minister. No one was willing to succeed him. Eventually, in May 1891, Matsukata Masayoshi from Satsuma was appointed, it being Satsuma's turn to form a new cabinet.

Mutsu was immediately aware that the second session was heading for trouble, and embarked on creating a platform based on a consensus among cabinet members. The effort resulted in a voluminous document called *Naikaku giketsusho* (内閣議決書, A guideline on cabinet decision-making), which aimed to unify the statements the cabinet made to the Diet as well as to the press—a common practice nowadays, but a novelty then.

Opposition to this came from Home Minister Shinagawa Yajirō, whose views on Diet proceedings differed radically from those of Itō and Mutsu. Shinagawa did not regard the compromise during the first Imperial Diet as a breakthrough but a disgrace. Far from wanting to improve the way the government functioned, he was violently opposed to any further concessions to the anti-*hanbatsu* parties, believing that the Diet should be dissolved as many times as it would take to eliminate the opposition should they reach a stalemate.

Mutsu next proposed to establish an Office of Parliamentary Affairs (Seimubu, 政務部) within the cabinet. This office, which would be led by a cabinet-level director and staffed by senior officials from the various ministries, was designed as a channel through which relations with parliament could be maintained when the cabinet itself was unable to do so. Again, Shinagawa, who might have been expected to chair it, was opposed. Mutsu, having shown in the first Diet that he was almost alone in effectively dealing with a divided parliament, was pressed into taking the job himself. He repeatedly declined the offer, afraid of resentment from the *hanbatsu*, but finally accepted after constant persuasion by Itō.

The creation of the Seimubu was reported to Emperor Meiji on August 13, 1891. On August 17, the emperor summoned Matsukata and presented him with a formal request to unify the cabinet's efforts in dealing with state affairs. Less than a month after the imperial message was conveyed, however, Mutsu resigned as director, allowing the Seimubu to become virtually extinct.

Mutsu was disappointed at the way the institution had been treated by other cabinet members. They largely ignored the Seimubu and did as they pleased. He was not provided with a secret budget for political maneuvering. Some complained that he acted high-handedly. Shinagawa, for example, told him, "If you have to be so critical, why don't you become home minister yourself?" He earned the nickname "Razor Blade," with one colleague saying in a letter to Itō, "I don't think the cabinet is using its razor properly."

Mutsu had a history of being one step ahead of people, creating predictable antipathy: when he undertook to have the *han* abolished; when he built up a modern army; and when he tried to make the *Genrōin* a de facto legislature.

Despite these setbacks, he continued to take new initiatives. He had nothing to be ashamed of, as most of what he did later proved to be effective. Others were simply not as quick-witted.

But this time, even Mutsu accepted that the situation was hopeless. The innovation was a good one, but the prime minister had not acknowledged its significance and wasn't resourceful enough to supervise it anyway. It was not until the next arrival of the Itō cabinet that Mutsu was able to demonstrate his parliamentary skills.

Imperial Diet Dissolved

Along with the failure of the Seimubu, it became apparent that the Matsukata cabinet would collapse if left unattended. Mutsu tried to persuade Inoue to save the situation, but the latter was pessimistic: "They don't feel a sense of urgency, and won't listen to advice. We might as well let them learn a lesson from their own mistakes."

Mutsu also tried to encourage Itō to take some action, sending him a letter on October 3 saying, "I don't think you can sit by and watch the government sink into disarray. We've come this far in twenty-four years since the Restoration." But Itō too, had run out of patience. Toward the end of October, he wrote to Inoue: "In a letter addressed to various people including yourself as well as Yamagata, Kuroda, Itagaki, and Ōkuma, I have made it clear that I can no longer be bothered by state affairs, and that everyone should go their own way." This provoked an unhappy reply: "I hate being included in the list of recipients of your letter. I would rather be among those who refused to support the cabinet."

By this time, Itō had started to consider seriously organizing his own political party. Although he had been an earlier advocate of a "transcendental cabinet," he had soon come to terms with the true nature of a parliamentary system and accepted that party politics was the only viable option for Japan. He had already foreseen that no fundamental solution could come from any remedy attempted under the Matsukata cabinet.

Nevertheless, Mutsu refused to give up and continued to propose various possible strategies. One was that the government submit an overinflated budget that would include six to seven million yen of unnecessary expenditures; they would then be able to cut the surplus in response to demands from the opposition. Of course, this strategy would require a secret deal with leaders of the opposition parties beforehand, but it might save the government.

Mutsu was the kind of person who was always willing to put duty ahead of personal preferences. He drafted Japan's first budget under Ōkuma whom he despised. Later, he wholeheartedly supported Ōkuma in the revision of the unequal treaties. But, in spite of his efforts, the second Imperial Diet was doomed without Itō's cooperation. Although a budget was submitted on November 30, none of the newly proposed projects were approved by the Diet, quickly resulting in its dissolution on December 25.

Government Intervention

According to *Kensei kaikoroku*, the dissolution of the Diet was when Japan's constitutional politics began to go seriously astray:

> After the anti-*hanbatsu* government parties had delivered a crushing blow to the government by forcing a nearly ten percent cut in government expenditures during the first Imperial Diet, they carried out thorough policy research during the one-year interval which allowed them to give another decisive blow to the government during the second Diet. These actions immensely harmed the pride

of the *hanbatsu*, causing it to stigmatize the anti-*hanbatsu* parties as nothing more than rebels. By this time, the government was convinced that there was no other choice than to dissolve the Diet and hope that the public elected as many pro-government moderate representatives as possible in the next election. The government used a budget cut equivalent to approximately one-sixth of the previous year's budget as an excuse to dissolve the second Diet.

Although the Diet was initially established by an ideally implemented election, it was dissolved arbitrarily by the government during the second Imperial Diet. There was no chance of carrying out a fair election as the government had every intention to intervene from the very beginning.

As expected, the second general election resulted in a chaotic political battle between anti-*hanbatsu* government and pro government parties, with incidents involving murder, assault, and intimidation. On the part of the government, Home Minister Shinagawa Yajirō, an old-fashioned politician with retrograde views on people's rights and freedom, led the election campaign. Shinagawa ordered prefectural governors and local police chiefs to suppress the anti-*hanbatsu* government parties and support the pro-government parties. Backed by the minister's order, the governors and chiefs, who themselves were obsessed with petty feudal official mentalities, intervened radically in the election.

Police chiefs leading a band of outlaws in threatening anti-*hanbatsu* government parties were among the most innocent of the incidents. Some governors even wielded their sword canes and led radical anti-*hanbatsu* campaigns themselves, resulting in hundreds of cold-blooded killings and injuring more than four hundred people. In constituencies where anti-*hanbatsu* government party candidates were prevailing, pro-government supporters even forged or destroyed ballots. When ballot forgery was discovered in Tosa and legal action was taken by anti-*hanbatsu* government parties, pro-government groups threw the ballot boxes into the sea to conceal the evidence of their crime en route to the Osaka courthouse.

Furthermore, pro-government groups urged local dignitaries to stand in the election by offering them campaign funds and other benefits, establishing the basis for future corruption.

Shinagawa made his position clear in a public statement:

> During the second Imperial Diet, the opposition made spurious claims that ran contrary to the authority of the emperor [presumed to mean the demand to cut the budget], resulting in an imperial order to dissolve the House of Representatives. Believing that another win for these rabble-rousers would jeopardize the state's security, I decided as home minister to resort to all possible means to intervene in the general election and replace miscreants with loyal and conscientious people. I promise that I would interfere again in future elections to cut out this blight should a similar situation emerge.

Shinagawa was an authority on the Confucian Wang Yangming, and a former student of Yoshida Shōin. To those on the lookout for a strong man of firm beliefs who saw the radical opposition as "public enemies" disloyal to the emperor and the state, he made good sense.

Mutsu Standing Fast

Mutsu expressed his firm opposition to the dissolution of the Diet and official interference in elections in his autobiography:

> On March 14, the twenty-fifth year of Meiji, I resigned from my cabinet post.... The government dissolved the House. I was strongly against this happening without any clear future plan, but the majority of the cabinet would not listen. The public was infuriated by illegal interference in free elections, which again I openly deplored. So I resigned.

In point of fact, Mutsu had wanted to resign ever since standing down as director of the Seimubu. But the cabinet kept him on out of concern that he would become a bastion of dissent if he was discharged. It had taken real courage to stand up against his colleagues almost singlehandedly, without any support from the oligarchs.

According to Takekoshi Yosaburō's (竹越与三郎, 1865–1950) *Heishū josanki* (萍聚絮散記, Tales of great people from the Meiji era), when he was advised to be a little more tolerant as a cabinet minister, Mutsu was grateful for the suggestion but replied, "I have no backing from my masters. I have nobody but myself to rely on. If I compromise on my principles even an inch, I cease to exist." He had a firm idea of how parliamentary politics should operate. He had no reason to be bothered with unenlightened cabinet members. He wasn't going to prevaricate, even if it made him numerous enemies.

One principle of this, which causes no surprise today and stemmed presumably from his knowledge of Western politics, made him urge the prime minister to ensure that officials who had allegedly tampered with the previous election be investigated and duly punished if proven guilty. It is no surprise, either, that Matsukata refused. Mutsu tendered his resignation immediately after this proposal was rejected.

A Remote Cause of Decline

The following quote from *Kensei kaikoroku* might digress a little from the subject of this chapter, but it gives some clue as to the underlying cause of the decline of prewar democracy, the main reason for which is assumed to be corruption. No other book seems to give a more accurate account of the development of representative government and a more despondent view of its degeneration.

> Despite official interloping, an anti-*hanbatsu* coalition in the second general election won a landslide victory over a party that secured less than one-third of the seats. The outcome reflected a loathing of the oligarchy that enabled its opponents from the very beginning to fight against it.
>
> Although political infighting continued to impede the development of Japan's constitutional politics until the First Sino-Japanese War, the process of candidate selection and fund raising in the anti-*hanbatsu* parties was conducted in a reputable way, maintaining the standards of the first election. In my own case—a second

candidacy, having won the by-election held in response to Mutsu's resignation—my campaign expenses were limited to setting up a campaign headquarters in Wakayama city.

In contrast, the pro-government parties spent a great deal to gain support for candidates running without being nominated by voters. These costs included fees for transportation and office rental as well as various gatherings and banquets. So-called election brokers, detested in today's elections (the 1930s), are an outgrowth of the pro-government campaign in the second election.

When did vote buying begin? It is impossible to pinpoint the date, but it must have begun soon after the second election in which the government trampled on the free will of voters in ways that included entertaining them with food and drink. The probity of elections was maintained over long periods of time in constituencies where the anti-*hanbatsu* parties prevailed, but corruption became rampant in areas where the two sides competed neck and neck.

Vote buying became nationwide during and after the 1914 general election staged by the Ōkuma cabinet. By then, the oligarchy bureaucrats unanimously believed that the Seiyūkai had abused its position as the majority party.... Intent on reining it in, Ōkuma dissolved the House of Representatives in December 1914 when the government proposal to increase army divisions was rejected by the House. Ōkuma and members of his party, the Rikken Dōshikai, had good reason to devote themselves to the election campaign: for Ōkuma, it was his first chance to lead a cabinet since his first one in 1898; and for his party, it was a great opportunity to take the lead over the Seiyūkai, on which they had long kept a jealous eye.

First, Ōkuma appointed Agriculture Minister Ōura as home minister with responsibility for using the police force, the pet tool of the cabinet, on their behalf. Two elder statesmen, Yamagata and Inoue, asked the big conglomerates for support and succeeded in raising a huge amount of campaign funds, establishing an unprecedentedly "inflated" election.

It was also around this time that the activities of election brokers became conspicuous. One began to hear rumors of how some had made enough money by embezzling election funds to build houses for themselves, while others were said to have used it to set up mistresses. And having tasted the forbidden fruit, they weren't inclined to stop. Candidates were aware that they were being drawn into wrongdoing, but continued to rely on the brokers rather than risk losing the election. This sometimes meant spending a tremendous amount of money. In extreme cases, it might mean withdrawing simply for lack of cash.

The *Kensei Kaikoroku* continued:

I believe that it was during the 1924 election under the so-called "cabinet of the three pro-constitution factions" (*Goken Sanpa Naikaku*, 護憲三派内閣) that a Seiyūkai candidate asked for the authorization fee to be paid by his party. Customarily, this happened the other way around. The request was like a tenant asking a landlord to pay his rent for him. The demand seemed ridiculous, but set a trend. One only has to look at the situation today to know.

While there are various views on the reasons for corrupt party politics, the primary cause is undoubtedly costly elections. Politics did not become expensive because of corrupt political parties; on the contrary, parties became corrupt because of expensive politics.

No matter how clever or virtuous a politician might be, he would not be able to run as a candidate or become influential in his party without any financial resources, forcing him to work hard to raise campaign funds. On the other hand, a politician would be in a position to have a controlling influence at a high level if he could provide the party with a sufficient amount of money during elections. Unlike earlier elections, today's cost several million yen, leading inevitably to inappropriate relations between political parties and corporate powerhouses.

In a climate where politics was seen to be all about money, it became tempting to think that only the affluent, no matter how unprincipled they might be, could afford to be elected. Ambitious politicians, rather than cultivating the qualifications appropriate in a representative, spent their time cultivating the rich.

A Canker in Parliamentary Democracy

In post–World War II Japan, at least until the 1980s, newspapers have often identified districts that have been awash with money whenever a general election or party presidency election has been held. They have carried stories about the rise of young legislators to become party president or prime minister with huge private assets acquired along the way. Weekly magazines have published photos of the lavish homes of members of both ruling and opposition parties that are miles out of reach of ordinary people.

What seems to be the direct cause of the problem, however, can be attributed to the early destruction of clean elections by people like Shinagawa with absolutely no appreciation of constitutional politics. Some might also argue that the limited suffrage of slightly more than one percent of the population contributed to the rectitude of the first election. But this was not necessarily so. For some thirty years until the introduction of universal suffrage, voting rights had only gradually expanded to the level of about five percent, though corrupt practices were now common during the same period.

Neither does mass politics necessarily breed corruption. Political crime is almost unheard of in the present United Kingdom, the birthplace of parliamentary democracy, as well as in countries that have inherited its parliamentary tradition, such as Australia and New Zealand, where it has remained untainted for over a century.

Does this imply that the Japanese are by nature liable to corruption? This seems unlikely. Most of the population are patently honest and upright people. Cheating a customer at a cash register just doesn't happen. The frugal lifestyles of its business leaders are unmatched elsewhere. Japanese judicial and administrative officials are among the most straight-dealing in the world. There have been exceptions, of course, but they are kept in hand by strict law enforcement organizations and condemned by the media.

If so, why couldn't a similar honesty be maintained in Japanese politics? Because the canker had set in so deeply that no one could think of a way to restore the political integrity of the late 1920s.

In 1935, Okazaki warned reform-minded bureaucrats that they were carrying out the same measures Shinagawa Yajirō had once done by enforcing discipline on elections in an attempt to "purify" them.

Parliamentary democracy is in essence based on the Anglo-Saxon concept of liberalism. Parliaments without the spirit of liberalism are as irrelevant as communist national assemblies. The meaning of parliamentary democracy is lost the moment governments or autocratic parties interfere in parliament. No matter how corrupt their systems have become, countries need to rely on their own self-cleansing powers to restore their politics rather than to resort to outside force.

Okazaki pointed out that the more governments meddled in elections in the hope of improving the standard of representatives, the worse they became. He implied that government intervention caused a deep repugnance for politics and elections in voters. His *Kensei kaikoroku* stated:

> The efforts made by oligarchy officials to reform the Diet by getting reputable individuals elected actually ended up degrading the Diet, undermining elections, and crippling constitutional politics. The results can't ever have been foreseen by self-righteous bureaucrats good only at toying with empty theories.

The book recorded that Emperor Meiji expressed grave concern to Itō at the time. Sending a message via Grand Chamberlain Tokudaiji Sanetsune (徳大寺実則, 1840–1919), the emperor asked, "What measures would ensure the election of as many honest Diet members as possible?" Itō, who was against government intervention from the beginning, replied, "With all due respect for your disquiet, it would be extremely difficult to have only honest representatives elected," and added, "This is because honest people are reluctant to be involved in unruly elections." In his straightforward way, Itō was criticizing Shinagawa and his followers for creating bedlam during the second general election.

Emperor Meiji, like Shinagawa, was an adherent of the Wang Yangming school, which emphasized the importance of personal improvement. And though he may not necessarily have approved of Shinagawa's expedients, he was conscious that politicians needed to have certain qualities.

This is the eternal problem for democracy: to find the right balance between maintaining a free-working regime and getting good representatives.

Without any doubt, the loss of probity established during the first general election due to later government interloping inflicted a deep wound. Satsuma-Chōshū conservatives showed no respect for democracy, which they believed would destroy a long tradition of loyalty and patriotism. They were convinced that any means, including vote-rigging and intimidation, was permissible to prevent the rise of democracy in Japan.

As a consequence, the country lost precisely those qualities that the samurai had prided themselves on for many centuries.

Even today, the population does not feel entirely comfortable about politics. To be sure, the same sense of discomfort can be found elsewhere, in America for example. But the degree of distrust seems to be stronger in Japan, where moral standards among the general public are fastidiously maintained.

It was this distrust that allowed militarism to gain power without any major resistance in the 1930s. People had high expectations of the moral values such as honesty and integrity that they invested military officers with. Their hopes, in a sense, were not off the mark, since neither Tōjō Hideki (東条英機, 1884–1948), the dictatorial leader before and during World War II, nor Itagaki Seishirō (板垣征四郎, 1885–1948), the lynchpin in Manchuria and Northern China, took advantage of their positions to get rich. They maintained simple, soldierly lifestyles.

As we know, the rise of militarism in the 1930s was also fueled by such factors as Japan's international isolation after the abrogation of the Anglo-Japanese Alliance, the threat of international communism, the danger of Chinese moves to counter Japanese national interests, and the impact of the Great Depression on rural villages. But the loss of trust in party politics due to misguided intervention had a much deeper effect than the independence of the Prerogative of Supreme Command (tōsuiken, 統帥権), which is supposed to have led to military rule (as will be discussed in later chapters), or the attack on Pearl Harbor.

XI

Revision of Treaties

Freedom from Half a Century of Humiliation

The Big Issue for Japan's Diplomacy

For nearly fifty years after the opening of Japanese ports to the Western powers, Japan's biggest diplomatic priority was to revise its treaties with these countries.

This was both a personal desire and a goal in other Asian countries including Turkey, Persia, Siam, and China, which had narrowly escaped colonization in the nineteenth century.

The legalized disparity between advanced and underdeveloped nations was permanently put an end to by decolonization after World War II. Nowadays, when even reverse discrimination is practiced, where advanced countries grant preferential tariffs on imports from developing countries, the very existence of such unequal treaties belongs to the remote past. But in the Meiji era the matter repeatedly gave rise to heated political controversy, sometimes resulting in a change of government.

The issue for Japan had two major components: elimination of consular jurisdiction, and tariff autonomy. From the perspective of the Western powers, it involved the safeguarding of their nationals overseas and the protection of domestic industries from imports.

Seeking to protect nationals overseas was not an entirely unjustified cause on their part, given the circumstances in some underdeveloped regions. Because Westerners came from very different cultures with different customs, they were unlikely to know what constituted a crime locally. Neither were they likely to know how bad conditions in local prisons were.

Where penal laws were clearly established, foreigners who violated them could blame their punishment only on their own ignorance. But in underdeveloped countries where the rule of law was not firmly established and the outcome of a trial was entirely in the hands of a judge, it might be hard for foreign residents to feel safe in their daily life.

In these circumstances, the nationality principle was applied, meaning that the party involved in a possible offense was subject to the laws of his own country. For example, when an American committed a crime in Japan, the U.S. consulate would have jurisdiction.

There were also cases where the security in a host country was so poor that its laws alone were not sufficient to protect foreign residents. This resulted in the permanent presence of foreign military personnel. In the case of Japan, the British and French troops stationed there toward the end of the shogunate led to a crescendo of anti-foreign sentiment. Sometimes, as in the Foreign Concessions in China, self-contained areas were set apart as de facto overseas territories.

A further complication was Japan's policy of isolation from foreign contact for two centuries. Then Foreign Minister Inoue Kaoru said in an 1884 speech:

> In hindsight, it is clear that Japanese people had a great dislike of foreigners. They gave them no welcome, even if they were determined to abide by our laws and live among us. The government also refused to let them live in local communities, preferring to confine them in small, restricted zones where they could be protected by their own laws.

Japan's special situation notwithstanding, the issue of consular jurisdiction was taken as evidence that the Western powers did not view their relations with Japan as being between civilized countries on an equal basis, which was humiliating as well as unfair. Consuls stationed in an underdeveloped country also tended to treat their own nationals with some indulgence and were known to let a suspect leave the country at the consul's own discretion.

"Natural" Exploitation

As for tariff discrimination, no defense for the behavior of the advanced countries can reasonably be made. Tariff rates favorable to them were unilaterally imposed, sometimes by force, on nations whose ignorance made them easily exploited.

During the 1880s, Britain forced India to accept imports of British products almost duty free, in the name of free trade. But it slapped tariffs on cotton textiles imported from India in order to protect Lancashire's growing textile industry. As a result, many Bengali fabric makers were driven out of business.

In Japan, only two years before the collapse of the Tokugawa shogunate, a crippled administration was forced to accept across-the-board tariffs of only five percent by the Western powers—a good example of the unscrupulousness typical of the age of imperialism.

As the then Japanese minister to Britain Ueno Kagenori (上野 景範, 1845–88) pointed out to the British government in 1878, average duties of more than ten percent were being levied on imports from Japan despite Britain's claim to have the lowest tariffs in the West and its advocacy of free trade. Japan imposed half that amount, generating only four percent of the country's revenue, while the same figure was as high as twenty-six percent in Britain.

The low income from tariffs, aggravating the already straitened situation of the Meiji government, led to the imposition of an export tax on Japanese products—scarcely a "protective" measure for domestic industries.

This was an age in which it was only natural for the strong to exploit the weak.

In the twenty-eight years between the opening of its doors in 1853 and 1881, almost all Japan's gold and silver accumulated over the past thousand years (an estimated $300 million or about $30 billion in today's terms) was drained away. Given the deficiency of the government's finances, a loss of this magnitude could have ruined the nation.

Unlike Japan, China and Persia sold various rights and interests to foreigners and mortgaged future tariff revenues in order to make up for the deficit, gradually reducing these countries to the status of semi-colonies.

The situation then was in stark contrast to that after World War II when many industrial countries conferred preferential import tariffs and offered economic and technical assistance to developing countries, while allowing them to levy prohibitive duties to protect their own businesses.

Meiji leaders deserve considerable respect for seeing through the modernization of their country in these circumstances.

Restoration of Tariff Autonomy

As early as January 1868, the leaders of the Restoration had already announced their intention to renegotiate with the Western powers, issuing an imperial edict stating euphemistically that "some treaties concluded by the shogunate have been disadvantageous."

Rather than being a mere observation tour, the purpose of the 1871 mission to the United States and Europe led by Iwakura Tomomi had also had this matter in mind. A clause in the 1858 Treaty of Amity and Commerce with the U.S. stated that the treaty could be renegotiated from 1872, although it became clear during the tour that the process would not be plain sailing.

It was during the tenure of Foreign Minister Terashima Munenori in the years 1873–79 that the Meiji government seriously started tackling the issue of treaty revision. Terashima decided to take a realistic approach. He set the issue of consular jurisdiction aside until the domestic legal system improved to the satisfaction of other countries, and concentrated on customs duties. The government chose to deal with the United States first, seeing that it had shown a favorable attitude toward the issue.

Negotiations went smoothly, and both sides reached an agreement in 1878 that America would grant Japan tariff autonomy on condition that other Western powers took corresponding measures.

This demand was only natural from the American standpoint, since its exports would be at the mercy of a high tariff if it was alone in granting Japan tariff autonomy. It now became imperative for Japan to conclude similar treaties with other Western powers.

Debate went back and forth within the government whether to pursue bilateral or multilateral negotiations. In the end, it was decided to negotiate bilaterally with Britain, the dominant global power and leader of world trade at the time, thereby determining the general direction of negotiations with other nations.

Rokumeikan

But it was the issue of consular jurisdiction that truly offended national pride. Given the status of the legal system in Japan, when neither Western criminal law nor civil law had been instituted, and in view of the nation's financial situation, Terashima's choice of priorities was understandable. But a public outcry against the acquittal by consular jurisdiction of a British national named Hartley, who was accused of smuggling opium into Japan, resulted in Terashima's resignation in 1879, and his replacement with Inoue Kaoru, whose eight-year tenure as foreign minister was saddled with both issues.

As a partial measure, Inoue advocated the lifting of restrictions on foreigners' areas of residence and movements. In those days, foreigners were segregated in certain places and needed special permission to travel outside them. Inoue hoped to obtain concessions in his wider negotiations by allowing foreigners to purchase real estate and live anywhere they liked.

The need to demonstrate that Japan was a civilized state on an equal footing with the West resulted in other endeavors. This was the beginning of the so-called Rokumeikan (鹿鳴館) era. The Rokumeikan was a French Renaissance-style banquet hall that the government used for receptions for high-profile guests. Everything connected with it was an imitation of Western court life, and people dressed like Western gentlemen and ladies rode to and fro in horse-drawn carriages through central Tokyo.

While the building no longer exists, a similar structure still stands in Thailand—a parliamentary mansion astonishing in the grandeur of its rococo architecture, its ceilings decorated by an Italian painter to look like the Sistine Chapel. One can imagine the cost and effort that went into constructing this attempt to show the outside world that Thailand was too civilized to be snapped up as a colony or semi-colony.

Itagaki Taisuke wrote the following commentary in his *Jiyūtō-shi*:

> Inoue seemed determined to do anything for the revision of the treaties, including all-out Westernization with the government's assistance if it helped this cause. The series of banquets at the Rokumeikan, day in and day out, set a bad example. There was a tendency to look down on anything Japanese and adore everything Western. From the Romanization Society to the restyling of plays, music, clothes, and food, nothing escaped the infantile imitation of foreign fashion. Some even went to the extreme of advocating racial reform by "improving" Japanese blood with some Caucasian stock.

He went on to document the resentment this caused among Japanese nationalists: "[The fad] made high-minded, patriotic people here absolutely furious. Regardless of their party affiliation, conservatives as well as progressives linked arms against the damage done by wholesale Westernization."

In retrospect, the desire among Asian and African people to become more like Caucasians was widespread. Even during the Pacific War when Japan tried to inspire its neighbors with Pan-Asianism, this urge remained intact. The pro-Japanese president of the Philippines, José Laurel, was an advocate of racial reform. The Phibun government of Thailand (1938–57), which formed alliances with Japan and Germany and tried to stoke up nationalism in the hope of reclaiming former Thai territories, also encouraged Westernization, and Thai women were encouraged to wear Western-style hats.

Inoue's efforts, however, ended in failure. After carefully preparing drafts of new treaties and laying the groundwork with Britain and other Western powers, Inoue convened a conference in Tokyo in May 1886. Here a concession was aired authorizing foreign judges to participate in Japanese trials in exchange for allowing Japan other equal rights. The concession infuriated nationalistic members of the public, eventually resulting in Inoue's resignation.

Because a time limit of twelve years was imposed on the treaty, the Japanese would only have had to put up with the presence of foreign judges for that limited period, by which time their own legal system should have become sufficiently developed; but many cabinet members were against the proposal, and Komura Jutarō, who later became foreign minister himself, took part in a hostile campaign despite being an official at the Ministry of Foreign Affairs. In the end, Inoue gave up and resigned as foreign minister.

His successor, Ōkuma, took on the same task. In the course of preparations, however, a draft treaty was leaked. One clause authorized a Western judge to preside in the Daishin'in (大審院, Great Court of Cassation, today's Supreme Court) at a trial in which the defendant was a foreigner. This again gave rise to violent dispute. Although Ōkuma would not give in and tried to obtain endorsement of the original draft, he was hospitalized after a right-wing activist, Kurushima Tsuneki (来島恒喜, 1860–89), threw a bomb at him, blowing off his leg. Shortly afterwards, his attacker committed ritual suicide in front of the Imperial Palace.

The leak was believed to have been sent to the *Times* of London by Komura during his tenure as head of the Foreign Ministry's translation bureau, in the knowledge that the disclosure was likely to derail further negotiations.

Naturally, it was entirely inappropriate for an incumbent diplomat to take this action, but nobody doubted that it was done from personal conviction, not self-interest. And it is interesting that Mutsu, a firm advocate of Westernization, later singled out Komura for an important post during the First Sino-Japanese War.

The Era of Nationalism

Mutsu's new life had started as a special assistant to Foreign Minister Inoue. By the time he was given the title of envoy extraordinary and minister plenipotentiary, it was exactly ten years since his disastrous mistake in connection with the Satsuma Rebellion.

Meanwhile, the general atmosphere in Japan had also greatly changed, marking the beginning of a period of nationalism. In the summer of 1886, China's Beiyang fleet (北洋艦隊), led by the massive battleship *Dingyuan*, made a port call in Nagasaki. Although it was officially a courtesy visit, there was clearly an intention on the part of the Chinese to demonstrate their military strength. During the visit, Chinese sailors became involved in a scuffle with local police, resulting in casualties on both sides.

Had the incident occurred ten years later, Japan might have severed diplomatic relations with China, sent troops to the mainland, and perhaps occupied a province or two. But the Japanese military at the time had no means of resisting the firepower of the *Dingyuan* and *Zhenyuan*, and the authorities were compelled to accept China's humiliating demand that Japanese police officers be banned from carrying swords.

This was only one of several affronts endured by a country that would inflict much worse on the Chinese and Koreans in the next century. In October 1886, the *Normanton* Incident involving the sinking of a British freighter off Wakayama took place. The *Normanton*'s captain and his British crew escaped safely, but all twenty-two Japanese passengers drowned. At a hearing at the British legation in Kobe, the captain was exonerated. The decision caused public outrage and intensified anti-foreign feelings. It was in the midst of this nationalistic atmosphere that Mutsu returned to officialdom.

Japanese Minister to the United States

In 1888, Mutsu was stationed in Washington, D.C., as the Japanese minister, or in today's terms as the Japanese ambassador to the United States. And in November of that year, only six months after his appointment, he succeeded in signing an equal treaty with Mexico.

Mutsu as Japanese minister to the U.S. (middle-back) and wife Ryōko (left)

It was a treaty stipulating that legal cases should be heard by the respective legal authority of the host country. In return, Mexican citizens were granted complete freedom of residence, travel, and business in Japanese territory. Because the status of most-favored nation was mutual in the case of tariffs, Japan had to wait until its other trading partners accepted Japan's tariff autonomy before it could gain any real benefit from this agreement with Mexico; but as far as the format was concerned, the terms were perfectly equal.

This was an important breakthrough. The impact would remain insignificant if Mexico alone signed the treaty, but if Germany, France, and Russia followed suit, Britain, which had remained the most uncooperative regarding revision of the treaty, would find its nationals at a serious disadvantage. Thus, as was expected, Britain opposed the freedom of residence and travel granted only to Mexico and attempted to persuade other Western powers to join its opposition, but failed to accomplish this. The reason may have been the conspicuous growth in Japan's strength as a nation along with the steady consolidation of its judicial institutions, which helped to eliminate concern about peace and order.

As soon as the treaty with Mexico was signed, Mutsu started

negotiating with the United States. Convinced that this would be a crucial turning point for the treaty negotiations as a whole, he took pains to prepare for confrontation with Secretary of State Thomas Bayard.

It was soon apparent, however, that this wasn't necessary. The American side declared that "it is our hope that Japan will be promptly granted the right of independence," and advised that a treaty should be signed before the end of February 1889, because a new administration would be sworn in in March owing to the defeat of the Democrats in the December presidential election. Thus, agreement was reached between the two sides with surprising ease.

Concerned that this would rankle with Great Britain, the Ministry of Foreign Affairs in Tokyo tried hard to get Britain's blessing before signing the treaty with the U.S. But since the British side would not take a clear-cut position on the matter, it became too late to sign the document before a new U.S. Congress got going.

The Final Battle of the Meiji Restoration

It was the second Itō Hirobumi cabinet (1892), with Mutsu as its foreign minister, that finally brought off the revision of treaties with the Western powers. Nicknamed the "cabinet of senior statesmen," it consisted of prominent leaders including Kuroda Kiyotaka from Satsuma and Yamagata Aritomo from Chōshū, who joined forces in what they called "the final battle of the Meiji Restoration."

The failure of the Matsukata cabinet was much on their minds. It had been a chastening example of how a government should not be run, with internal disagreement bringing constitutional politics to a dead end despite Mutsu's attempts to keep it going.

At that crossroads in Japanese parliamentary democracy, Itō agreed to take over the government again. Even before Matsukata had resigned, in fact, there had been a secret imperial instruction to appoint Itō as the next prime minister. Itō, however, had first declined the appointment, saying:

It is a huge challenge to put the new constitution into practice when our society as a whole is still unfit to adopt it. Whoever becomes prime minister is unlikely to last long. If he pushes his way through, he might be risking his life. While I wouldn't hesitate to give my own away, I wonder who would assist the imperial family in completing the transition in my place.

When he finally accepted, he managed to obtain an important concession from Emperor Meiji. Itō wrote the following to him:

I understand that my predecessor first consulted Your Imperial Majesty on every matter before submitting it to the cabinet. Now that I have been appointed to this important post, I would like most humbly to ask you to delegate authority on all decisions to me. Needless to say, I would ask for Your Imperial Majesty's instruction on major decisions. But, other than that, I would like to proceed on my own responsibility.

To this request, the emperor replied, "I agree. I have no intention of interfering in government decisions. I will present my own view only when asked to do so."

The imperial concession would later have important implications for the development of Japanese parliamentary politics, but at the time it served as a stepping-stone, allowing Itō to mobilize Mutsu, for example, and have him actively engage in state affairs.

Since the first year of Meiji, the Satsuma faction had loathed Mutsu. As Emperor Meiji was surrounded by aides from the former Satsuma domain, his attitude toward Mutsu, too, must have been influenced by them. The emperor had allegedly opposed his first cabinet nomination. While Mutsu was struggling to rescue the Matsukata cabinet, Grand Chamberlain Tokudaiji wrote to Itō that "His Imperial Majesty is deeply concerned about Mutsu's presence in the cabinet, fearing that he will be an obstruction to cabinet unity. We would like to have your response, taking His Imperial Majesty's misgivings into full consideration." In short, it was a request to discharge Mutsu and, whether he knew of this or not, he soon tendered his resignation. It is easy to imagine that the Satsuma faction had maneuvered and slandered in order to dismiss him.

It was obvious to everyone, though, that it would be impossible to deal successfully with the new Diet without the talent of someone like

Mutsu, who understood the workings of parliamentary politics and kept in close contact with the peoples' rights advocates from Tosa. This may well have been the reason why Itō, who had privately decided to take Mutsu on board, asked the emperor to let him have a free hand.

The newly formed Itō cabinet was able to survive the fourth session of the Imperial Diet thanks to well-coordinated efforts by Itō, Mutsu, and Speaker of the House of Representatives Hoshi Tōru.

When the government submitted a proposal to carry over a portion of the military budget from the Matsukata cabinet and, in addition, proposed an expansion of the Imperial Navy by building two new battleships, opposition parties immediately hardened their stand. Deciding not to resist the general inclination of the Diet, Speaker Hoshi rejected the budget proposal and authorized passage of a cabinet impeachment bill. At this point, Itō requested an imperial edict urging popular support for the construction of the battleships in return for a voluntary cut of ten percent in the private expenses of the imperial family for the next six years, as well as a ten percent salary cut for all government officials. With the issuing of this edict, the atmosphere in the Diet changed completely. The budget proposal passed, and the Itō cabinet had weathered the crisis.

Enlightenment vs. Nationalist School

On joining the Itō cabinet, Mutsu applied himself to the revision of the treaties, but rather than resort to multilateral negotiations or tactics to bypass Britain, he decided to take the orthodox approach of dealing directly with the British.

Revision of a treaty requires two fronts of negotiation—with the signee and with the domestic opposition. In the past, although foreign ministers Terashima, Inoue, and Ōkuma had all managed to reach a certain level of agreement with their negotiating partners, they eventually faced setbacks due to patriotic resistance at home.

Japan's modern diplomacy, throughout the Meiji, Taishō, and Shōwa eras, always involved confrontation between what might be called the enlightened and the nationalist schools.

Members of the former group, often with firsthand experience of life abroad, were an absolute minority, an elite in both number and distinction, even among the cabinet itself. In the Diet, where the overwhelming majority were of the nationalist persuasion, any hardline argument against a foreign country immediately found support, regardless of party affiliation.

Unlike today, when anyone in Japan can travel overseas, those who had benefited from study abroad became the target of envy, and tended to provoke antipathy for affecting a "Western style." When the frustration of the population as a whole peaked, as in the 1930s, the "enlightened" were easily drowned out by public opinion and the press, which favored a nationalist approach.

Itō and Mutsu's maneuvering in the Diet on the treaty issue was typical of this dichotomy.

The draft treaty with Britain was based on equality between two nations, to be effective within five years of signing with the proviso that a system of laws be completed in Japan within that period. Even if this draft had been leaked as before, there was no element in it that should have provoked homegrown resentment. Opposition to it, therefore, was concentrated on the ownership of land by foreigners and their freedom of economic activity.

Ostensibly, the opposition's antagonism took the form of a movement to promote the rigorous enforcement of the clauses of the existing treaties. By that time, restrictions on foreigners' activities outside their authorized zone had been considerably relaxed. Making it much more inconvenient for them to live and move about in Japan would, in theory, make them aware of the disadvantages of the current international treaties. But the ulterior motive was to force the government to take a hardline stance vis-à-vis other nations in general.

In response, Mutsu came up with a countermeasure that squarely confronted this movement. Declaring that the proposal went against the open-door policy instigated by the Meiji Restoration, he demanded its withdrawal, saying that refusal would lead to the immediate dissolution of the Diet

Historic Speech

In defense of his motion, he gave a speech reviewing Japan's recent history and its future ambitions.

> The purpose of the revision of the treaty, and, moreover, the objective of our diplomacy, is to ensure that Japan is granted its due rights and fulfills its due duties. In a sense, the revision is to demand special treatment from the Western powers, which other Asian countries are not entitled to receive, even though our empire is located in Asia. Japan, therefore, must demonstrate a progressive stance not shared by other Asian countries by pursuing special policies and actions.
>
> The priority of our diplomacy today is to join the club of civilized powers through self- and mutual respect, slighting or fearing no one.

He went on to look at the modern history of Europe and Asia, in the course of which he referred to the way some Asian states, despite an overt deference to Westerners, despised and remonstrated against them at home. Their ambivalence led them into armed conflict with Western powers, resulting in humiliating defeats that often changed the very fate of their own countries. This pointed reference to the experiences of Qing China and other Asian nations was Mutsu's way of sending a warning to his own people.

> A country's foreign policy often reflects the disposition of its people. In the past, the Tokugawa shogunate retreated behind a policy of restricting contact with foreigners. It takes an enterprising nation to adopt an open-minded foreign policy.
>
> On behalf of the government, I wish to say that the proposal for stricter enforcement of the treaties and other accompanying acts goes counter to the national policy of Japan since the Restoration. The government stands against anything that runs counter to that principle.

One thing that distinguishes Japan from Western civilization is the lack of the Greco-Roman tradition of moving people with rhetoric. In ancient Rome, commanders often inspired their soldiers by delivering a speech before a battle, while Chinese generals would shout "Right and justice are on our side!" to their warriors in the battlefield. But this was almost unheard of in Japan. There was no speech by Tokugawa Ieyasu, for instance, before the Battle of Sekigahara. Even today, hardly any speeches by prime ministers deserve to be quoted for posterity.

In this sense, Mutsu was untypical of his country. His speech was acclaimed both at home and abroad. The acting British minister to Japan, for instance, wrote to him saying: "Your Excellency's speech clearly shows that your government is sincere in its pursuit of a progressive policy."

Completion of the Treaty Revision

But Mutsu's eloquence failed to change the opposition parties' attitude, and Itō dissolved the Diet.

Mutsu, meanwhile, pressed on with negotiations with Britain. These progressed to the point where both parties had reached agreement on the substance of the draft treaty, but formal endorsement was pending. While the Japanese side tried to push the process forward, the British seemed reluctant to make a full commitment. They would not accept the Japanese argument that opening mainland Japan to the British was already a major concession. Further inquiry revealed that what the other side wanted was the offer of an island for use as a military base or, failing that, the government's pledge that it would not provide Russia or France with a similar site. While Russia's Siberian Railway was steadily advancing eastward, the British interest had already shifted from merely the content of the treaty to strategy vis-à-vis Russia in the Far East. The tide of international politics in the area, which led to the Anglo-Japanese Alliance within eight years and the Russo-Japanese War in ten, was rising.

In response, the Japanese government reassured the British by announcing that "we would resist any such request from Russia or France even if meant turning the whole land to ashes." This pledge also succeeded in limiting the British side's request to permission for British vessels to use the port of Hakodate. Thus the last hurdle before the signing of the treaty was cleared.

In the general election, the opposition party Kokumin Kyōkai (国民協会, National Association), which had been behind the reinforcement of the existing treaties, fared badly, and a resolution denouncing the government for having dissolved the Diet without allowing it to offer a counter argument to Mutsu's speech was defeated by a slim margin thanks to his persuading the Jiyūtō to cooperate. "Persuasion," however, had not involved resorting to illegal intervention or a Bismarck-style use of authority, despite the Prussian flavor of the constitution.

Through inattention, however, the Itō cabinet drove into trouble with the Diet again, while Mutsu himself was too involved with the completion of a new treaty and the handling of the situation on the Korean Peninsula to pay much attention to politics at home. With the eruption of the First Sino-Japanese War, the government was forced to dissolve the Diet yet again in order to buy time.

This was the limit of the two men's management of domestic politics. Once the war started, however, a wave of patriotism brought about an abrupt shift toward cooperation with the government, allowing the first phase of parliamentary politics to survive and take hold without the suspension of the constitution.

The new treaty with Britain was signed in London on July 16, 1894. As soon as Mutsu received the news by telegram, he gave thanks in a little private ritual and went straight to the Imperial Palace to report. He also sent a telegram instructing the Japanese delegation to convey his gratitude to the British foreign minister, Kimberly, who commented that "this treaty is much more significant for Japan than victory over China."

Tariff autonomy was realized in 1911 after a transitional period of twelve years as stipulated in the treaty, which brought to completion half a century's endeavors "to level the score"

It was only eight days after this that the Battle of Pungdo (豊島沖海戦) at Feng Island was fought, opening the First Sino-Japanese War and raising the curtain on Japan's own imperialism.

XII

Rivalry on
the Korean Peninsula

One Imperialism vs. Another

The Road toward the First Sino-Japanese War

In his *Rokujūnen-rai no Chūgoku to Nihon* (China and Japan in the past sixty years, 1932), the Chinese journalist Wang Yunsheng (王芸生, 1901–80) wrote, "The First Sino-Japanese War originated from the Imo Incident (壬午事変, 1882)." Wang, a leading scholar of Sino-Japanese relations, based this comment on a thorough study of diplomatic documents from the Qing dynasty that were disclosed in 1911.

We need to briefly review the situation on the Korean Peninsula leading to the 1882 incident Wang referred to.

The Korean Peninsula was the terminal point for the Western powers in the Far East. Geographically, it is located in the shadow of China and Japan, and was known as "the Hermit Kingdom." Moreover, its configuration served as an antidote to gunboat diplomacy: its eastern seaboard is lined with steep cliffs, defying access from the sea, while its western shore is an unsafe beach with powerful tides. Attacking vessels might be able to advance into the bay at high tide, only to be stranded at low tide.

A Russian battleship approached the east coast first in 1865; a French fleet attacked the west coast in 1866; and an American fleet followed in 1871. The Joseon dynasty (朝鮮王朝) was then under the leadership of the Daewongun (大院君), acting as regent during the early years of King Gojong (高宗), and its successful defense from French and American incursion, helped by its geographical features, boosted its sense of insularity.

By contrast, without the benefit of geography, Japan was unable to repel the foreign battleships that appeared off its shores. The American fleet in 1854 sailed unopposed into Tokyo Bay, opening the country's gates to the rest of the world. Korea's resistance to foreign intrusion allowed it to stay intact, but the delay in opening up the country later proved fatal. When the Restoration government sought diplomatic relations with Korea, the regent's preoccupation with the threat of encroachment led to Japan being given the cold shoulder, which provoked possible retaliation (as discussed in the *Seikanron* debate).

When King Gojong came of age in 1873, the Daewongun resigned. Two years later, after an episode involving the Japanese warship *Un'yō* (雲揚) at Ganghwa Island, and following the advice of Qing China, Korea decided to end its closed-door policy and establish diplomatic relations not only with Japan but several other foreign powers.

The clan of Queen Myeongseong (informally known as Queen Min, 閔妃) took over power at the royal court and attempted to modernize the country along the lines of the Meiji Restoration. While a modern army was being trained under the guidance of the Japanese military, officers of the old school who had lost favor rose in mutiny. The Daewongun, hitherto ostracized from the center of power, took advantage of the confusion to reinstate himself. The resulting coup d'état later became known as the Imo Incident.

With the Daewongun's anti-foreign attitude as its backbone, the coup took on a xenophobic character. Japanese officers were killed, and the Japanese legation was burned down. Japan had legitimate reason to make a hardline response, and some in the government were strongly in favor of military action; but lack of military preparedness resulted in diplomatic negotiations instead, with only the dispatch of one battalion as a backup.

The Qing dynasty's response to this situation was quick and skillful. Two thousand soldiers were sent to the peninsula, the Daewongun was arrested and taken to Tianjin, and the queen's clan was restored to power, thus preempting any move by Japan while demonstrating China's position as Korea's suzerain state.

Competition with China

Although the relationship between Qing China and Joseon Korea was nominally that of suzerain and tributary, the former had never interfered with the latter's internal affairs for three hundred years. And because the Daewongun had carried out the coup d'état without any foreign assistance, the change of government was essentially a domestic affair that defied external intervention. But by subsequently violating the tradition and intervening in Korea's politics to prevent Japan's own intervention, China put itself on a footing of imperialistic rivalry with Japan.

Qing China is usually regarded as a failed state that had been thoroughly abused by the West ever since the First Opium War. After it lost Hong Kong to Britain in 1842 and Primorye (Primorsky Krai) to Russia in 1860, however, it reformed its domestic politics and modernized its military in the Tongzhi Restoration (c. 1860–74), earning itself the image of "a sleeping lion" among apprehensive onlookers. It wasn't until its devastating defeat in the First Sino-Japanese War and the destitution caused by the huge reparation payment that foreign powers realized how vulnerable Qing really was. And that was the beginning of half a century of humiliation for China.

In early Meiji days, however, Qing was seen as a threat to Japan. The sense of menace was evident in Fukuzawa Yukichi's article in the daily *Jiji Shimpō* dated December 12, 1882:

> Even today, the Chinese navy is three times more powerful than our own. Theirs is a wealthy country under autocratic rule, and is able to do whatever its ruler wishes. If it decides to add to its military

buildup and dares to annex Korea and reclaim the Ryukyu Islands, Japan will have to go to war with it.

The outcome of a modern war is determined by weapons, not courage. Just imagine for a moment Japan's defeat by superior military equipment—however courageous its soldiers.

Ships loaded with troops would invade Tokyo Bay.... Tokyo would be bombarded. Thousands of helpless citizens would die in agony, or be left to grieve. Through clouds of black smoke, pigtailed soldiers would then advance, raping, looting, and putting children and the old to death.... No property would survive untouched by those inhuman hordes....

Fukuzawa had previously been convinced that modernization was a top priority for Japan, but his awareness of a possible threat from China made him begin to argue for a military buildup, despite the constraints and extra tax burden it would entail.

Fukuzawa's fantasy was not wholly unrealistic. There were those in the Qing court who recommended "conquering the East [meaning Japan]." Immediately after the Imo Incident, Zhang Peilun (張佩綸, 1848–1903) of the Hanlin Academy (翰林院) reported to his emperor:

Post-Restoration Japan, after initial attempts to restore feudal rule, is now subject to a peoples' rights movement. The economy relies heavily on government bonds, and the public use paper money as currency. Yet they are still occupying the Liuqiu [Japanese: Ryukyu] Islands and have insulted Your Majesty by declaring that Korea does not belong to us. If we censure Japan's conduct in Liuqiu and Korea and strengthen our navy to obstruct its trade on the seas, Japan, in response, will have to expand its military spending, which would drain the country's resources. Then would be our chance to attack. One battle should be enough to defeat it.

If, however, we remain indecisive, even that little island nation will become a major concern for us.

According to the Chinese administrative system, it was General Li Hongzhang's (李鴻章, 1823–1901) job to respond to this advice to the emperor. In a lengthy reply, Li commented that, while agreeing with the analysis, he felt that it would be unwise to speak of "conquering the East" before making due preparations for it, in case Japan was compelled to prepare for its own defense. It would be necessary first, he argued, to secure an adequate military budget.

The Essence of Imperialism

Among the Qing staff officers dispatched to the Imo Incident were two talented people, Zhang Jian (張謇, 1853–1926) and Yuan Shikai (袁世凱, 1859–1916) who rose to be emperor of the Chinese empire.

Zhang Jian argued in his *Six Plans for Korea* that Qing should divide its military into three parts, attack Japan to recover the Ryukyu Islands, and annex Korea, which had once been a province of the Han dynasty (202 B.C.– A.D. 220). His advocacy of war met with Emperor Guangxu's approval when it reached his attention.

General Li Hongzhang remained as cautious as he had been in responding to Zhang Peilun's report, prompting a memorandum from Zhan Jian complaining that Li's "cautious attitude will misguide the state." (One can't help being impressed how bold and open the debate on national strategy seems to have been.)

Yuan Shikai, who befriended Zhang Jian and was influenced by his ideas, later took the initiative in his country's Korean policy and attempted to establish Chinese's authority there. These policy makers, therefore, were themselves the product of the age of imperialism.

To say that China's imperialism was an act of self-defense against Japan's designs on the Korean Peninsula is perfectly valid.

When the Japanese government forbade the kingdom of Ryukyu from dispatching a tributary envoy to China in 1878, He Ruzhang (何如璋), the first Qing minister to Japan (and a man of prominent literary fame), sent a warning to his home government saying, "After subjugating the Liuqiu kingdom, Japan will next invade Korea." Actual developments proved these predictions, including Zhang Peilun's conjectures at the time of the Imo Incident, to be surprisingly accurate. Under these circumstances, China's attempt to tighten its control of the Korean Peninsula can indeed be considered an act of self-preservation.

But all this is part and parcel of the practice of imperialism. And exactly the same argument can be applied to Japan's position in the First Sino-Japanese War and the Russo-Japanese War.

It was predicted that, once the Siberian Railway was completed, Russia would make a full-scale drive into the Far East. In order to defend Japan's independence, it was thought imperative not only to protect territories under Japan's sovereignty but to safeguard the Korean Peninsula—the "line of interest" that Japan regarded as critically important for its own sovereignty. And this was the argument on which Yamagata Aritomo's speech *Gaikō seiryakuron* (外交政略論, A view on diplomacy and political strategy) in 1890 was based.

Some historical studies by Japanese leftists after World War II claimed that Russia at the time was incapable of conquering Korea, and that it only meant to secure the territorial integrity of Korea. This opinion was founded on an analysis of Russian official documents during the First Sino-Japanese War. The studies concluded that Japan's policy was based on a misinterpretation of Russian intentions. But the perspective is too narrow.

When the Japanese government annexed the kingdom of Ryukyu in 1879, there was no indication that it planned to do the same to Korea, nor was it capable of doing so. Moreover, no such intention can be found in official documents of the time. Judging from Japan's way of thinking and its future goals, Qing policy makers were convinced that its next target was Korea—and subsequent historical analysis proved them correct. But just as convinced were the Japanese in the early twentieth century that Russia would advance on Korea and that the peninsula was a vital "line of interest."

To survive the law of the jungle of imperialism, one had to be the first to appropriate what lay between oneself and one's opponent.

The years between the Imo Incident and the First Sino-Japanese War were a period of rivalry in the arena of the Korean Peninsula between two power-aspirants—China, just awakened to imperialism, and Japan, recently awakened from almost three centuries of seclusion. It was not about which side was right or wrong. Each vied with the other to survive the competition. History shows that Qing China had won an easy decision in the first and second bouts—the Imo Incident and the 1884 Kapsin Political Coup—while in the third Japan won by a knock-out, catching its opponent off-guard.

Humiliation in the Kapsin Coup

In Korea, after the opening of Japan to Western trade and constructive change, the Gaehwapa (Enlightenment Party) group of reformers led by Kim Okgyun (金玉均, 1851–94) and Pak Yonghyo (朴泳孝, 1861–1939) had taken a pro-Japanese and pro-modernization stance in competition with Queen Myeongseong's clan, which was under the protection of China. Gaehwapa was also known as the Independence Party, seeking freedom from its dominant neighbor.

With China's defeat in the Sino-French War of 1884–85, the Gaehwapa group staged an attempted coup, hoping to be assisted by Japanese troops stationed in the kingdom's capital. Since the Imo Incident, however, the Japanese military presence had been reduced in number. Although two hundred Japanese soldiers tried to defend the palace, a much larger Chinse force intervened and immediately subdued the coup. The Japanese diplomatic mission was destroyed, and the Japanese minister as well as Gaehwapa leaders narrowly escaped on board a steamer to Japan.

Choosing diplomatic settlement rather than military conflict, the government dispatched Itō Hirobumi to China, where he cosigned the Treaty of Tianjin with Li Hongzhang in April 1885, which nominally put both countries on an equal footing in the peninsula and stipulated that each must be kept informed of the movement of troops there in future. About a decade later, this stipulation triggered the First Sino-Japanese War.

The failure of the pro-Japanese Kapsin Coup, together with this treaty, incensed public opinion in Japan. Ozaki Yukio (尾崎行雄, 1858–1954) of the former Kaishintō was among the most radical advocates of war, and former members of the Jiyūtō were active in organizing volunteer forces. It was reported that Itagaki Taisuke mustered more than a thousand volunteers in Kōchi prefecture on his own.

Some postwar history books have expressed disappointment that the Jiyūtō (particularly its left-wing element) became an advocate of imperialism. They lamented that it hadn't remained loyal to an "anti-war, anti-imperialistic, anti-colonial" creed. But this attitude fails to grasp the true nature of historical events and their participants. The people of the Meiji era poured their energy not only into the pursuit of freedom and rights but into the enhancement of national prestige. Both mattered to them.

Kim Okgyun's Final Days

After fleeing to Japan, Kim Okgyun continued to associate with former members of the Jiyūtō and firebrands like Okamoto Ryūnosuke in the hope of making a comeback. But the government, in line with Korea's requests, had Kim confined on the Ogasawara (Bonin) Islands and Hokkaido. Although soon released, he was constantly under threat of assassination by Korean agents.

In the spring of 1894, on the eve of the First Sino-Japanese War, Kim went to Shanghai to meet General Li Hongzhang. His purpose was to win support for cooperation between the three East Asian countries in the modernization of Korea. But it turned out to be a trap set by the Korean government, and Kim was murdered there. He had known of the danger, but decided to take a chance. It was an end befitting a courageous revolutionary.

Kim's friends and acquaintances in Japan, intent on giving him a suitable burial, sent Okamoto Ryūnosuke to Shanghai on their behalf, but it was too late. His remains had already been shipped home. There the body was cut up into six pieces and discarded in different parts of the country; his head and torso were attached to a gibbet on the roadside between Seoul and Incheon, while his limbs were scattered in various provinces with signboards declaring, "The corpse of Kim Okgyun, traitor." Stray dogs gnawed at his flesh.

This episode gave the Japanese public the impression of a cruel, intolerant regime stuck in a backward past. Many felt a responsibility, as Korea's neighbor, for reforming the place, and throughout the subsequent war with China, they consistently took a more hawkish stance than the government.

Foreign Minister Mutsu had a detached view of these developments, as indicated in his memoir *Kenkenroku* (蹇蹇録, *Kenkenroku: A Diplomatic Record of the Sino-Japanese War, 1894–1895*):

> There was a consensus, both in the government and among the general public, that Japan should help its neighbor even at the risk of some hardship, and if necessary wage a war in a bid to suppress the strong and help the weak, regardless of the outcome. This diplomatic issue was debated as if it derived from a moral not a political cause.
>
> While there may have been some expansionists who wanted to take advantage of the situation ... what predominated was the argument supporting a chivalrous attitude toward an adjacent country.
>
> At the beginning, I didn't pay too much attention to Korea's domestic political situation, and I was skeptical of its ability to carry out satisfactory reforms.... But I have to admit that it was most convenient for our foreign policy that public opinion was united in support of change in Korea. So I decided to use the situation as a means to turn the gloomy clouds over Sino-Japanese relations into either pouring rain or a clear blue sky.

The level-headed realism of Mutsu's diplomacy should be obvious from the above quotation. It was no wonder that in reference to his attitude, Wang Yunsheng commented that "the author makes no bones about the aims and methods of the Japanese government." The document is indeed very plainspoken—an unemotional monologue rarely found in the sentimental culture of Japan.

The Era of Imperialism

It is beyond doubt that the national strategy Mutsu pursued at the time of the First Sino-Japanese War was imperialistic in nature and that he made full use of every available maneuver to achieve Japan's goals. Mutsu himself didn't even bother to hide his intentions.

From a post-Wilsonianism historical viewpoint, imperialism is evil. But in the advanced nations of the late nineteenth century, individual and collective acts that brought glory to one's country were meritorious, even if they inevitably meant sacrifice of some kinds. Any military action in pursuit of this was applauded, and the act of self-sacrifice for the benefit of one's country was extolled. It would not be an overstatement to say that almost without exception the people of Meiji Japan were imperialists, including followers of the Freedom and People's Rights Movement and members of the opposition parties. And once the battle with China began, the Imperial Diet, which had been stubbornly anti-government, made a sudden volte-face to offer full cooperation.

It is only after accepting this overall picture that one can go on to decide, among the imperialists, who was more radical, more cautious, more rational or emotional. Only then can one also appreciate whose diplomacy was more skillful and whose more valid.

Japan's imperialism before 1945 inflicted unspeakable suffering on the Koreans and Chinese, and resulted in disaster for its own population. That population is now disgusted with it. Given the domestic and international situations, it seems highly unlikely that such policies will ever be pursued again.

But this may not be the way the rest of the world views Japan. Knowing how the country had once thrown its weight around and profited from its own season of expansion, it may well sound unconvincing for its people to say, after their defeat, "Well, it's over now, so let's all live happily together from now on." There are still too many states in today's world whose dissatisfaction or impatience makes them volatile.

The world evolves. Legitimacy that once seemed unshakeable has been lost, regained, and lost again. The age of imperialism may be over, but no one knows how long it will remain this way.

One doesn't have to think far into the future to appreciate this. Even today, it would be hard to insist that what China and Russia are doing in Tibet and Chechnya is not imperialistic.

Looking back over modern history, I believe that the Japanese owe a lot to the people of the Meiji period, who managed to weather the tensions of a competitive world. The generation that followed misjudged the realities of international politics and left a legacy of devastation. And yet our current living standard is due in part to the social system, education, technology, and, most of all, the spirit of independence and self-respect that accrued from the Meiji era.

At least, we should be grateful to it for not leaving to subsequent generations a colonized or semi-colonized country, or one deprived of a large part of its historical territory.

XIII

THE DONGHAK PEASANT REBELLION

Is Korea a Tributary to Qing China?

Peasant Uprising

Donghak was a typical Oriental socio-religious movement, the term "Donghak" (東学, Eastern learning) being the antithesis of "Western learning," or Christianity.

In contrast to established religions that promise happiness in an afterlife, many new religions promise benefits in this world. Donghak was founded by Choe Je-u (崔済愚, 1824–64), who claimed to have received divine revelation in 1860. The new cult, it was believed, had the power to heal any disease if the sick chanted the Donghak incantation or swallowed the ash of a piece of paper with a written incantation on it.

When a new religion becomes popular among a large number of ordinary people, it begins to function as a medium to siphon off and give vent to other frustrations and dissatisfaction.

Examples of cult-related incidents in Chinese history include the Taiping Rebellion (太平天国の乱, 1850–64) and the Boxer Rebellion (義和団の乱, 1898–1901) in modern times, as well as the Yellow Turban

Rebellion described in the *Sanguozhi pinghua* (三国志平話, Story of the Records of the Three Kingdoms). All were evidence of a similar social phenomenon.

According to Wang Yunsheng, resentment of misrule was so widespread in Korea in the late Joseon dynasty that the following verse from the tale of the *Chunhyangjeon* (春香伝, The Story of Chunhyang) was popular:

> Not wine in the golden cask
> But the blood of thousands
> Not food in the jade bowl
> But the flesh of thousands more
> Tears fall like candle wax
> While our rulers sing
> And we mourn and hate.

A tendency for some new cults was to capitalize on people's anti-foreign feelings. Donghak, too, started organizing anti-foreign meetings and putting up xenophobic posters in Seoul around 1893, one year before the First Sino-Japanese War started. All foreign residents in Seoul felt vulnerable, and Japanese inhabitants began sending their women and children back to Japan while they themselves wore swords when they went out, even during the daytime. Unsurprisingly, the Japanese government decided to dispatch troops to Korea on the pretext of "protecting our people there" at the time of the Donghak Peasant Rebellion in 1894.

Once again, China took the initiative ahead of Japan. At the request of its diplomatic mission in Seoul, the Qing court decided that the situation provided a good opportunity and had two battleships, the *Laiyuan* (来遠) and the *Jingyuan* (靖遠), sail over in a display of strength. The Korean government took advantage of the presence of these ships to tighten control.

In 1894, however, a peasant rebellion led by Donghak's Jeon Bongjun (全琫準) broke out in the province of Cholla-do (全羅道) and soon spread like wildfire to various regions. Rebels raided provincial government offices, returned crops that had been paid as tax to the original growers, and stole weapons from arsenals. By June of that year, the capital city of Cholla-do, Jeonju (全州), was under their control.

The Korean government in Seoul sent eight hundred troops to Gunsan (群山) in Cholla-do, on May 6, 1894, with the help of a Chinese cruiser, *Pingyuan* (平遠). Although these were relatively well-trained soldiers of the Royal Capital Army (京軍), they had been hastily dispatched without sufficient financial backup or food. As a result, their morale was low and half of them ended up deserting.

The commander of the Royal Capital Army asked for reinforcements, but he clearly had no confidence in his troops' ability to suppress the rebels, and on May 23 he reported back to the royal court that they had no choice but to "rely on foreign troops."

Meanwhile, Queen Myeongseong's people had been in close communication with China's Yuan Shikai who was stationed in Seoul, and the Qing government was prepared to dispatch its troops the moment it received a formal request.

A quick response from the court, however, was not forthcoming. The Korean government in those days was generally perceived as a caucus of feuding factions without any larger national vision—a cowardly institution reliant on foreign support. But in point of fact, the majority of court ministers were opposed to China's help for a reason that was all too obvious to anyone who cared about the country. To have foreign soldiers kill your own people alone was appalling. It was also easy to imagine that they would commit other atrocities. Asking China for military assistance would give other foreign powers, including Japan, reason to intervene.

Toward the end of May, Jeonju was on the verge of falling, and it became painfully obvious that the Korean army was unlikely to prevail. But court elder Kim Byeongshi (金炳始, 1832–98) stood against the other option to the very end, claiming "The rebels' crime may be unforgivable, yet they are our own people. They must be suppressed by our own forces. If we use foreign soldiers to do it, how can we justify our conduct to the public?"

Considering how militarily powerless and financially ill-provided Korea was in those days, the patriotism expressed in these words is moving.

Nevertheless, the influence of the pro-Qing faction, supported by Yuan Shikai, was such that the court eventually assented. On June 7, as soon as China received an official request, General Li Hongzhang notified the Japanese government of its intentions and dispatched some three thousand troops to Asan (牙山), in the southern suburbs of Seoul, for a fortnight through June 25.

It must have been beyond the imagination of Li, Yuan, or anyone in the Korean court that this incident would provide Japan with a pretext to start a war that heralded half a century of triumph for the empire of Japan, the humiliating colonization of the Korean Peninsula, and the semi-colonization of China.

Relations between Qing and Korea

Qing's relationship with Korea had been a thorny issue for Japan since the Ganghwa Island incident (江華島砲台事件) in 1875 and the Treaty of Ganghwa (日朝修好条規, Japan-Korea Treaty of Amity) the following year.

When Japan sought diplomatic relations with Korea in the after-math of this incident, the latter maintained that it couldn't authorize such an arrangement owing to its status as a tributary of the Qing court. The Japanese government then sent Deputy Foreign Minister Mori Arinori (森有礼) to Beijing to negotiate. To sidestep Japan's demand, China insisted that the peninsula was not part of China proper and that it had never interfered with Korean affairs, although it exercised suzerainty over it. China was therefore not in a position to make it take any action.

Wang Yunsheng, an authority on modern Sino-Japanese relations, noted that this reply gave Japan verbal evidence that Korea was an independent state, and asserted that the subsequent conflict over the peninsula could all be traced to this imprudent statement. What followed was twenty years of verbal tug-of-war concerning Korea's status, until the issue was finally settled by war.

Mutsu had, in fact, already been deeply interested in the international legality of a suzerain-tributary relationship, and had tried to explore the issue during his study trip to Europe, as his notes from those days reveal. In the last nine pages of his notebook labeled "The History of Constitutional Law and Politics" (憲法及び憲政史), he made the following comment, specifically on relations with Egypt, but perhaps with the Korean Peninsula in mind.

> After defeating Egypt in 1882, Britain has maintained de facto control of the country. What complicates the result of this military action is that, theoretically, Egypt has been part of the Turkish empire with which Britain has maintained peaceful relations...."

When a nation has nominal suzerainty over another but cannot control the conduct of the latter, how should this relationship be treated in international law? In another note, which appeared to be a sequel to the above quotation, he elaborated:

> There are semi-independent countries in the world which do not have equal relations with their suzerain states. Many legal experts submit that they should also be regarded as sovereign nations and full participators in international law. The term "semi-independent" is considered contradictory. According to Austin, they belong to one of three categories:
> 1. a country that accepts the law of the suzerain nation of its own volition, i.e., a full-fledged sovereign state;
> 2. a country that is compelled to accept the law of the suzerain nation, i.e., a tributary country that is subordinate and therefore not a sovereign state; or
> 3. a country that shares its sovereignty with a suzerain nation, i.e., a co-sovereign state....

Here, Mutsu appeared to have found a clear-cut answer to his question.

From the viewpoint of international law, any nation must be declared either fully sovereign or dependent. A sovereign nation must be responsible for its own conduct, while a suzerain state should take responsibility for its dependency. It is not justifiable to remain unclassified and take whichever position is convenient at the time.

Mutsu, it seems, while in Europe in 1883, had already formed the opinion that Korea could not be anything but a fully sovereign state.

When the Qing court decided to deploy troops in Korea, it sent an official announcement to Japan on June 7, 1894, which included the following:

> The Korean government has written to us saying, "The Donghak Rebellion has not been brought to an end and, if left unattended, might cause you problems. Since we succeeded previously in keeping the Imo Incident and Kapsin Political Coup under control with the assistance of soldiers of the Qing court, we humbly request that your troops be dispatched again. Once the rebels are suppressed, we would be grateful if your heaven-sent[*17] support could be repatriated promptly lest the troops suffer from a prolonged stay on foreign soil." Acknowledging this request as reasonable and having given military support in the past … we intend to help to restore peace and order in our tributary state and ensure the safety of foreign traders there. We wish to inform you, however, that as soon as the rebellion is put down, all our soldiers will be withdrawn.

The tone was condescending. In particular, the expression "to restore peace and order in our tributary state" would have been unacceptable to Mutsu. On the very day it was received, he sent the following succinct reply:

> I acknowledge receipt of your announcement. However, I wish to make it clear that our government has never recognized Korea as a tributary of your state, as referred to in your note.

A Swift Countermove

The dispatch of Japanese troops to Korea was in fact decided at a cabinet meeting five days before the message from the Qing court. This meeting was originally arranged to ask the emperor to sanction a

---

*17 The same term was used to describe relief columns the Ming court sent to counter Toyotomi Hideyoshi's (豊臣秀吉) invasion of Korea.

dissolution of the House of Representatives. It so happened, however, that a telegram from Sugimura Fukashi (杉村濬, 1848–1906), acting Japanese minister to Korea, reached the meeting with the information that the Korean government had finally asked for the mobilization of Chinese troops.

Mutsu wrote of Sugimura that he "has been stationed in Korea for quite some time and is remarkably knowledgeable about the situation there. The government has full confidence in his reports." Sugimura had been interested in Korea ever since he was a newspaper reporter, and had written extensively about the country. On joining the foreign services, he had specialized in Korean affairs. It is worth noting that, at the time war broke out, Japan's Foreign Ministry had in Sugimura a competent specialist on the spot who, being close to Yuan Shikai, knew almost immediately about the Korean request.

The formal request had actually been completed on June 1, but, owing to resistance from members of the Korean cabinet right up to the last minute, it wasn't transmitted until June 3. Because the Japanese government had learned of the Korean decision on June 1, it made its own decision a day later, before the petition had even reached the Qing court.

Mutsu's thought at this point was that "the already lopsided balance of power between China and Japan on the peninsula would be further tipped in China's favor, and Korea would become entirely at its mercy." Thus he suggested that "when China decides to send in its troops, whatever the pretext might be, Japan should also dispatch a substantial force to redress the balance between the two states there." The cabinet, including Prime Minister Itō, agreed.

Everyone in the cabinet was still painfully conscious of having been outdone by China, in terms of speed of deployment, during the Imo Incident and the Kapsin Political Coup. While it took a steamer only twelve or thirteen hours to transport Qing troops from the mainland to Incheon, it would take more than forty hours for Japanese troops to sail from Ujina Port (宇品港), the rail terminus in those days, to that destination.

The government moved quickly. Ōtori Keisuke (大鳥圭介, 1833–1911), on leave as minister to Korea, was ordered to immediately board a battleship, accompanied by members of the marine corps, and return to his post. At the same time, an expeditionary force was organized from among the 5th Division, ready to leave at a moment's notice. Mutsu wrote, "though it was an abrupt decision, we were able to undertake all the necessary preparation extremely quickly. And since it was a confidential decision, our activities were largely unnoticed by anyone outside the government. In fact, we were criticized by those not in the know for being too slow."

The swiftness of Mutsu's reaction at the outset certainly determined the direction of the entire war, as Wang Yunsheng noted critically in his review of the episode.

Admittedly, this was by no means an instant decision. Ever since the Donghak Rebellion, Mutsu had closely followed developments on the peninsula, relying on information provided by Sugimura and contemplating appropriate measures as the situation evolved. The military had also been prepared for a prompt response.

All this was in stark contrast to the clumsiness that Japan had demonstrated at the time of the Imo Incident and the Kapsin Political Coup. Of course, the shift in military balance caused by Japan's steady military buildup in the last ten years or so was a factor. But if either Itō or Mutsu had suggested that the country should wait and see how things developed, as common sense usually dictates, the course of the First Sino-Japanese War might have been very different. It was thus hugely significant for Japan's future that it had Mutsu as its foreign minister and Itō as prime minister at this critical moment.

Kenkenroku

Mutsu recorded his decisions and actions around this time in his memoir, *Kenkenroku*. In the preface, he wrote:

> Needless to say, the content of much of this memoir is based on official documents in the Ministry of Foreign Affairs. It should be noted, however, that in diplomatic correspondence the true

intention of the government often lies between the lines. Simply reading them literally would give one the feeling of chewing sand. Here, I intend to be more revealing.

An official document can be compared to a map drawn only with contour lines. Viewing it on its own gives one little idea of the actual features—of mountains and rivers—unless there are pictures showing the landscape as it is. The aim of this memoir is therefore to create a detailed map of foreign policy as drawn from real experience.

His description of *Kenkenroku* as an illustrative work is justified by the creative diplomacy he exercised at the time. What follows is based on his writing.

Preparedness to Fight Determined

Since such a major decision was involved, a consensus among government leaders on the future course of action was called for. A "basic policy" was adopted at a cabinet meeting, resulting from consultations between Itō and Mutsu, and submitted for imperial approval.

There was a preamble stating "now that both Japan and China have decided to send troops to Korea, the prospect is unpredictable, but if it leads to conflict, we must of course do our best to attain our initial goal." Then a list of priorities was drawn up:

Our aim is to:
1. maintain Japan's honor without disrupting peace and keep parity between Japan and China on the Korean Peninsula;
2. make sure that we remain a reactor, not the initiator; and
3. confine the confrontation between our two states and avoid the intervention of a third country.

In actuality, however, all three points turned out to be empty words.

Maintaining parity on the peninsula was precisely what China would adamantly refuse to accept, making a peaceful settlement impossible.

When China realized it lagged behind Japan, it looked for a peaceful settlement rather than military action. Therefore, Japan eventually took the initiative to start the war, ruling out its position as a reactor.

And because China's last hope for the prevention of war was foreign intervention—which China would plead for with the Western powers—foreign interference in the Korean situation was inevitable.

In the end, the only resolution in the "basic policy" that proved to be valid was the message behind the line in the preamble: "if it leads to conflict, we must of course do our best to attain our initial goal." In fact, it appears that Mutsu had already foreseen this eventuality, as hinted by the following sentences in the first chapter of *Kenkenroku*: "This was how our government was determined to conduct itself. It is doubtful, however, that the Qing government had the same resolution as we had, and that it would go directly to war with us."

When Wang Yunsheng discussed the diplomatic exchange between the two countries before the fighting began, he claimed that no expedient could change the course of events because "Japan had already made up its mind to fight." In retrospect, this assessment seems correct.

Some historians have argued that Mutsu and the Ministry of Foreign Affairs had no intention of starting a war; that they were pushed into it by the military; and that at least Itō was a pacifist. Personally, I think it is a waste of time to discuss this sort of anti-military argument. The lens through which it looks at actual facts is out of focus.

It might apply after World War II when the difference between pacifist and non-pacifist became more of an abstraction. But the ultimate concern for Itō and Mutsu was definitely to promote the national interest. Both war and peace were alternative means to accomplish this goal, and what mattered was that the chosen recourse should serve to attain it. One only needs to read the first chapter of *Kenkenroku* to understand this.

Naturally, it would have been ideal if a balance on the Korean Peninsula had been achieved without resorting to war. The possibility of this was close to zero. It would only have been feasible if China had accurately ascertained Japan's determination to go to war if necessary.

During the Cuban Missile Crisis of 1962, the Soviet premier Nikita Khrushchev was able to accurately ascertain U.S. President John F. Kennedy's determination to start a nuclear war, if necessary, and ordered Soviet missiles to be promptly withdrawn from Cuba. In contrast, China underestimated its opponent's intention and capability at every critical point and was forestalled and dragged into a war underprepared.

To be sure, some in the Qing court were aware of their shortcomings. Zhi Rui (志鋭) in the Chinese Foreign Ministry for example, submitted a letter to his superior on June 15, 1894:

> If we could show Japan that we were ready and in earnest, we might be able to arrest the flow toward war. But if China continues to make concessions and allow Japan's encroachment in the hope of averting war, the chances of doing so will be all the more reduced.

This was an excellent letter, pointing out the truth that only the resolve to fight could preserve peace, but it failed to help his leaders take a different course of action.

Summarizing the situation, Mutsu had the following to say:

> While the government was willing to play a passive role at the beginning, nevertheless it didn't hesitate to go to the other extreme if there seemed no other choice. China, however, appeared to believe that it could restrain Japan with a show of defiance short of provoking a war and Western intervention. It seemed to lack resolution. And this was not limited to China alone. Out of respect for the great Qing dynasty, the Korean court never even dreamed that China could be defeated by Japan, a misperception that Korea held on to until the fall of Pyongyang and the Battle of the Yalu River (黄海海戦) in September 1894.

Simply put, Mutsu concluded in *Kenkenroku* that it was the difference in initial preparedness that determined the overall course of events. And, objectively, in this he was right.

XIV

THE EVE OF THE FIRST
SINO-JAPANESE WAR

Tenacity

Dispatch of a Composite Brigade

Japanese Minister to Korea Ōtori Keisuke arrived in Incheon on June 9, 1894, soon after receiving his orders. He was followed by a composite brigade of about seven thousand men.

Historians believe that the deputy commander-in-chief, Kawakami Sōroku (川上操六, 1848–99), deceived the prime minister by saying that only one brigade would be sent. Itō would have assumed this meant a standard brigade of some two thousand soldiers; in actuality, it involved a composite brigade, which could be up to four times that size. A single brigade in peacetime comprises two regiments of one thousand men each, plus a few auxiliaries. A composite brigade is almost as powerful as a division, but falls numerically short of full division status. Kawakami is thought to have shipped over a force several times larger than he led Itō to believe.

This may well be true, but neither Itō nor Mutsu recorded any complaints about the military's conduct at the beginning of the conflict, including this mobilization order. Further inquiry into the issue would be of little purpose. Even if Itō was initially misled, the discovery of Kawakami's ruse probably provoked little more from him than a certain wry surprise.

Arriving in Korea, the Japanese troops found themselves in an unexpected situation: around Seoul and Incheon, things were quite calm.

In the south, where the battle to suppress the rebels was being fought, the morale of the Korean government forces had been buoyed by news of the dispatch of the Chinese. Korean soldiers soon recaptured Jeonju Castle, and the situation had begun to settle down even before China's troops landed in Asan. The Donghak rebels had run rampant through Seoul the previous year, but order had already been restored in the city.

Under the circumstances, the appearance of some seven thousand Japanese soldiers must have come as a shock. Mutsu wrote:

Our troops were well disciplined and the local people were never maltreated, which earned the admiration of Seoul's foreign residents. But there was no disguising the fact that these were armed men in large numbers, stationed between Seoul and Incheon when the Qing troops were in the less conspicuous region of Asan. As a result, they were suspected of having an aggressive purpose and, if the situation allowed, overrunning Korea; and the residents' sympathies lay more with China than Japan....

When news of the Donghak Rebellion first reached Yuan Shikai, he had seen an opportunity to reassert China's dominance in the region and persuaded his superiors to send troops into the country with the approval of its government. He learned to regret this decision, however, on the arrival of the Japanese forces, and began trying to maneuver the Korean government into demanding their withdrawal.

But Ōtori had already been negotiating with the Korean court on the basis of an official directive to pursue a "peaceful settlement." Observing the situation in Seoul and the reaction of foreign powers, he advised the Ministry of Foreign Affairs that the dispatch of Japanese troops should be limited in number.

Despite this advice, Mutsu maintained his commitment to the

original plan. In *Kenkenroku*, his cool-headed comment was clearly influenced by past experience:

> The decision to send a large contingent had already gathered momentum at home, making it impossible at that point to reduce the size of the operation. Furthermore, China's diplomacy was suspected of being deceptive: we had received intelligence that it was prepared to send in reinforcements. Ōtori's advice was reasonable, but there was no knowing how the situation would develop. Once a confrontation began, military strength alone would determine the outcome. We therefore decided that it would be safer to stick to the original numbers.

From Acted-Upon to Actor

Meanwhile, negotiations between Ōtori and Yuan for the joint withdrawal of troops progressed to the point almost of an exchange of diplomatic notes between the two governments.

At this stage, however, the acting minister, Sugimura, began to have second thoughts, reasoning that Tokyo would not have sent such a large force to Korea without an urgent purpose. To agree to reduce the number of Japanese troops simply because they were so visible and controversial might go against that purpose.

Sugimura's meeting with Brigade Commander Ōshima, who had landed in Incheon on June 16, only deepened this conviction. Returning to Seoul on the same day, he immediately briefed Ōtori on his interview with the commander, and advised against a formal exchange of diplomatic notes.

Sugimura had read Mutsu's intentions intelligently. At a time of crisis, when telegrams were expensive and necessarily brief, his intuition made a definite contribution to the favorable development of the situation for Japan.

At the same time, the negotiations between Ōtori and Yuan may have had the effect of delaying China's decision to send in reinforcements by raising hopes for a joint withdrawal.

In any event, the Japanese government decided not to cut the planned number of troops. The question of what to do next, however, presented difficulties, as Mutsu explains:

> The cabinet's "basic policy" was to remain diplomatically passive but always to make the first move militarily. For this reason, the officials who were involved all took pains to maintain the delicate balance between diplomatic and military action until the last minute. Even now, it makes me nervous thinking back on the situation.
>
> Both countries had troops on Korean soil, but there was no possibility yet of a direct clash since they were in different areas. The Donghak Rebellion also appeared to have subsided. So the two sides maintained an uneasy standoff in which suspicion mingled with hope. A joint withdrawal through diplomatic negotiation seemed unlikely, but there was no imminent danger of combat. Armed conflict could not begin without a reason, even if only a superficial one. So there seemed no way to break this impasse without using diplomatic ingenuity to drastically change the situation.

After frequent consultation with Mutsu, Itō eventually came up with a strategy. The handwritten document submitted to a cabinet meeting on June 14 would play an important part in future developments. It contained two key factors:

1. Cooperation between Japanese and Chinese troops in suppressing the rebellion; and in its aftermath,
2. the formation of a standing commission, with both China and Japan sending representatives to monitor the situation on the peninsula. The goal should be to help reform Korea's domestic politics, rebuild its finances, improve its bureaucracy, and restore peace and order.

As Mutsu frankly acknowledges in the excerpt above, the ulterior motive of this policy was to provide an excuse for Japanese troops to remain in situ. It was not, however, a departure from the orthodox position vis-à-vis Korea. The pro-modernization Gaehwapa (Enlightenment Party) had carried out a successful coup d'état during the first stage of the Kapsin Political Coup, until its suppression by China. With the presence of crack Japanese troops now in Seoul, a second opportunity was at hand.

Historically, Western hegemony was at its height. The colonization of certain regions was justified in the name of bringing civilization to backward areas—a project commonly known as the "white man's burden." The goal of raising the level of social and political conditions in Korea was sufficient reason, it could be argued, to keep an army in place.

Although other cabinet members were receptive to Itō's suggestion, Mutsu asked for the final decision to be deferred by one day so that he could sleep on it—a rare occurrence for this usually decisive person. Presumably, although in basic agreement with Itō's ideas, he felt that the implications were so significant that the proposal should be fleshed out in more detail.

Mutsu himself had this to say on the matter:

> Although I had nothing against it in principle, its adoption would make Japan the actor rather than the acted-upon. At the same time, we had to consider how to maintain our diplomatic strategy in the face of China's objections, which were easy to imagine. It also seemed to me that the prime minister had some deeper intention, not mentioned at the cabinet meeting.
>
> Back at home, I gave it further thought overnight and came to the conclusion that we had no choice but to resort to diplomatic duress.
>
> While the Chinese government was very unlikely to agree to it, we should remain determined to help carry out the reform of Korea's domestic politics unilaterally if necessary. Otherwise, the future course of Japanese diplomacy might be blocked every time we have a disagreement with China.

If the government was to adopt a proposal as daring as Itō's, he felt, it must be prepared to accept the consequences and follow through.

At the next day's cabinet meeting, he suggested adding two points, which were duly included in the final decision:

1. Refusal to withdraw Japanese troops until negotiations with China started to take effect; and
2. unilateral pursuit of domestic political reform in Korea if China rebuffed Japan's proposal.

One wonders, however, why Mutsu insisted on this point-of-no-return proviso, though he knew how hawkish the public was and suspected that Itō had secretly endorsed the hardline approach.

"It Is Not Our War"

One reason for Mutsu's firmness must have been the need to take a stance that would not be shaken by changes in circumstance such as foreign intervention. Another apparent factor, however, was Emperor Meiji's restraint.

In the time between the fateful cabinet decision and the outbreak of war, the emperor, through Grand Chamberlain Tokudaiji, sent a variety of inquiries to the Itō government about the unsettled situation on the Korean Peninsula. The common thread in these communications was the emperor's desire to restrain Japan's foreign policy, which he feared was rushing toward military confrontation.

On June 21, for instance, he asked the following question:

I have read the telegram reporting on China's preparations to dispatch further reinforcements to Korea. I have also been told that the situation in Korea is calm and that China has demanded the withdrawal of our troops. Is it not possible that the idea of Chinese reinforcements is mere speculation, unsupported by solid evidence?

Similarly, on receiving Ōtori's July 19 telegram claiming that Korea's refusal to accept Japan's agenda left them no option but coercion, the emperor sent a message the same day asking, "Did Ōtori really exhaust all means of persuasion? Is it truly hopeless?"

On July 23, the day Japanese troops set out for Asan, the emperor inquired, "If the reform of domestic politics is pursued under the banner

of the Daewongun, doesn't this make it unnecessary to resort to force?"
When war finally broke out, he said, "This is not our war; it's our cabinet ministers,'" and remained discomposed for days, even refusing at
first to send the imperial messenger to report the outbreak of war at Ise
Shrine. A *waka* he wrote around the same time is indicative of his true
opinion:

> We believed we were surrounded by friends
> Why, then, are the seas so rough?

There is no need to defend the imperial family from the post–World
War II attribution of responsibility. The relative pacifism of the emperor
during the Meiji era and throughout the imperialistic period is simply an
objective fact. Indeed, during the imperial conference of September 6,
1941, at which Japan effectively decided to plunge into the Pacific War,
Emperor Hirohito asked for an opportunity to speak—a highly unusual
occurrence—and recited his grandfather's poem when given the floor.

War is a dangerous venture for a monarch. Military rulers like Napoleon and Alexander the Great apart, an aversion to risk generally makes
pacifists of kings. The houses of Hapsburg, Hohenzollern, and Roma-
nov, none of whom were shy of involvement in military affairs, were all
overthrown after World War I.

The matter is more complicated for an elected cabinet, which must
not only demonstrate political competence but also respond to public opinion and, at times, take serious risks for the sake of the nation.
Lorenz von Stein once told Mutsu that "since a monarch only has to
worry about the long-term fate of his kingdom, being aloof from public
opinion and domestic politics, he can serve as a curb on national policy."
There seems to be a certain truth in this.

Bismarck, whom Itō looked up to, succeeded in unifying Germany
after the Austro-Prussian War; but before that conflict, he had struggled
to persuade his initially reluctant king to agree to open hostilities.

Although Germany and Japan had similar constitutions, the Japanese emperor wielded less power than his counterpart. The reasons for
this can be found in the historical development of the two countries.

In Japan, direct administration by the emperor ended after the Nara period, when real power was held by the *sesshō kanpaku* (摂政関白, first secretary and regent) or *seii taishōgun* (征夷大将軍, shogun). While the emperor's wishes were often ignored in this system, it did have the benefit of releasing him from political responsibility, which surely contributed to the uninterrupted continuation of the imperial line. As a result of this tradition, even after the promulgation of a constitution based on the Prussian model, Japan retained something similar in nature to Britain's system where "the king reigns, but does not govern."

This explains why the Itō cabinet was able to start a war despite the emperor's opposition—a move that would have been unthinkable in Prussia.

In his *Kawakami Sōroku den* (川上操六伝, A biography of Kawakami Sōroku), Tokutomi Sohō (徳富蘇峰, 1863–1957) argues that Mutsu and this officer were responsible for the essential direction of the First Sino-Japanese War, with "the likes of Itō and Yamagata … more or less dragged into it."

Mutsu appears to have had a tacit understanding with Kawakami, who was known as a handsome, mild-tempered, and polite individual— more "good listener" than "heroic warrior," which would have endeared him to the foreign minister.

Kawakami's post at that time was army second-in-command, but though the actual commander-in-chief was Prince Arisugawa Taruhito (有栖川宮熾仁, 1835–95), who had led the Imperial Army against the last partisans of the shogunate in the Boshin War, Kawakami acted as de facto commander. After personally observing military training and materiel in China between April and July 1893, he returned convinced that Japan would prevail if war broke out. It was at least partly due to his practical advice that Mutsu's diplomacy during the ensuing war was so successful, seizing every opportunity, making no mistakes.

Kawakami was also an excellent judge of character. As deputy commander-in-chief, he had built up the foundations of the Imperial Army by bringing in talent from all over the country.

Mutsu died in 1897 at the age of fifty-four; the First Sino-Japanese War had taken a toll on his health. Kawakami died in 1899, aged fifty-three, exhausted by the same war.

Kodama Gentarō (児玉源太郎, 1852–1906) was another senior officer who died young, passing away in 1906 at the age of fifty-five, one year after victory in the Russo-Japanese War. Given the poor living conditions at the time, these men must have known that their strenuous, day-and-night routine, with no time for rest or recuperation, would probably shorten their lives. But they carried the country's future on their shoulders.

The Art of Imperialist Diplomacy

If Bismarck's foreign and military policy was a model for the age of imperialism, this was no less true of Itō and Mutsu's diplomacy. In *Kenkenroku*, immediately after the reference to the proposal for Korean reform quoted above, the author wrote:

> We reached a critical moment in our diplomatic quest.... Should China reject our proposal, we couldn't let it have its own way. Eventually, direct confrontation with China became unavoidable, forcing Japan to carry through an initiative implicit in the decision to take troops to Korea.

"The skill with which Japan switched its diplomacy from a passive stance to an active one was impressive," Wang Yunsheng commented. The Japanese proposal sparked a verbal contest with China, which argued that, with the rebellion at an end, there was no need for cooperation in suppressing it. As for political reform, China announced its intention to stay out of Korea's internal affairs, and urged Japan to respect Korea's sovereignty and do the same. Pointing out that the Treaty of Tianjin stipulated bilateral withdrawal once the uprising was defeated, China proposed that both countries recall their troops immediately.

In itself, this was a reasonable retort. As Wang Yunsheng observed, however, "Clear and rational though China's arguments were, Japan was already determined to enter into a war with it, and could not be turned from its course by this repudiation." Here too was an accurate analysis.

If China refused to participate in a joint commission, then Japan would undertake a reform program on its own. The Itō cabinet drafted a detailed plan for redevelopment and wired it to Minister Ōtori on June 28, 1894.

This document included some reasonable proposals such as "Courts must be impartial," and "Revenue and expenditure should be rigorously managed." In short, the cabinet was advocating that Korea be governed as Japan had been since the Meiji Restoration.

But the Korean government was also reluctant to comply. It was unclear how long Japan would be able to maintain its position in Seoul; Chinese troops could regain the upper hand overnight. Given this state of affairs, the Korean administration decided to stall the Japanese while formulating a plan, in close consultation with Yuan Shikai as well as the diplomatic missions of the Western powers, to force the prompt withdrawal of Japanese soldiers.

Japan's mission in Seoul was the first to detect these machinations and realize that, even if a directive to carry out political reform came from Tokyo, their hands would be tied.

In his memoir, Sugimura wrote:

> Even without the presence of our troops, those old foxes in the royal court who were so dependent on China would have detested Japan and clung to the Middle Kingdom anyway. They seemed firmly convinced that China would come out on top even if our troops were in temporary control. It seemed to me, therefore, that our reform proposal would only be accepted if we defeated the Chinese forces in a direct confrontation.

No sooner had the expected directive arrived from Tokyo on June 28 than Minister Ōtori wired his opinion back to the home office. His telegram was almost identical in content to Sugimura's comments in his memoir, suggesting that it had in fact been drafted by Sugimura. It read:

> Determined on the withdrawal of foreign armies from its soil, the Korean government has not only wired requests for help to both Yuan Shikai and Li Hongzhang, but sought mediation by the Western diplomatic missions. Yuan resorts to all kinds of malicious

schemes to turn the Korean court against us and make it rely more heavily on China. He insists, for example, that China would emerge the victor in a direct clash with Japan. He also fabricates telegrams designed to accuse us of having hopes of subjugating Korea. In view of this, we cannot expect to carry out any reforms there unless we contrive, and win, a military engagement with China.... At this point, we should put pressure on the Korean government to induce China to withdraw the forces it sent to "protect its tributary state," or commence political reforms.

Mutsu wrote about this telegram in *Kenkenroku*, pointing out that, although he found Ōtori's argument initially rather radical, its main thrust did not go against the "basic policy" adopted at the cabinet meeting. Accordingly, the cabinet decided to let Ōtori use his own discretion as to how the issue was handled.

Okamoto Ryūnosuke

This is where Okamoto Ryūnosuke, the most notorious political activist of his time, entered the scene.

Having been purged from every official post he held, military or civilian, for his involvement in the Takebashi Incident (竹橋事件) immediately after Mutsu's imprisonment in 1878, Okamoto had involved himself in national politics only as a "concerned citizen," without relying on any official assistance.

When Kim Okgyun and Pak Yonghyo visited Japan, Okamoto had volunteered to look after them, along with other members of the Gaehwapa party, in consultation with Gotō Shōjirō and Fukuzawa Yukichi. After the abortive Kapsin Political Coup, however, he withdrew from the Korean revolutionary movement, seeing it as premature, and entered the Nichiren Buddhist (日蓮宗) priesthood. There is no denying the courage and seriousness of the man.

Okamoto gave Kim Okgyun shelter when the latter sought asylum in Japan afterwards, and strongly opposed Kim's visit to Shanghai out of concern for his safety. When news of the assassination reached him, Okamoto went to Shanghai on behalf of Kim's comrades in Japan to negotiate for the burial of his friend. Being an independent with no official role, Okamoto could be useful on such occasions.

After returning from Shanghai briefly to meet with Mutsu, he traveled to Korea to gather intelligence there in cooperation with Sugimura. When Ōtori Keisuke was sent to Seoul as Japanese minister, Mutsu entrusted to him a message for Okamoto that read, "The success of Ōtori's appointment depends very much on your generous assistance."

Behind this were certain new developments. The Korean government announced that it would willingly reform its domestic politics only if Japan withdrew its troops first. But withdrawal would remove the pressure on Korea to effectively change. In Japan's eyes, the sole way of breaking this stalemate was the establishment of a more cooperative government via a coup d'état. The Gaehwapa had lost its influence after the deaths of Pak and Kim; and none of its members now had the authority to become the leader of a coup. The only person in Korea who might was the Daewongun, the former regent, whose hold on power had been broken by China after the Imo Incident. The Daewongun, however, was known for his anti-modernization position and aversion to Japan. In the end, it was none other than Okamoto who took on the task of persuading him to enter the fray.

On July 19, 1894, Ōtori issued a highhanded demand for a response from the Korean government by July 22. Korean officials gave no indication of intending to meet this deadline.

The Japanese side had made plans to capture the royal palace at dawn on July 23, immediately after the expiration of Ōtori's time limit. The raid would be coordinated with the coup d'état. This left Okamoto and a few associates in a desperate effort to win the Daewongun round from the evening of July 22 until daybreak.

Hearing no good news from Okamoto, Sugimura paid a visit to the Daewongun himself. It was some indication of what this elderly, conservative Korean thought of Okamoto when he apparently pointed at him and said: "This is a brave man. He says he will commit harakiri if I don't agree to lead the coup."

Nevertheless, though his visitors continued the attempt to persuade him to cooperate, they had little success. Finally, the Daewongun sat up straight and demanded that they answer a question: "If you are sincere in claiming that this proposal derives from the goodwill of your government, can you promise me on behalf of His Imperial Majesty that Japan will not deprive Korea of an inch of land should the coup d'état succeed?" Sugimura, on behalf of Minister Ōtori as the Japanese representative in Korea, then put his response in writing: "The government of Japan, having only the best of intentions in the action it proposes, hereby guarantees that it will never deprive Korea of even an inch of its territory after the success of this undertaking." At this, the Daewongun finally agreed to lead the coup. The episode is evidence that he was motivated by more than just a desire to restore his own authority.

At long last, the Japanese were able to have a Daewongun-led administration abolish various treaties with China. They also managed to make it appear as if the Korean king had formally requested that they use their troops to expel the Chinese forces from Asan. According to Sugimura's memoir, this agreement was finalized at eleven o'clock on the morning of July 25. Considering that the composite brigade had started to move south that same morning, after the first shots of the Battle of Pungdo were fired three hours earlier, these negotiations were concluded just in time.

On August 1, 1894, the imperial mandate on the declaration of war was made public. It had been walking on a tightrope, but Japan finally had its war with China.

One notable aspect of all this was the degree of mutual understanding among not only leaders like Itō and Mutsu but also figures like Sugimura and Okamoto, imperialists though they all were. Even when communication was difficult, each appeared to know exactly what to do, as if part of a well-tuned machine. Perhaps the experience of earlier setbacks had helped to form a perfect consensus on how to handle tough conditions. Whatever its cause or background, it was a fine display of teamwork.

XV

A WAR OF DIPLOMACY

Keeping the Western Powers at Bay

The Problem of Foreign Intervention

Japan's determination to "avoid the intervention of a third country" notwithstanding, it was inevitable that the Western powers would take an interest in the rising tensions on the peninsula. In the end, direct appeals from Korea and China were what spurred Britain, the United States, and Russia into action. The Korean court, shocked by the presence of so many Japanese troops on its soil, had asked every diplomatic mission in Seoul to press Japan to withdraw; and China, knowing that it would not prevail in any armed conflict, also hoped to use foreign pressure to achieve a peaceful settlement.

But the Western powers were bound to get involved of their own accord eventually. In the nineteenth century, intervening in the affairs of other countries was a way to demonstrate power and influence. Yet some interventions were more serious than others. After Prussia's unexpectedly rapid triumph in the Franco-Prussian War of 1870–71, for example, Britain was quick to declare its opposition to the ceding of French territory. But, with the outcome of the war already determined, Prussia simply ignored this objection, and Britain let the matter drop.

The question in any intervention, then, is whether the country behind it has both the inclination and military capacity to insist on its position, or whether it simply wants to remind the parties to the conflict of its interest in the region. Mutsu decided it was safe to ignore the objections of the Western powers at the outbreak of the First Sino-Japanese, but by its final stage he would become convinced of the seriousness of the Tripartite Intervention, and decide to consent to it. History has proved his judgment correct on both counts.

Russia Makes Its Move

Following an appeal Li Honzhang made to the Russian minister in Beijing, Russia became the first Western power to enter the dispute. Russia's minister in Japan, M. A. Hitrovo, met with Mutsu to convey his government's hopes for a prompt settlement and to ask if Japan would agree to recall its troops if China did the same. Mutsu's reply was firm:

> While your suggestion is understandable, I must remind you that our distrust of China is not groundless, given that nation's history of meddling in Korea's domestic politics and repeated misrepresentations to Korea and Japan alike. Accordingly, we will retire our forces only if China's withdrawal is accompanied by a guarantee of either cooperation on domestic political reform in Korea or non-interference while we address the matter ourselves.

It was Mutsu's foresight in securing the cabinet's agreement to resist foreign intervention and pursue Korean reform with or without China's participation that allowed him to respond to Hitrovo so decisively.

Recognizing Japan's determination, Russia decided to shelve the idea of mediation between Japan and China and unilaterally address Korea's appeals instead. On June 30, Hitrovo conveyed the following message from his government:

> We urge you to accede to Korea's request that both your own and Chinese troops leave the country. Should you refuse to do this in

concert with China, we must advise you that it would place a heavy responsibility on your shoulders.

By insisting that responsibility for the outcome of the situation lay solely with Japan, Russia was reserving a free hand for itself in Korea. This was a serious diplomatic threat—indeed, it foreshadowed the Tripartite Intervention itself.

Mutsu, realizing the gravity of the situation, rushed over to the prime minister's residence in Isarago, Tokyo. He summarizes their conversation as follows:

> Without offering an opinion of my own, I presented Russia's warning to Itō and asked for his thoughts. He considered the communiqué for a moment, then said calmly, "Having come this far, how could we comply?"
>
> "I quite agree," I told him. "Finding a way through whatever lies ahead will be a 'heavy responsibility' the two of us can share. There's nothing more to say."
>
> I promptly took my leave and, on my return, immediately wired our representative in Russia to explain the situation and how we intended to respond to it. I sent a similar telegram to our minister in Britain so that he could brief the British government before Russia spoke to them.
>
> Even today, it still makes me break out in a sweat remembering all this.
>
> My talk with Itō consisted of that single exchange. No more was necessary when we knew ourselves to be in full agreement. I wonder, though, what would have happened had our views differed. Would Japan still have the esteem internationally it enjoys today?

Public opinion in Japan was surely one factor behind their decision. The Diet and the newspapers took a much more aggressive attitude than the administration throughout the First Sino-Japanese War—so much so that it was often difficult for Mutsu to reconcile public opinion with the policies actually called for by the situation in Korea. He usually tried to steer a popular course until things became too dangerous, when he would ease off. Mutsu called this "navigating," and had frequent recourse to it.

It is hard to imagine that Itō and Mutsu would have accommodated the public outlook in this case had they seen real danger in the Russian intervention. But Russia was obviously still unprepared for military action in the Far East, and Britain and Germany seemed likely to keep it in check as well. Indeed, historians have established that Russia had been reluctant to divert troops to its eastern frontier with the threat of a newly emerging Germany in the west.

Itō and Mutsu's response to Russia's overtures may have been a gamble, but the odds were in their favor.

Shrewd Assessments, Bold Decisions

After his meeting with Itō, Mutsu didn't waste time before drafting a reply to Russia. After cabinet consultation and receiving imperial approval on July 1, the letter was handed to the Russian minister on July 2. It read:

> Your diplomatic note was of such importance that we needed time to think about it.
>
> We have seen reports that the Korean government has notified diplomatic missions in Seoul of the rebellion's suppression. Our own reports, however, inform us that the fundamental causes of unrest have not been eliminated, and the rebellion itself—the initial reason for our military deployment—continues.
>
> Japan has absolutely no territorial ambitions on the Korean Peninsula. We openly declare, therefore, that our troops will be withdrawn once the rebellion is completely quelled and the nation's future is no longer in doubt.
>
> We are grateful for your cordial advice, and, given the bonds of friendship and trust between our nations, we hope that you will recognize the sincerity of this declaration.

Though courteously put, the reply made clear that Japan would not retreat unless "the fundamental causes of unrest" were removed—in other words, until the reform of Korea's domestic politics had begun.

Having rejected the Russian proposal in this way, the Japanese side anxiously awaited the reply. It came on July 13:

> His Imperial Majesty the Emperor of Russia is pleased to learn that Japan has no intention of invading Korea and intends to repatriate its troops once the danger of a recurrence of the rebellion is precluded. At this juncture, the Russian government urges the governments of Japan and China to confer together and conclude a peace agreement as early as possible.
>
> Korea being a neighbor of ours, we cannot remain mere spectators to any upheaval that might take place there. Nevertheless, we hope that your government understands that our conduct is inspired by a wish to forestall conflict between your nation and China.

Direct intervention had successfully been averted. Russia had left open the possibility of future action, and would no doubt continue to follow developments closely, but for the time being it had agreed to stay out of the dispute. Most importantly, it had expressed only a wish to "forestall" Japan starting a war with China. Itō and Mutsu's gamble had paid off.

The speed in decision-making Mutsu showed in this episode would serve him throughout the war. As early as June 2, when informal reports of Chinese soldiers entering Korea were received, Mutsu had persuaded the cabinet to send in Japanese forces in response, and had completed an operational plan in consultation with Kawakami Sōroku before the evening was out.

Several weeks later, when the Qing court rejected Japan's Korean reform proposal, he replied with a lengthy note, later known as the "first ultimatum," the next day. The missive refuted China's arguments one by one, and ended:

> As Japan's foreign minister, I have spoken plainly, without reserve. Let me emphasize again that, while our views differ from those of the Qing court, Japan will not withdraw the troops it currently has stationed in Korea.

His "second ultimatum" came immediately after he learned that British-mediated negotiations had broken down in Beijing. When Britain sent a letter on July 21 outlining its intentions in the Korean situation, Mutsu replied on July 22.

In the course of the whole war, Mutsu made decision after decision on which the fate of Japan rested. None of them seem to have been misjudged, despite the speed at which he made them—bolstered by the trust that he and Itō had in each other and his ability to accurately predict developments and obtain cabinet approval in advance.

As a former member of the foreign service myself, I can't help being impressed by the wording of the documents Mutsu produced, some of which he must have stayed up all night to get done. It would be difficult, if not impossible, to duplicate this in today's Ministry of Foreign Affairs. The current system of repeated consultation from a senior level all the way to the top is neither fast enough nor conducive to prose of an equivalent quality.

Aided by a succession of victories early in the war, his work helped keep China at bay while arranging a fait accompli before Russia could prepare for war in the Far East.

Thwarting the British

The British intervention was of a rather different nature.

Russia, which had its own designs on Korea, had hoped to forestall a Japanese incursion until it could complete the Siberian Railway and make ready for possible war itself. Britain, on the other hand, sought to maintain the status quo in order to protect its vested interests in the region. "The British appeared strongly opposed to any disturbance of the peace in East Asia, whatever the cause," was Mutsu's assessment. Accordingly, rather than stake out a claim on the peninsula in its intervention, Britain offered only an impeccably professional attempt at mediation between Japan and China through diplomatic channels.

When the British minister to China, Nicholas O'Connor, was asked by the Qing court to help them reach a settlement with the Japanese, he doubted Japan's willingness to play along. But unlike Russia's more authoritarian approach, he hoped to find room for compromise. In this case, the most realistic scenario appeared to be an agreement combining cooperation on political reform with the repatriation of Japanese troops.

Itō and Mutsu, however, had already agreed, after their meeting with the Russian minister Hitrovo on June 25, that it was too late to change course now. This attitude had not escaped the notice of Hitrovo, a shrewd diplomat and keen observer of the Korean situation. He reported as much to his home office after the meeting, saying, "Korean affairs are the subject of heated debate in Japan today, and in my opinion the Itō cabinet is too deeply involved to make any concession without a plausible excuse or the appearance of victory."

Later, reflecting on an interview with Mutsu on June 30, he wrote:

> If we could persuade the Korean government to organize a tripartite committee for political change with Chinese, Japanese, and Russian representatives, combined with a request for Japan to pull out, Japan would be denied any justification for maintaining a military presence there.... The Japanese public are in such an overexcited state that their government could not withdraw even if it wished to unless we provide a credible pretext that doesn't wound their pride.

But the expansion of Russia's influence in Korea which such a committee represented would have troubled both China and Japan, and the Russian government decided not to interfere in Korea's politics, so the proposal was never formally made.

On June 30, Minister O'Connor paid a visit to China's Foreign Ministry (総理衙門) to suggest a deal: the British government would join with other Western powers in pressuring Japan to remove its troops if China would agree to support Korean reform and respect that country's territorial integrity. Seeing no harm in this proposal, the Chinese accepted on the condition that the fundamental suzerain-tributary relationship was not affected.

This condition, unfortunately, doomed the attempt from the start. Suzerainty might have been non-negotiable for China, but it was unacceptable to Japan. Anyway, in the end the point was moot: the agreement was nullified when China reneged on its pledge to compromise on reform, partly in the hope that Russia would be able to force Japan's unconditional retreat.

Japan accepted the British offer of mediation as well. Despite its "basic policy" of rejecting foreign attempts at intervention, it could not dismiss out of hand a proposal that included Korean political reform. However, when Japan's acting deputy minister in Beijing, Komura Jutarō, visited the Foreign Ministry there on July 9, he was informed that discussions would not even begin until Japan had pulled out of Korea. Recognizing the futility of further argument, Komura ended the meeting and went to complain to O'Connor.

On July 12, O'Connor visited the Foreign Ministry himself to request clarification from Yikuang, Prince Qing (慶親王). Rescinding China's previous commitments, the prince was adamant that Japanese withdrawal must precede any other negotiation.

"This incident alone is sufficient to prove the ministry's lack of experience," Wan Yungsheng wrote later. "Not only did they disappoint the British minister, who had begun the mediation out of goodwill, they also gave Japan further excuse for its own actions."

Mutsu's supposition was that China had acted in expectation of Russian intervention:

> The Qing court's acceptance of the original British proposal was, it seems, a pretense in anticipation of another development. They never had any intention of keeping faith in their dealings with foreign governments, and did not realize that ignoring a fundamental rule of diplomacy would only isolate them further. It is particularly regrettable to see such behavior from one as experienced, insightful, and broad-minded as Li Hongzhang.

China's mistake was, in fact, attributable to its internal circumstances at the time, which divided authority for foreign policy between Li and the Foreign Ministry.

Following the collapse of the British attempt at mediation, Mutsu issued a second ultimatum to the Chinese government, laying "all responsibility for future developments" at its feet. And Japan began to prepare for war in earnest.

Britain, still hoping for a peaceful solution, approached Mutsu with a new proposal. This time, however, rather than securing the approval of the Chinese in advance, the British had simply drafted an agreement they considered fair and appropriate. Even if Japan accepted it, there was no guarantee that China would follow suit. At this point, Britain appeared to be siding more with China in the dispute, trying to persuade Japan to back down.

But Mutsu was already determined to go to war. He responded with a hard-nosed counterstatement, explaining that the circumstances had changed. Disappointed, the British sent back a strongly worded diplomatic note on July 21 saying "if Japan's hardline policy should lead to war with China, all responsibility for the consequences will lie with the Japanese government."

When Mutsu immediately replied on July 22 to explain Japan's position, the British government must have realized that war would be inevitable. Its reply, dated July 23 stated, "In case of the eruption of a war between Japan and Qing, the British government requests that Japan agree not to enter into battle in and around Shanghai, which is the center of British interests in China."

The matter was settled. Ever pragmatic, the British would accept war as long as one particular area was spared. Gratified by this de facto acceptance, the Japanese government assented to Britain's request.

That very day, Japan succeeded in persuading the Daewongun to act as a figurehead for the coup d'état it had plotted, even as Japanese troops seized the royal palace. The last obstacles to war had been eliminated, and Mutsu's prescient diplomacy had maintained Japan's position in the global community as the conflict widened.

Reading the Americans

The American attempt at intervention was of little consequence as war approached, but Mutsu's response to it is instructive.

On July 9, after a direct appeal from the Korean court to the

American minister stationed in Seoul, the U.S. government issued a strong warning to Japan, deploring its refusal to withdraw along with China now that the rebellion in Korea was over and frowning on the attempt to impose radical reform on Korea's government. The president of the United States, the missive stated, would be gravely disappointed if Japan were to victimize a defenseless neighbor and start an unjustified war.

By claiming neutrality and framing the warning as friendly advice, however, the U.S. was effectively announcing that it did not intend to impose any sanctions on Japan should it go ahead. This was just one more example of the U.S. making a declaration of principles with no intention of enforcing it.

As former Japanese minister to Washington, D.C., Mutsu knew this aspect of American policy better than anyone on the Japanese side, and his comments reveal as much:

> The United States has long maintained close relations with Japan and regards us as a friend. Meddling in the Far East would also be against their national policy. It is clear that their message was motivated solely by a common human desire for peace and their reluctance to entirely ignore a request from Korea.

Explaining Japan's position to Edwin Dun, U.S. minister to Japan, and asking that he convey this to his home office, was sufficient to end the American "intervention."

Mutsu's time in Washington and his reading on world history while in prison had left him with full confidence in America's goodwill, which he saw as part of its national character. He also admired the country's achievements. In a poem written during his imprisonment, he described the Declaration of Independence as being "like fresh air on tired eyes." It is no coincidence that, later, as the war drew to a close, Mutsu would accept the U.S. offer of mediation first.

THE BATTLE OF PUNGDO

Dawn of an Empire

Naval Engagement

On July 25, 1894, just nine days after the revision of the unequal treaty with Britain, Japanese and Chinese ships exchanged fire near Pungdo Island off the west coast of the Korean Peninsula. The Battle of Pungdo was both the opening salvo in the First Sino-Japanese War and the dawn of the empire of Japan, which would last until its defeat in the Pacific War fifty years later.

An account of the battle can be found in *Nihon no senshi: Nisshin sensō* (日本の戦史：日清戦争, A military history of Japan: The First Sino-Japanese War). According to this work, written by the General Staff Office of the Imperial Army and reprinted in condensed form after World War II, the cruisers *Yoshino* (吉野), *Akitsushima* (秋津州), and *Naniwa* (浪速) of the Grand Fleet's First Mobile Squadron encountered the Chinese cruiser *Jiyuan* (済遠) and gunboat *Guangyi* (広乙) in the offing of Pungdo Island early in the morning of July 25. The commander of the Japanese fleet decided to sail past the Chinese ships in accordance with peacetime naval procedure, but ordered the crews to prepare for action just in case.

When the distance between the two sides had narrowed to about three thousand yards, the *Jiyuan* suddenly fired on the *Yoshino*. The Japanese fleet returned fire immediately, and the battle was underway. Visibility soon dropped as exhaust and gun smoke mixed with the morning mist.

When the air cleared, the *Guangyi* was disabled and drifting as the *Jiyuan* fled. The *Naniwa* gave chase, and the *Jiyuan* soon hoisted a white flag along with the ensign of the Rising Sun in surrender.

At this point, the British commercial ship *Kowshing* (高陞) arrived on the scene. It was carrying Chinese soldiers under the escort of the Chinese gunboat *Caojiang* (操江), which promptly surrendered. The *Naniwa*'s crew boarded and searched the *Kowshing*, and the *Jiyuan* took the opportunity to attempt another escape.

Ordered to accompany the *Naniwa*, the *Kowshing*'s British captain agreed to comply, but the soldiers on board objected. Arguing that the ship had left China before the outbreak of hostilities, they insisted on being returned to a Chinese port. After four hours of futile disputation, Tōgō Heihachirō (東郷平八郎, 1848–1934), commanding officer of the *Naniwa*, issued one final warning before sinking the *Kowshing* along with its crew and passengers. The lives of three officers, including the captain, were spared.

The General Staff Office's anodyne description of the battle conceals one key fact: the first shots were actually fired by the Japanese side. Japan had seized on China's troop deployment to Korea as the opportunity it needed to start a war it had been paving the way for through diplomatic and strategic means ever since the decade of humiliation following the Imo Incident and the Kapsin Political Coup. Mutsu, Navy Minister Saigō Tsugumichi, Admiral Itō Sukeyuki (伊東祐亨, 1843–1914), and Tōgō Heihachirō, captain of the *Naniwa*: all had known what the consequences of the engagement would be. The First Sino-Japanese War was a conflict that Japan intentionally provoked.

Should this seem proof of naked imperialism and aggression on the part of Meiji Japan, this book can offer no counterargument. Intellectual integrity demands that the truth be told—just as it requires acknowledgment that, in spite of the arbitrary judgment of the International Military Tribunal of the Far East, responsibility for starting the Second Sino-Japanese War of 1937–45 lies squarely on China's side.

At the time, however, Japan was unwilling to admit that it had started the Battle of Pungdo, or the reasons it had had for doing so. This was part of a pattern of secrecy regarding strategy that would have lasting consequences.

Cui Bono?

The events that sparked the Battle of Pungdo were disputed right from the beginning. Japan claimed that the Chinese fleet had opened fire unprovoked, and most of its later military histories took that view as well. China maintained that the Japanese fleet had blocked and then fired on the *Jiyuan* and *Guangyi* as they approached Pungdo Island to rendezvous with the *Kowshing*. Neither side could produce conclusive evidence, however, because the battle had taken place at sea without any entirely neutral witnesses.

But, for a historian, there are areas in which common sense is more useful than dogmatic insistence on the primacy of evidence. The beginning of the Korean War of 1950 is one example. There can be no doubt that North Korea's initial maneuvers were planned; its successful advance almost to Pusan at the peninsula's southern tip shows this. Arguing over which side's rifles fired the first shots is pointless. And yet, until quite recently, the mainstream of Japanese academia maintained that it was impossible to determine which of the two Koreas had started the war—a position also adopted by Japan's major newspapers. Emphasizing the lack of evidence was little more than leftist bias in disguise.

What does common sense tell us about which side had more to gain from the outbreak of war?

The Battle of Pungdo on July 25 was soon followed by the first land engagement, the Battle of Seonghwan (成歓の戦い) on July 29. These two encounters were in fact connected: both hinged on China's presence in Asan.

More than a month earlier, around June 10, some three thousand Chinese troops had been sent to Asan at the request of the Korean government. As relations with Japan worsened, China decided to send in reinforcements: 1,200 soldiers on July 21, and 1,300 more on July 23.

Japan had a force of over six thousand in Korea by then, but Seoul could not be left unguarded; the risk of losing the upper hand in the city should the royal court and the inhabitants turn against Japan was too great. As a result, only three thousand men could be spared for the southern front.

The Chinese general Nie Shicheng (聶士成) had led his two thousand men to Seonghwan, a strategically important point on the highway, to create a defensive line against the Japanese army marching south from Seoul. A thousand more men were stationed in reserve in nearby Cheonan (天安) under the command of General Ye Zhichao (葉志超). The two sides in the battle were therefore more or less evenly matched, with roughly three thousand foot soldiers and eight cannons each. Had the 1,200 soldiers and thirteen cannons on board the *Kowshing* arrived as China intended, things might have gone quite differently.

As the war progressed, China's soldiers would be demoralized by a series of defeats and show a tendency to retire without putting up much resistance, but in their first clash with Japan at Seonghwan they put up a good fight, perhaps cheered by the memory of their decisive victory over Japan during the Kapsin Coup.

China was desperate to get its reinforcements safely to Asan. With cost no object, the decision was made to use a British commercial vessel flying a British flag. Japan, meanwhile, was determined to prevent their arrival—making it more than obvious which side had reason to open hostilities off Pungdo Island.

The Japanese fleet had even obtained permission for the attack beforehand. On July 19, following Britain's second attempt at intervention, Japan had demanded a reply from China to its brusque counterproposal within five days. It had also declared it would regard any deployment of additional troops to Korea as an act of hostility. On the same day, according to *Kenkenroku*, Navy Minister Saigō asked Mutsu whether it would be "diplomatically controversial" to engage with Chinese forces immediately on encountering them once the five days were up (the assumption being, apparently, that no reply would be received).

"As regards official procedure," Mutsu replied, "that would cause no difficulties at all": tacit approval for an attack on the Chinese fleet, so long as it was after July 25.

Kabayama Sukenori (樺山資紀, 1837–1922), Chief of the Naval General Staff, left Tokyo for Sasebo the following day, and gave sailing orders to the Grand Fleet there on July 22. Any attempt on China's part to deploy reinforcements, he stressed, was to be interpreted as a hostile act and dealt with by "immediately destroying" China's armored and transport ships.

The Grand Fleet set sail on July 23 under the command of Itō Sukeyuki, headed for the western coast of the Korean Peninsula; early in the morning of July 25, the First Mobile Squadron would be deployed near Pungdo Island.

Tōgō's Strategic Thinking

The three ships of the First Mobile Squadron had a total displacement of 111,000 tons, and the *Yoshino* and *Akitsushima* in particular were state-of-the art vessels. China, on the other hand, had two aging craft with a displacement of 3,900 tons, which, in combination with the fact that traditional Chinese military strategy emphasized winning through intimidation rather than combat, adds to the improbability of their attacking first.

It is conceivable that lax control could have accounted for an unprovoked attack from the Chinese side, but the question is as academic as who fired the first shot in the Korean War. Japan was committed to a full-scale offensive, and would have embarked on one eventually whatever China's ships did. In all probability, the two sides only met in the first place because the Grand Fleet was searching for a Chinese convoy to destroy it; similarly, it was surely Tōgō's expectation that an additional transport ship would be in the area that allowed the *Naniwa* to find and, after due process, sink the *Kowshing*.

Falsifying history muddies the waters for later generations, often to their detriment. In his *Senryaku Nichiro sensō* (戦略日露戦争, A strategic appraisal of the Russo-Japanese War), Shimanuki Shigeyoshi (島貫重節) records a conversation with Lieutenant General Mori Takeshi

(森赳, 1894–1945) in an air-raid shelter in August 1945. (Mori was commander of the Imperial Guard Division who would later be shot and killed by a subordinate demanding that he continue fighting after Japan had decided to surrender.)

> Our military knew nothing of the wider strategy that lay behind the Russo-Japanese war. The leadership of the Imperial Army underestimated the importance of knowledge because they were ignorant of strategy, and they were ignorant of strategy because it had consistently been excluded from reference works for reasons of confidentiality. Worse yet, the army was not even aware of its ignorance.

Mori was correct about this deficiency in Japan's military documents. Today, disclosing strategic planning and permitting public debate on it is usually seen in a free society as a means of ensuring that everyone involved in a war understands what it concerns. In prewar Japan, however, military strategy was given a top secret classification. It was not recorded in the official histories, and the tactical thinking in the First Sino-Japanese War was undisclosed even before the Russo-Japanese War a decade later. Thus the generation that fought these wars failed to pass on the lessons of their experience to their successors.

Without knowing that Japan's aim in the Battle of Pungdo had been to prevent Chinese reinforcements from reaching Asan, Tōgō's decision to detain the *Kowshing* while allowing the *Jiyuan* to flee is difficult to understand. And in preventing its future leaders from engaging with this facet of military science, the Japanese military ensured that they would learn only the importance of numbers and morale.

During the Pacific War, the Imperial Navy tended to ignore convoy transport ships in favor of fleet-to-fleet battle with armored vessels. The U.S., however, was careful to escort its own transports, while using its submarines to attack Japanese merchant ships. The damage this did to Japan's supply lines, already no match for those of the U.S., hastened its defeat.

The command of the sea that comes with victory in a fleet-to-fleet clash is meaningless if not used to protect friendly convoys and interfere with enemy ones. As a result, the U.S. tactic of pursuing this goal from the start proved more effective than Japan's narrow focus on combat.

The aftermath of the First Battle of the Solomon Sea, fought by American and Japanese cruisers on August 8, 1942, is one example in this regard.

The Imperial Navy lived up to its reputation for martial prowess and achieved an overwhelming victory, reminiscent of the Battle of Tsushima. However, it did not pick off the accompanying merchant ships after the battle, almost in a throwback to the samurai ethic against attacking members of the unarmed merchant class. The convoy safely continued on to Guadalcanal, and the reinforcements and supplies it carried would contribute to a string of subsequent Japanese defeats. Strategically speaking, for Japan the aftermath of the battle was disastrous.

Nowadays, most historians agree that Japan initiated the naval engagements that began the First Sino-Japanese and Russo-Japanese wars. Even histories of the Korean War now acknowledge that North Korea started the conflict. Truth in history cannot help but be uncovered.

Sometimes this even happens earlier than expected. Tabohashi Kiyoshi (田保橋潔) wrote his *Kindai Nissen kankei no kenkyū* (近代日鮮関係の研究, A study of modern Japan-Korea relations) in 1940, as militarism and chauvinism reached their height at home, but his view of events at Pungdo was unclouded: "Contradictory reports from the two sides notwithstanding, from a tactical viewpoint it should be obvious which fired first," he noted, and the rest of his account takes it for granted that Japan was the aggressor.

Diplomacy after the *Kowshing* Episode

Japanese leaders had expected the navy to intercept China's reinforcements, but the involvement of a British vessel seems to have come as a surprise, if the consternation of Prime Minister Itō on hearing the news is any indication. All of Mutsu's skills would be needed in the days to come.

Using the *Kowshing* as a troopship had been a deliberate ploy. Li Hongzhang was so confident that Japan would not attack the vessel for fear of making an enemy of Britain that he sent the reinforcements in defiance of Mutsu's ultimatum.

Even if the troops did not arrive safely in Asan, the sinking of the *Kowshing* could be used to drag Britain into the war. Li wired China's Foreign Ministry the very day he heard the news; the British, he said, could not possibly overlook the incident. At China's naval base in Weihaiwei, a toast was drunk to the prospect of an alliance with Britain.

It is interesting to note the difference in attitude between China and Japan here. If a thousand Japanese soldiers had been drowned by the enemy, the Japanese would have sworn vengeance. The Chinese, however, saw the possible advantage in what they described as "a totally unexpected interception."

The British empire was still preeminent at this time. Public opinion would not allow the sinking of a ship flying a British flag to go unanswered. All of Fleet Street denounced the barbaric conduct of the Japanese and demanded satisfaction for the insult to the red ensign. Those who offered a dispassionate defense of Japan from the standpoint of international law were subjected to stinging personal attacks.

In London, Minister Aoki Shūzō (青木周藏, 1844–1914) wired Tokyo to suggest appeasement before the British government began demanding reparations. Japanese newspapers called for Tōgō's punishment, and his immediate dismissal was said to be among the measures Itō allegedly instructed Navy Minister Saigō to take in order to placate the British.

Mutsu had responded to news of the sinking by inviting the British acting minister to visit him at the Foreign Ministry. He promised that Japan would investigate the "tragic incident" thoroughly, adding that the government was prepared to pay the necessary reparations should its own side be found at fault.

This done, however, he refrained from taking any further measures prematurely. He knew the British well enough to realize that making amends or dismissing those responsible for the incident before a proper investigation could be concluded would only lower their estimation of Japan. As he had expected, the British government welcomed the commitment Mutsu had offered their interim minister and temporarily settled the issue by announcing that it would contact Japan after all the facts were known and it had decided on its response.

Mutsu was not the only one familiar with the British approach. Yamamoto Gonbei, superintendent at the office of the navy minister and one the most powerful men in the service, shared Mutsu's assessment. Summoned by a grim-faced Itō to explain himself, Yamamoto's cool reply was that it "could have been worse." If Japan had sunk a Russian vessel, who knew what they would have demanded in return? "We were fortunate that the ship belonged to a civilized country like Britain," Yamamoto said, "which is by nature inclined to prefer a thorough inquiry before passing judgment. I don't think we should worry too much."

Public opinion in Britain remained a concern, but this too calmed down under the influence of authoritative commentators like Thomas Holland and John Westlake, who insisted that under international law Japan had not been in the wrong. Privately, Wang Yunsheng also wondered if "the British public, seeing Japan win battle after battle, simply became less inclined to go against this powerful nation."

Had Japan lost those early battles, its behavior off Pungdo Island would doubtless have been denounced as barbarism. But Japan had the upper hand from the earliest stages, and experts like Holland and Westlake were prepared to offer their "objective" legal opinion that, since the war had begun with the Battle of Pungdo two hours earlier, Japan had been entitled to search, capture, and, if necessary, use force to overpower the *Kowshing*.

It was fortunate for Japan that the British transport arrived after the *Jiyuan* and *Guangyi*. If the *Kowshing* had been at the head of a small fleet instead, Japan might have sunk it before the war had officially begun, making things much more difficult for Mutsu. Even in that case, though, a series of subsequent victories could still have vindicated Japan in retrospect. For better or worse, the principle of "might makes right" has held throughout history. As Tōgō Shigenori (東郷茂徳), foreign minister at the beginning of the Pacific War, wrote before dying in prison as a war criminal:

Now listen, children,
Never go to war
But if you must fight
Don't ever forget
To make sure you win.

XVII

JAPAN SAILS TO VICTORY

China's Strategic Dilemma

The Battle of Seonghwan

The Japanese had prized martial prowess since feudal times, but the Battle of Seonghwan was their first opportunity to demonstrate it in a modern international arena. China's goal in the battle, on the other hand, was merely to stop the Japanese offensive in its tracks south of Seoul until major reinforcements arrived from Pyongyang.

The two sides were well matched in numbers and guns when the battle began, but the Chinese had the advantage of the terrain. They were waiting behind the defensive line they had prepared when the Japanese arrived. Nor were Japan's forces in the best of condition. Horses and conscripted local laborers had run off, and flooding on the roads due to bad weather and high tides had drowned a number of soldiers. The men who did arrive were exhausted after three days and nights of hard marching.

The odds appeared to favor China, and the Koreans shared this assessment, making them unwilling to collaborate with the other side. But when the Japanese began the battle with concentrated close-range fire and repeated charges, the Chinese couldn't hold their positions. Morale was still quite high, and the resistance they offered was effective in places, but they simply could not withstand the waves of charging infantry. Once the Chinese troops had been driven back, they abandoned any attempt at organized defense and made for Pyongyang in disarray. Their opponents returned to Seoul in triumph and prepared to push north.

The Battle of Seonghwan was Japan's first application in modern warfare of this tactic of head-on attack in waves, which would see extensive use right up to the end of World War II, delivering both success and failure in different circumstances.

The formal declaration of war on China came on August 1, 1894, immediately after the Battles of Pungdo and Seonghwan. Moving north, Japanese forces on September 16 attacked Pyongyang. Following the Imperial Navy's victory at the Battle of the Yalu River a day later, which gave it complete command of the sea, soldiers crossed the Yalu River (鴨緑江) and kept going, occupying Jiuliancheng (九連城) in Chinese territory on October 26. Other troops transported to the Liaodong Peninsula (遼東半島) by the navy proceeded to take Dalian Bay (大連湾) on November 8 and Lüshunkou (旅順口, Port Arthur), known to the West as Port Arthur, on November 21.

The First Army Corps pressed on into Manchuria and occupied Haicheng (海城) on December 3. The Second Army Corps, which had landed on the Liaodong Peninsula, advanced to the Shandong Peninsula (山東半島) and forced the surrender of the Beiyang Fleet based in Weihaiwei on February 12. Finally, in spite of peace negotiations that were already underway, the army occupied the Penghu (or Pescadores) Islands off Taiwan on March 26.

What explains this succession of Japanese victories? The answer is not equipment, in which department Japan and China were almost evenly matched, but tactics.

Every confrontation between the two sides unfolded in the same way: after a long buildup, during which minor skirmishes occasionally broke out while troops were being positioned, the battle itself would be settled in a day or two at most.

1894	25 JULY	1. Battle of Pungdo
	28 JULY	2. Battle of Seonghwan
	1 AUGUST	DECLARATION OF WAR BETWEEN CHINA AND JAPAN
	15–16 SEPTEMBER	3. Battle of Pyongyang
	17 SEPTEMBER	4. Battle of the Yalu River
	10 OCTOBER	5. Invasion of Manchuria
	25 OCTOBER	6. Capture of Jiuliangcheng
	6–7 NOVEMBER	7. Siege of Lüshunkou (Port Arthur)
	21 NOVEMBER	8. Fall of Lüshunkou
	10 DECEMBER	FALL OF KAIPENG (MODERN-DAY GAIXIAN)
1895	20 JANUARY– 12 FEBRUARY	9. Battle of Weihaiwei
	12 FEBRUARY	10. Fall of Weihaiwei
	5 MARCH	11. Battle of Yinkou, Manchuria
	23 MARCH	OCCUPATION OF PENGDHU (PESCADORES) OFF THE WEST COAST OF TAIWAN
	17 APRIL	SIGNING OF THE TREATY OF SHIMONOSEKI

Chronology of the First Sino-Japanese War, 1894–95

The Chinese forces would begin these battles with an impressive display of defiance, but their lines invariably collapsed under the relentless onslaught of their opponents—often much sooner than the latter expected.

China's last stand on its southern front was made at Pyongyang when the Imperial Army converged on the city from several directions on September 15. The defenders fought bravely, making trouble for the Japanese side where they could, but morale dropped among their leaders when they realized they were surrounded. By four o'clock in the afternoon, they had either raised the white flag or fled further north.

Things took a similar course at Port Arthur several weeks later. This was the stronghold of the Beiyang Fleet, and China had invested a lot in its defense over a period of years. Li Hongzhang expected that the city's stockpiles of ammunition would allow it to withstand an enemy offensive for at least three years. But, following a siege by Japanese forces, Port Arthur fell on November 21 after barely a day of fighting (not including the fierce battles prior to the attack on the city itself). Observers concluded from the relatively small number of Chinese soldiers lying dead in the streets that many of the troops stationed there had retreated by sea or along the western coast as soon as fighting began.

Strengths and Weaknesses

Watanabe Ikujirō (渡辺幾治郎, 1877–1960), seeking to explain Japan's startling success in the war, quotes from an article in the January 18, 1895, issue of the *Hōchi Shimbun* about a Major Saitō of the 15th Regiment and a Chinese officer Saitō recognized by his bearing among the prisoners captured by his regiment in Jeonju. In accordance with samurai etiquette, Saitō addressed this officer, saying:

> I offer my sympathies as a fellow soldier. I can imagine how painful it must be to become a prisoner of war. Perhaps I should free you, to do battle with us again.

But the other man shook his head, saying pessimistically:

> We would never win. For one thing, there are your charging tactics. Our method is to pick off enemy soldiers with guns and cannon before they can close with us, but your men move too quickly to be dealt with in this way. Every soldier we hit has another right behind him to continue the charge. And we haven't managed to counterattack even once.
>
> Another reason we can't win is your open-order deployment. By never crowding in one place your troops are less vulnerable to gunfire. Ours, however, can only fight in line formation. If they spread out unsupervised, a lot of them would desert. So we stick to our lines even though we know this makes us an easy target....

Carl von Clausewitz, author of the famed *Vom Kriege* (On War), witnessed how effective skirmishes in open-order formation could be during the Napoleonic Wars. In conventional engagements, two sides of uniformed soldiers lined up in closed ranks opposite each other. Open formations had obvious advantages in terms of protection, but were not practical for the mercenary armies of the time, since few hired soldiers would willingly advance ahead of their fellows.

But the French forces in the Napoleonic Wars were not the usual mercenaries hired by the royal family. They were a people's army under the tricolor, and open-order deployment was just one of the things that made them unconventional.

The hostilities between Japan and China had many parallels with the war between Napoleonic France and its European neighbors a century earlier, and Japan's repeated victories, too, echo the series of successes that Napoleon had.

China was also held back by its own strategic thinking, far older than Japan's, the essence of which was to win without actually fighting. Enemies were to be outwitted in the field or outmaneuvered diplomatically; to defeat them in pitch battle was the crudest of victories. And since no one in their right mind would willingly provoke an unpredictable, possibly dangerous opponent, the shrewdest approach was to weaken the enemy's will to fight by demonstrating military preparedness. Mutsu's observation in the *Kenkenroku* that China seemed to lack the resolve to actually go to war and appeared to believe it could restrain Japan by combining posturing with Western intervention was not incorrect.

The same approach, by all accounts, is visible in everyday disputes as well. The first stage is a heated argument between two parties, each claiming to be in the right. As the two sides edge toward physical confrontation, they begin to compare their strength. If there are four people on one side and five on the other, the former will try to add a couple more. This goes on until an obvious difference of power emerges, at which point the weaker side probably gives in. This is Chinese military strategy applied in miniature, with voice and posture standing in for military force—a fact endorsed by a comment made by the Foreign Ministry's Zhi Rui once war with Japan was imminent:

If China sends in sufficient reinforcements and shows that it is just as ready for war as Japan, the potential humiliation of defeat should make Japan think twice about it. Showing a determination to fight could save us from actually needing to fight.

Naturally, the Chinese army had its share of heroes. When headquarters gave the order to surrender Pyongyang and fall back, General Zuo Baogui refused to obey, heading out through the Chilsung Moon Gate to die in a charge on the enemy. During the Battle of the Yalu River, Captain Deng Shichang (鄧世昌) of the cruiser *Jingyuan* (経遠) recognized that the odds were against China and tried to ram his ship into the *Yoshino* in a last-ditch attempt to level the score. The *Yoshino* was just fast enough to avoid the collision, and the *Jingyuan* was blown up and sunk by fire from the Japanese side.

And then there were cowards. At the Battle of Pungdo, Captain Fang Boqian (方伯謙) of the cruiser *Jiyuan*, from the safety of a heavily armored part of the vessel, ordered his deputy to hoist the white flag and the Rising Sun in surrender. Two angry sailors defied Fang's orders and fired at the *Yoshino* from the stern of the ship, striking it on the bow as it approached to board and search them. The resulting confusion allowed the *Jiyuan* to slip away. Then, at the Battle of the Yalu River, after his command had taken a few shells, Fang again turned tail, hoping to escape with the *Jiyuan*'s escort *Guanjia* to Port Arthur. This infuriated the captain of the battleship *Zhenyuan*, who ordered that a warning shot be fired across *Jiyuan*'s stern, but Fang made good his escape. Not having the *Jiyuan* and *Guanjia* on hand weakened the Chinese considerably in a battle that had begun with twelve ships on each side, and it comes as little surprise to learn that Fang was later court-martialed and executed by firing squad.

Learning the Wrong Lessons

The experience of the First Sino-Japanese War had a lasting influence on Japan's military leadership, up until the end of the Pacific War. It led them to believe that going on the offensive was always the best policy, regardless of the balance of power beforehand, for the debilitating effect it had on the enemy. More dangerously, they came to assume that victory in battle meant access to supplies: Chinese soldiers fleeing Pyongyang and Port Arthur left provisions and ammunition in such abundance that Japanese troops were able to rely almost solely on them afterwards.

I once spoke to a distinguished prewar graduate of the Imperial Army War College who explained that every examination included a scenario where differences in combat capability, terrain advantage, and supplies seemed to favor either temporary withdrawal or a defensive operation. Students who ignored these indications and advocated going on the offensive instead were always awarded the highest marks. In this way the military cultivated a contempt for intelligence and balance, along with an obsession with offensive operations, that characterized its performance during the Pacific War.

The underlying issue was a failure to realize why these tactics had worked during the First Sino-Japanese War. They were only effective against an enemy that was likely to fold because of them. From the Battle of Baekgang (白村江の戦い) in 663 to the clash with U.S. Marines at Guadalcanal in 1942, every time the Japanese faced a stronger opponent who resisted intimidation, they were annihilated, just as military doctrine would predict.

Other lessons, too, were forgotten. Sending wave upon wave of infantry on the attack was not the only tactic employed even in the First Sino-Japanese War. Most of the time, Japanese forces followed their German military textbooks in first gaining supremacy with firepower before initiating a charge of any sort. Japan's soldiers were better trained in firearms than China's, and this approach proved effective. Charging was not simply used as a way to compensate for inferior firepower with heroism.

Just as China was in thrall to traditional strategic thinking, Japan came to overvalue the dividends of combat. Our most dangerous weakness often lies concealed in our greatest strength, and this is no less true for nations than individuals.

Charges were not carried out only on land. At the Battle of the Yalu River, the Japanese *Matsushima* (松島), *Itsukushima* (厳島), and *Hashidate* (橋立) faced down China's advanced *Dingyuan* and *Zhenyuan* battleships, both equipped with four 12-inch Krupp guns. Each of the Japanese vessels was armed with a 12.5-inch Canet gun, but lack of funds for construction had left the ships too small to use them reliably, making them prone to mechanical failure when they were fired. Their main weapons were all but unusable.

The *Dingyuan* began firing on the *Yoshino* early in the battle, when the distance between the two fleets had narrowed to about six thousand yards. The first shot was followed by fifty more rounds, sending up clouds of spray around the Japanese battleship. According to Chinese military doctrine, this should have driven the Japanese into retreat. Few on the Chinese side can have imagined that the *Matsushima* and its companions would draw even closer to fire at the *Dingyuan's* deck with 6-inch guns and 4.7-inch rapid-fire cannons. The sailors must have felt just like the army when faced with charging infantry on land.

The Chinese strategy of intimidation was not inherently flawed, but it could only bring victory if overwhelming superiority was maintained. China did have the resources to achieve this when facing Japan. During the Kapsin Political Coup, it had defeated a Japanese company of two hundred men by deploying three battalions of fifteen hundred soldiers. Things might have gone the same way at the Yalu River if China had acquired what later became the *Yoshino* from Armstrong Whitworth instead of allowing the Japanese to do so. But, complacent after past victories over Japan, China failed to recognize the importance of expanding its military capabilities, and this, as we shall see, ensured its defeat.

The Naval Arms Race

The Japanese were aware of the importance of technology in military affairs. "The outcome of a modern war is determined by weapons, not courage," was how Fukuzawa Yukichi put it in that article he wrote in 1882 for the *Jiji Shimpō* daily newspaper. Warning of the misery that defeat in war would entail, he recanted his former belief that modernization should be the nation's first and only priority and called for a rapid military buildup.

Japan's naval development did indeed lag far behind China's at the time. The Chinese Navy had bought both the *Dingyuan* and *Zhenyuan* in 1882. These were ultra-modern turret ships, each displacing 7,300 tons,

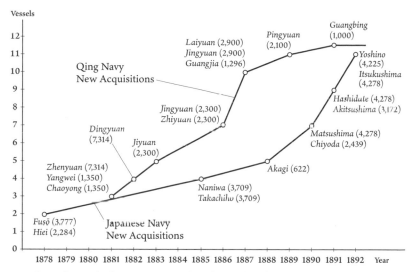

Vessels

Guangbing
(1,000)

Pingyuan
(2,100)

Laiyuan (2,900)
Jingyuan (2,900)
Guangjia (1,296)

Qing Navy
New Acquisitions

Yoshino
(4,225)
Itsukushima
(4,278)

Hashidate (4,278)
Akitsushima (3,172)

Jingyuan (2,300)
Zhiyuan (2,300)

Dingyuan
(7,314)

Jiyuan
(2,300)

Matsushima (4,278)
Chiyoda (2,439)

Zhenyuan (7,314)
Yangwei (1,350)
Chaoyong (1,350)

Akagi (622)

Naniwa (3,709)
Takachiho (3,709)

Fusō (3,777)
Hiei (2,284)

Japanese Navy
New Acquisitions

1878 1879 1880 1881 1882 1883 1884 1885 1886 1887 1888 1889 1890 1891 1892 Year

Number of Vessels that Participated in the Battle of the Yalu River

Notes: Japanese steamer *Saikyō Maru* (4,100) is excluded. If included,
it would put the total number of vessels on a par at 12.
The numbers in parentheses are tonnage.
Source: Based on *Kindai Nihon sensō-shi* (Dōdai Keizai Konwakai)

armed with four 12-inch main guns, and protected by 14- and 12-inch
armor on their turrets and broadsides respectively. Japan's *Fusō* (扶桑)
displaced a mere 3,800 tons and was barely armored at all, its most powerful armament being four 240-mm guns with obviously limited range.

Japan became determined to consolidate its military, but the problem, as Chinese observers were aware, was that the nation was still
too poor to do much building. When the Imperial Diet, then in the
grip of the Freedom and People's Rights Movement, refused to fund the
proposed construction of two battleships in 1893, a pledge was made
to deduct three hundred thousand yen annually for six years from the
imperial family's budget. Additional funding was secured by cutting all
government salaries by ten percent. When these measures were made
public, the proposal passed unanimously.

By contrast, after China had unnerved the Japanese with the *Dingyuan*
at Nagasaki in 1886 and completed the battle formation of its Beiyang

Fleet the following year, it stopped increasing its naval power entirely. Empress Dowager Cixi (西太后), who held the reins of power at the time, had little interest in military affairs and left them in the hands of Li Hongzhang. Li, though brilliant, was concerned chiefly with protecting his own position, and in accordance with the empress dowager's wishes devoted more time to suppressing the rise of nationalistic young bureaucrats than naval acquisitions.

Cixi's lukewarm attitude toward the military was partly self-serving. She was planning an extravagant celebration for her sixtieth birthday in 1894, including the construction of the Yiheyuan (頤和園, Summer Palace) on the outskirts of Beijing, and was reluctant to support programs that would compete for financial resources. Indeed, when funding for the Summer Palace came up short, thirty million silver taels were taken from the naval budget to make up the difference. This was a tremendous sum, equivalent to forty-five million yen in Japan, which shows just how wealthy China was at the time. Li Hongzhang was forced to cancel the purchase of two high-speed battleships from Britain, one of which was later acquired by the Imperial Navy using Emperor Meiji's one million eight hundred thousand yen donation and named the *Yoshino*.

A ship-shaped marble pavilion on the lake of the Summer Palace is said to have been built for a banquet intended to appease senior officers who objected to the lavish spending on the palace at the expense of the British ship deal.

The chart on page 273 reveals how a hard-up Japan managed to scrape together enough resources to build a fleet on a par with China's by the outbreak of the war.

The Ships That Won the War

In May 1894, two months before the war began, China held a grand naval review in honor of the Beiyang Fleet's sixth anniversary.

Li Hongzhang's effusive address at the event nevertheless contained a note of warning toward the end:

Even the small country of Japan has wisely cut back on other expenses and expanded its naval armaments every year. We, however, have added not one warship since the Beiyang Fleet was established. I am deeply concerned about the future of the Qing empire.

He was right to be concerned. After the Battle of Pungdo, the Beiyang Fleet would permanently retreat to the Bohai Gulf (渤海湾), allowing the Japanese navy to set up base in Incheon and travel freely off the west coast of the peninsula. When the court condemned Admiral Ding Ruchang (丁汝昌) for incompetence and ordered Li to bring the Beiyang Fleet out of hiding, he gave the following reply:

> When we acquired our warships a decade ago, fifteen to eighteen knots was considered fast. Today's warships sail faster than twenty knots. The Japanese navy's current acquisition program has given them a ship that can do twenty-three. As I have explained before, these high-speed vessels make it well nigh impossible for us to defeat them on the open sea. The more prudent course of action is to keep our navy in the area around Weihaiwei and Lüshun; this should discourage Japan from attacking us out of fear of our own ironclads, the *Dingyuan* and the *Zhenyuan*.

During the Battle of Pyongyang, however, the fleet was obliged to leave its haven to escort a transport full of reinforcements to the mouth of the Yalu. There it was spotted by the Japanese side and dragged into what would become the Battle of the Yalu River.

Had China acquired the *Yoshino* as planned, it would have won at Yalu. The ship had a world-leading top speed of twenty-four knots and twelve state-of-the-art rapid-fire cannons—technology that China lacked entirely. The *Yoshino* devastated the Beiyang Fleet, depriving the *Dingyuan* and *Zhenyuan* of their firepower by bombarding them until they burst into flames.

Meanwhile, for personal reasons, the empress dowager was still hoping to end the war quickly. Some in the Qing court suggested that her plans be scaled back so that more money could be diverted to war preparation, but Emperor Guangxu only lamented that "nothing that went against filial piety" could be done. Cixi's fury with those who dared defy her was well known. "Who displeases me today," she said, "I shall never please, as long as he lives." The court could only obey.

And so, war or no war, the celebration went ahead as planned. Weng Tonghe (翁同龢) of the Grand Council wrote the following account in his diary on November 5 (the tenth day of the tenth month, by the lunar calendar still in use in China at the time)—the very day Japanese troops seized the walled city of Jinzhou and pushed on toward Dalian (大連):

> Everyone stood outside the Gate of Imperial Supremacy. At nine o'clock, a palanquin arrived.... The empress dowager appeared in the Palace of Imperial Supremacy.... I led a group of courtiers in making the full obeisance. At eleven thirty, we entered the theater, but I couldn't stay long due to the emergency in Dalian....

The following day, he added:

> I entered the theater intending to enjoy the play, but left immediately after bowing formally. I simply couldn't bear to sit there as if nothing was wrong.

Precarious Victory

Japan won both the First Sino-Japanese and Russo-Japanese wars by applying intense pressure in the first stages and then pushing for peace negotiations while its adversary was still in disarray.

When Japan's offer of peace in exchange for two hundred million taels arrived at the Qing court, the hawkish contingent argued that it made more sense to continue fighting: the sum Japan was demanding was more than six times the thirty million taels originally earmarked for modernizing China's navy. But if money could end the war, that was the solution the empress dowager preferred, and so peace negotiations began.

A similar pattern would be followed at the end of the Russo-Japanese War. The Russian army had sent a stream of reinforcements on the Siberian Railway to prepare for a counteroffensive, but when General Nikolai Linevich reported to Tsar Nicholas II that all was in place, the tsar was so tired of fighting domestic revolutionaries that he ordered the general to sue for peace instead.

Japan's victory in both cases was only possible because China and Russia elected to end the war rather than redouble their commitment. The converse of concentrating the full power of Japan's military in an initial burst of action was that nothing was held in reserve, leaving no margin for error. In the Pacific War, this proved disastrous when the United States not only failed to back down but actually increased its capacity to fight five- or even tenfold, decisively crushing Japan's ambitions.

Patriotism on the Home Front

The patriotic fervor raised on the home front was greater than anyone had expected. The military was immediately flooded with recruits. Hundreds of former samurai from Tosa and Mito organized themselves into sword squadrons and offered their services, and a yakuza in the Kantō area named Ishisada rallied a thousand "urban knights" around Tokyo. The government was forced to issue an imperial edict stating that no more soldiers were needed and urging citizens to return to their usual occupations.

Intellectuals, critics, and newspapers supported the war unanimously. Even the prominent Christian Uchimura Kanzō (内村鑑三), who later opposed the Russo-Japanese War, was a vocal proponent of this conflict as a "just war" (gisen).

At the seventh extraordinary session of the Imperial Diet held on October 15 in Hiroshima City, all military expenditure bills were passed without amendment in five minutes—an astonishing reversal of the struggles Itō and Mutsu had with the Diet several months earlier. Tokutomi Sohō, a journalist giant of the time, pointed out to Kawakami Sōroku that this decision at the Imperial Diet was more effective than reinforcing a whole division, to which Kawakami wholeheartedly concurred.

Before the end of World War II, Japanese history books all praised the Diet for abandoning its anti-government stance in favor of enthusiastic cooperation on the outbreak of war. This unity in the face of crisis, historians agreed, was a display of the best side of the Japanese people.

This opinion was not necessarily empty patriotism. Compared to any other people in the world, nationalism does seem particularly strong among the Japanese. It is difficult to say why this should be so, but common sense suggests that a homogeneous people speaking one language and inhabiting a secluded archipelago since the beginning of history would tend to have a stronger sense of national identity than usual.

The question is why this nationalism was expressed so strongly at the time. Part of the reason may be simple naivety on the part of the general public, who had yet to be exposed to exogenous ideas like liberalism, individualism, and socialism. But reviewing the debates at the Imperial Diet from its establishment up to the time of the war clearly reveals why the mood of that body in particular changed.

Before the war, criticism from parties in opposition was invariably based on a hardline attitude toward foreign relations. The right wing attacked the government for its weak-kneed diplomacy while the moderates held their peace. This was the convergence of a variety of factors, including an exclusionism that dated back to the last years of the Tokugawa shogunate, the expansionist orientation underlying the enthusiasm for invading Korea, an aversion to the unequal treaties, and an imperialism rooted in modern enlightenment thinking. Against this background, it is small wonder that a national consensus formed immediately at the beginning of actual contention.

Marxist historians of the postwar era deplore the opposition parties' sudden change of heart. Their premise is that the Freedom and People's Rights Movement should have been allied with pacifism and incompatible with imperialism; but I question the validity of this opinion. It seems merely to reflect a simplistic view that what is considered good should be fundamentally at odds with what is considered wicked.

Even today there is no shortage of statesmen around the world who are liberal in domestic affairs but hawkish internationally. This combination may be even more common than consistency across the two fronts. The liberal leanings of Japan's opposition parties reached a high point with the movement demanding that a parliament be established, but external crises like the Imo Incident, the Kapsin Political Coup, and now the First Sino-Japanese War brought hardline preferences on foreign policy to the surface. It might not be unreasonable to identify a shift from civil rights to sovereign rights in the sociopolitical realignment of the day, but it would be incorrect to conclude that the Freedom and People's Rights Movement or the Liberal Party had undergone some essential transformation.

XVIII

THE FINAL PHASE OF
THE WAR

A Race Against Time

The Looming Threat of Foreign Intervention

Japan's unbroken streak of wins soon brought it within range of its strategic goal: a prompt and favorable end to the war as a whole.

The *Kimitsu Nisshin senso* (機密日清戦争, Classified documents on the First Sino-Japanese War), compiled by Itō Hirobumi after the war but only made public posthumously, opens with a memorandum to the emperor in which Itō, apparently writing immediately after war was declared, stresses the importance of diplomacy alongside military operations. "A sovereign nation determined to go to war must recognize that difficulties in diplomatic relations with other countries are sure to arise"—a perceptive observation for the leader of a country still inexperienced in foreign affairs after two and a half centuries of self-imposed isolation.

Itō acknowledges Mutsu's success in deflecting the initial interventions from Britain and Russia and allowing Japan to start the war unimpeded, but predicts that "neither Britain nor Russia will stand idly by for long. Let there be no doubt that further attempts at interference are forthcoming." Moreover, he added, "actual coercive measures" rather than just words would be employed next time, and other great powers were sure to follow suit. He concluded:

> It is of the utmost urgency for us to defeat China quickly and decisively, pressing our demands on it before the Western powers have time to intervene jointly. This might prevent us from accomplishing all our goals, but it would secure a better position for us and allow us to plan for the future without risking our prestige or honor as a nation. Instead of relying solely on military force, we must constantly and accurately monitor the situation to determine whether we should keep advancing or stop where we are. Our country will be in grave trouble if diplomatic relations with the Western powers are not handled with faultless skill at all times.

Itō is sometimes viewed as little more than an adroit powerbroker, but he had a genius for disentangling issues, identifying the essential matters at stake, and presenting a clear vision and strategy in response. Here he appears to foresee not just the Tripartite Intervention and subsequent ideology of *gashin shōtan* ("persevering for redress"), but also the Russo-Japanese War ten years later. The document ranks alongside his 1880 memorandum on the establishment of a national parliament as some of Itō's best political writing; his simple, direct style is both sophisticated and persuasive.

The imperial edict issued shortly afterwards appears to accept Itō's arguments, declaring that "a master plan must be drawn up with care and thoroughness through close consultation between the military and civilian branches of the government." Article 5, toward the end, reads:

> It should be borne in mind that the gains and losses of a warring nation are not determined by the outcome of battles alone. Intervention by other countries is inevitable more often than not, making it crucially important to plan and coordinate diplomatic and military efforts to bring the war to a conclusion.

Accordingly, Itō and Mutsu were both included in the war council at Imperial Headquarters (originally restricted to army and navy staff officers), giving them a de facto role in political and strategic planning.

All of this stands in stark contrast to the military's intractable conduct during the Shōwa era, when the Meiji constitution was held to guarantee the autonomy of the armed forces. Needless to say, the rise of Japan's military dictatorship before World War II cannot be blamed on the constitution per se.

The accomplishment of this grand design was predicated on swift military victory, which the tenacity of the advancing troops soon delivered.

Chapter 12 of *Kenkenroku* vividly describes the domestic and international situation after these early events:

> Following the triumphs at Pyongyang and the Yalu River on September 15 and 17, foreign public opinion did a sudden about-face and Japan came to be regarded with either admiration or jealousy.
>
> The editors of the London *Times*, acknowledging that we had achieved a military success of some consequence, argued that Japan should be recognized as a significant power in the Far East and was not to be underestimated.
>
> Another newspaper summarized the reaction in France:

> People love a winner, and Japan has won over Europe as convincingly as it has defeated China. It has become an independent nation that can do as it pleases, including encroaching on the territory of other countries just as the other great powers do. Its conduct is no longer subject to restrictions by the nations of Europe.

> And amid all this near-excessive praise, the Russian government was busy bringing its fleet through the Suez Canal and on to the Far East.

Mutsu goes on to discuss the impact of the war from a sociological point of view:

Our adept use of modern military methods and understanding of international law awakened the Western powers from the delusion that civilization can take root only in Christian nations. An exuberant Japanese public, however, had no interest in anything but pressing onward. Voices urging moderation were denounced as cowardly and forced into silence. Patriotism is unobjectionable in itself, but if mishandled it can work against the good of the nation....

To satisfy people at home, the government decided it should advance the war effort as quickly and thoroughly as possible, only changing course diplomatically when the international situation became hostile.

With these considerations in mind, on October 11 I wrote to Prime Minister Itō (then staying in Hiroshima) with a warning. My letter read in part:

> As the Western powers begin to meddle in the war, I believe it vital that our troops be urged to take whatever objectives they can before foreign interference makes this impossible— although I am sure Your Excellency has long been aware of this and needs no reminder from me.

The unexpectedly swift fall of Port Arthur toward the end of November, however, opened new options for Japan which would affect the progress of the war as a whole. Mutsu wrote to Itō on November 26 as soon as he heard the news, which came shortly after an offer from the United States to act as a mediator.

> So far our policy has been led by the army and navy, but from now on it will be imperative for the military to act in accordance with our diplomatic needs.
>
> I believe we should accept the American offer of mediation while the capture of Port Arthur is still fresh in people's minds. But if China's response is unsatisfactory, we should immediately strike another blow. The specific direction of this action being the prerogative of Imperial Headquarters, I wouldn't presume to interfere in its planning, but I hope that you will be prepared to order our army and navy into action straight away should the diplomatic need arise.

On December 4, Itō wrote a proposal for "attacking Weihaiwei and seizing Taiwan," thus implementing the principle elucidated by Mutsu of gaining as much ground as possible before the war ended. Building on their aim of destroying the Beiyang Fleet in order to ensure favorable conditions for a decisive battle near Beijing, the proposal observed that the flexibility this would allow Japan would leave Taiwan and the Penghu Islands ripe for capture.

The Second Army Corps, led by Ōyama Iwao (大山巌), was shipped from the Liaodong to the Shandong Peninsula where it besieged the Chinese position around Weihaiwei. China's land troops were defeated in due course, but the Beiyang Fleet was protected by islets in the bay as well as its own armor and firepower and refused to surrender. To break the standoff, torpedo boats sneaked in to pick off Chinese vessels one by one. Admiral Ding Ruchang faced mutiny from the fleet's sailors and was forced to concede defeat on February 12 before later committing suicide by poison.

The prolonged engagement with the Beiyang Fleet, together with the Imperial Navy's reluctance to divide its forces before the move on Beijing, unexpectedly delayed the invasion of Taiwan. Politically speaking, it might have made more sense to prioritize the accumulation of gains before peace talks began, but military leaders preferred to focus on preparing for the decisive operation against China's capital.

As a result, Itō's proposal was only partly realized. The Penghu Islands were occupied on March 26, but Japanese troops still had not landed in Taiwan when peace negotiations started. Li Hongzhang protested that it would be absurd for China to cede an island that had not even been occupied, and Itō could only lamely reply that Primorsky Krai had been ceded to Russia under similar circumstances.

The scale of the forces Japan positioned around Beijing in preparation for the final battle was impressive. The Third and Fifth Divisions had marched northward through the Korean Peninsula and formed the First Army Corps by that time. The Second Army Corps was joined on the Liaodong Peninsula by the First Division in October and the Second and Sixth Divisions in January. The Imperial Guard Division and the Fourth Division were transported to Dalian Bay while peace talks were underway.

Japanese planners estimated that around two hundred thousand Chinese troops might be concentrated around Beijing. China may well have had that many soldiers, but only a fraction could be mobilized for actual combat: thirty thousand plus five thousand from the Beiyang and Fengtian units respectively. Small as these forces were, they had been sufficient to defend the mainland, as Li Hongzhang had predicted, so long as the Beiyang Fleet's presence in the Bohai Gulf had left the Japanese no access route except via a northward march through Korea.

Once Japan seized control of the gulf, however, the balance shifted. With seven army divisions at the ready, if a temporarily negotiated truce was lifted the fall of Beijing would be only a matter of time. China was backed into a corner. Its only remaining option was a guerilla war that would lure Japanese troops deep inland while the Chinese worked—and spent—furiously to reconstruct their military strength.

As it turned out, even after the signing of the Treaty of Shimonoseki, the calls within China for the continuance of the war were so vehement that the Qing court delayed ratifying the treaty and sent an imperial messenger to both Liu Kunyi (劉坤一), imperial commissioner in Shanhaiguan, and Wang Wenshao (王文韶), acting viceroy of Zhili, to inquire about their willingness to continue fighting.

Liu Kunyi assured the court that over a hundred thousand men were prepared to fight to the death in defense of Beijing rather than accept the conditions in the treaty. Even at that late stage, China's cumulative war expenditures were less than half the amount Japan was demanding. The Japanese army, Liu argued, was too far from home to last long; all China had to do was somehow defend Beijing and turn the war into an endurance contest. He was strongly in favor of continuing the war.

Wang Wenshao's position was more ambivalent. Like Liu, he found Japan's demands outrageous and hoped to keep fighting, but he warned that China's soldiers were unlikely to fight to the bitter end. Reading between the lines, he appears to have been pessimistic about their chances but afraid to defy the mood sweeping the nation.

Yi Shunding (易順鼎), a section chief at China's Censorate, also submitted a long report to the court on the subject. Predicting, like Li, that Japan's troops could not continue much longer, he suggested that China could still win through skillful "maneuvering"—i.e., retreating—and defense. While retreat and defense was certainly not a high level recourse in traditional Chinese strategic theory, it was a respectable middle one, superior to the low option of reparations and territorial concessions.

China's thinking was coming into focus. There was no need to bring the war to a hasty conclusion: the longer it lasted, the greater China's advantage over Japan's expeditionary force. The strategy that would torment Japanese soldiers in 1937–45 was already emerging here, almost half a century earlier.

A war that becomes a contest of endurance can only be won with the support of the population. It seemed unlikely at first that the Qing court—a conquering dynasty of a different ethnicity—would be able to inspire the Chinese people to this extent, but the disclosure of Japan's humiliating demands seemed to ignite a blaze of nationalism; as contemporary reports to the Qing emperor explained, the Chinese people now bristled at any slight by the Japanese. China might indeed have been able to put up a stronger resistance, delaying Japan's triumph to some extent. The situation showed remarkable similarities between the proposals of the more hawkish element in the Qing court and Mao Zedong's later tactic of endurance supported by an upsurge of patriotism.

But these arguments failed to persuade a majority of the Qing court, which finally opted to ratify the peace treaty. It was obvious that failing to do so would have put the country at an overwhelming disadvantage militarily, at least in the short term, with the fall of Beijing an inevitability.

China appears to have believed that foreign intervention would eventually allow it to retrieve the Liaodong Peninsula ceded to Japan as stipulated by the treaty. In the event, the Chinese were forced to pay even larger sums to Japan in exchange for the peninsula's return, only to be deprived of it shortly afterwards by Russia—one of the very nations on whose intervention China had counted. At the time of the signing of the treaty, however, short-term diplomatic maneuvers still seemed preferable to military resistance.

XIX

THE TREATY OF
SHIMONOSEKI

Li Hongzhang in Japan

The Inevitability of Intervention

The words "Tripartite Intervention" aroused strong emotions in Japan for many years after the end of the war. The intervention was both humiliating and infuriating, particularly as Russia occupied the Liaodong Peninsula immediately after insisting that it be returned to China in the name of regional stability; but the sheer intensity of emotion it provoked does suggest a certain political naivety.

In the age of imperialism, geopolitics was subject in many respects to the law of the jungle. Just as a smaller predator might be deprived of the spoils of its hunt by a larger one, states with territorial ambitions attracted attention and interference from others. Japan was by no means an exception.

Even Russia, leader of the Tripartite Intervention and a big player in the post-Napoleonic age, was repeatedly thwarted by Britain in its attempts to encroach upon Turkey. One would be justified in saying that without the nineteenth-century deterrence by the British, the Soviet Black Sea Fleet might have sailed whenever it liked through the Dardanelles into the Mediterranean during the Cold War.

Itō and Mutsu were both well aware that foreign involvement in their dispute with China was inevitable, as the *Kimitsu Nisshin sensō* shows. For Japan, the war was a race against time; China, on the other hand, had been waiting for the West to step in since the beginning of the war.

Li Hongzhang and Russia

The nature of Li Hongzhang's connection with Russia gradually came to light later, as the Russo-Japanese War loomed. Li was almost certainly bribed at the coronation of Nikolai II, one year after the First Sino-Japanese War, to conclude a secret treaty allowing Russia to build a railway through Manchuria. But he appears to have been favorably disposed toward Russia from a much earlier date for reasons that remain unknown.

In 1879, during China's border disputes with Japan and Russia over the Ryukyu Islands and Xinjiang respectively, Li argued in a report to the Qing emperor that the nation should prioritize a settlement with Russia. "Since Japan lacks the power to defend the Ryukyus from them," he wrote, "the wiser course seems to be making concessions to the Russians in exchange for their assistance in restraining Japan." He offered similar arguments during the 1886 debate on Korea, concluding that collaboration with Russia was the best way to discourage Japan's ambitions on the peninsula.

It was common wisdom that Russia was China's most dangerous external threat, with Japan in second place. "Playing one barbarian against another" (*yi yi zhi yi*) can be a shrewd strategy, but it is unclear whether Li had any idea of the price China would pay for involving Russia in its struggle against Japan. It may be that he thought it futile to resist Russia and simply sought a way to derive at least some benefit from the relationship. Still, it is difficult to be certain what Li was thinking with Russia's seizure of the north bank of the Amur River and insistence on the cession of Primorsky Krai so recent.

Within the Qing court, as well, some questioned the advisability of Li's outlook. On the eve of the Battle of Pungdo, Wen Tingshi of the Hanlin Academy submitted a report to the emperor that read in part:

> Russia's designs on Korea are far stronger than Japan's.... Korea's position in the Far East is comparable to that of Turkey in Europe. Just as Turkey's location at the mouth of the Black Sea means that its conquest is necessary to obtain freed passage to the seas around Europe, Russia cannot operate freely in Far Eastern waters unless it controls Korea at the mouth of the Yellow Sea. In constantly seeking an opportunity to attack Korea, Russia is a greater threat to us than Japan—which, fully aware of Russia's ambitions, contrives its endless intrigues on the peninsula compelled not only by rivalry with China but also fear that Russia will advance on Korea first.
>
> Domestic and international circumstances suggest that, as things are, the Western powers would not intervene in a war between China and Japan, but would turn a blind eye as the Japanese seized whatever they could. If, however, we were to emphasize the protection of Korea as a way to block Russia's southward advance, our foresight would impress Britain and Germany, which countries might lend their support to maintain the status quo in the Far East. If this kept Russia at bay, even Japan would have to abandon its ambitions and cooperate. We must proceed in full cognizance not just of our own interests but the entire situation that surrounds us.... Beiyang Minister Li Hongzhang is reportedly inclined to rely on the Russians, but they are not be trusted.

Such a clear-sighted grasp of international politics was rare in nineteenth-century China. But, unsurprisingly, Wen's arguments were never endorsed by Li, and came too late to change the course of events in any case.

It is no exaggeration to say, as Wen very nearly does, that it was Li who originally invited Russia to intervene. Mutsu's comments on the matter foreshadow much of what came after the war—Western occupation of the leased territories, the semi-colonization of China itself, and Russia's immediate advance into Manchuria:

Invited or not, the Western powers were bound to get involved sooner or later. Yet China rashly opened its gate to these ravenous beasts, rolling over in submission with no regard for its own dignity…. Should the Far East become an area for contests between the nations of the West, it will all result from the present war. China can only be said to have invited this crisis itself.

Even in the age of expansionism, however, it was difficult to intervene in a conflict unless at least one of the warring parties was receptive to the idea. If China had followed Japan's lead in stonewalling the Western powers from the start, it might still have lost the war, but at least it would not have gone to the brink of being divided up by the West immediately afterwards. In this respect, Li lacked the foresight of a Saigō Takamori or Katsu Kaishū, who rebuffed British and French interloping at the demise of the Tokugawa shogunate.

The best strategy for China would probably have been to build up its military strengths and settle the dispute with Japan directly rather than relying on external assistance. Had it failed to prepare sufficiently for war, another conceivable approach would have been to form an alliance with Britain and involve Germany and Japan in dealing with Russia directly. In any case, it should have been obvious that waging war on Japan while hoping for foreign involvement—and from Russia, at that—was ill advised, but Li did not seem to share this view.

British and American Moves

As expected, Britain was first to renew its attempts at intervention. The British had kept up their efforts to prevent the war until the very last minute, and when it had barely even begun their newly appointed minister to Japan told Mutsu that his government would soon propose a peace mediation plan.

Britain's motives in intervening were unremarkable. As the preeminent naval empire, it had the largest interest in China itself, and British goods were sold as far south as Korea through the Chinese merchant network. More generally, Britain frowned on any geopolitical intrigue it was not apprised of in advance. All things being equal, it preferred the status quo.

Any attempt at mediation is meaningless unless backed by the will and capacity to actually influence the situation. Britain's vast power made it impossible to ignore, allowing it to keep abreast of developments around the world. The Anglo-Saxon countries have remained at the center of the global information network for over four centuries in the same way.

The British presented their mediation proposal on October 8, just after Japan's victories at Pyongyang and the Yalu River. They offered only two basic principles: 1. Korea's independence should be guaranteed by the Western powers, and 2. China should pay reparations to Japan.

As the Japanese side mulled this over, Britain endeavored to clarify the intentions of the other Western nations. This was premature, however: the war was still evolving, the moment too volatile for anyone to take an interest in a proposal that was really just a rehash of Britain's previous approach. Calm, unhurried discussion held little appeal now; war had broken out, and nothing could be done to stop it until an equilibrium had been reached.

This thinking is apparent in Mutsu's response to the British minister, prepared in consultation with Itō:

> We thank the British government for its kind offer. Our troops have won some battles already, but we believe that further military progress is necessary to ensure a satisfactory outcome in peace negotiations. We would, therefore, rather not specify conditions for peace just yet.

This was a blunt declaration of their intention to prolong the war before accepting mediation.

Before sending this response, however, Mutsu had written to Itō, arguing that the British offer should be interpreted as a way of informally probing our conditions for a settlement rather than a determined attempt at mediation. Still, forewarned is forearmed, and now that we have started down the road to peace, we need to plan ahead.

Mutsu presented three draft peace proposals to Itō for his opinion. All three reconfirmed Korea's independence and required China both to pay reparations and conclude an unequal treaty with Japan like the ones China had with Western countries. Where the proposals differed was in openness and the matter of territory.

Proposals (A) and (B) involved disclosing Japan's conditions for peace, while (C) called for saying nothing definite on the issue before hearing from China. Meanwhile, (A) demanded that China cede Lüshun (旅順) and Dalian to Japan as a guarantee not to interfere in Korea's domestic politics in the future. Japan had started the war on the pretext of promoting Korea's autonomy, so occupying these territories in order to eliminate China's influence on Korea's northeast border had a reasonable sound to it. Proposal (B), on the other hand, required the ceding of Taiwan in exchange for Japan's assent to a joint guarantee of Korea's independence by the Western powers. The theory here was that it would weaken Japan's position to insist on receiving Lüshun and Dalian even after Britain had offered such a guarantee.

Proposal (A) was Itō's first choice, because it would give Japan control of the Liaodong Peninsula, but he could see the advantage of (C), feeling that there was no need to offer a detailed response to the British yet.

Making a Choice

At first there was some disagreement between the two men on the matter of exclusion. Where Itō preferred to keep Japan's hand hidden, Mutsu was inclined to disclose their intentions with concrete proposals like (A) and (B). In Itō's judgment, the best scenario was a bilateral negotiation, with the terms of the settlement disclosed to the Western powers only once it was too late for China to renege. If other countries involved themselves in the peace negotiations—especially if they took China's side—reaching a favorable conclusion would be most unlikely.

We cannot say with certainty even today which of these approaches would have been seen better results. In the end, Itō opted for the bilateral approach, with Japan winning control of the Liaodong Peninsula in the final settlement—only to abandon it once more in response to pressure from the West.

How might things have turned out if Mutsu had prevailed, leading to backroom talks with the West before formal negotiations began?

In the best case, Britain might have accepted Japan's argument for acquiring the Liaodong Peninsula, recognizing that it would also restrain Russia's advance into the Far East.

If Britain had rejected the cession of Liaodong on the grounds that the Western powers would guarantee Korea's independence instead, Japanese operations on the Chinese continent would naturally have been constrained. With less ability to exert military pressure, the amount of reparations it could demand might have been significantly reduced, and Japan's claims on Taiwan rejected. On the other hand, secret negotiations with Britain might at least have prevented the Tripartite Intervention. Ultimately, as long as the British reaction was monitored carefully, proposals (A) and (B) were both less risky.

Mutsu's predictions often turned out to have been accurate in retrospect, but his very farsightedness isolated him among not only the public and parliament but even other cabinet members. Few had time for his cool-headed prescriptions when the general mood was so aggressive. Going all in and retreating only when necessary was a more appealing option, even if the outcome was exactly the same. Itō's preference for responding to the British only in vague terms was the pragmatic solution of a politician, allowing him to observe the development of events before making any firm commitments.

Once Itō had made his decision, Mutsu accepted it without complaint. "The outcome of such a delicate situation was beyond prediction," he writes. "The best of the three proposals would become apparent only in hindsight." Nevertheless, a choice had to be made, and Mutsu threw his support resolutely behind it, accepting that it prevented others from fathoming Japan's intentions until the last moment.

Indeed, when the Tripartite Intervention finally came about, it was Mutsu who successfully convinced first an indecisive Itō and then the rest of the cabinet to stick to the policy of forcing China to ratify the peace agreement first as decided in advance.

Itō summarized the basic direction he and Mutsu had agreed on in a report to Emperor Meiji on January 31, just before peace talks began:

> Whether the negotiations succeed or not, disclosing our conditions for peace would make foreign interference inevitable. Even the wisest statesman, however, could predict neither the nature of these interventions nor the resolve behind them. Should a powerful nation act coercively, we would be forced to either modify our demands or risk making a new and formidable enemy while war with China was still being waged. If and when this occurs, we hope to consult with Your Majesty on the right course to take.
>
> The most important thing for us, the civilian and military leadership, is to remain united in pursuit of our goals without revealing our intentions to other powers.

Notice the provision he makes for future adjustments.

In America We Trust

Next came a new attempt by America to intervene.

The U.S. government would undoubtedly be impartial, Mutsu felt, but China might not have experienced sufficient loss to agree to peace negotiations. Public opinion in Japan favored continuing the war as well. However, the war was bound to end eventually, and it might be convenient for Japan if one of the Western powers were to mediate peace talks—particularly if that country happened to be the United States.

Mutsu decided to turn down the American offer for the time being, while leaving open the possibility of accepting it at a later stage, using wording similar to his reply to Britain.

Along with a written reply, Mutsu met U.S. Minister to Japan Edwin Dun on November 17 to explain that while he had to decline the offer at present in case it encouraged other countries to cut in, he hoped that America would still be willing to mediate when China was ready to come to the table.

Dun promptly asked the U.S. minister to China what the Chinese leadership's intentions were. When Empress Dowager Cixi, who had been against the war from the beginning, learned of Dun's inquiries, she called for peace negotiations with Japan to begin at once.

Mutsu surely judged the American intervention the safest to accept, having never doubted the country's integrity. Even in *Kenkenroku*, for all its diplomatic machinations, his unshakable trust in the U.S. comes through clearly.

Testing the Waters

With the empress dowager hoping to end the war, and the British and American governments both expressing hopes for an early settlement, the Qing court warmed to the idea of peace talks. The subsequent involvement of the United States was unexpectedly well received, and before long it was agreed that a Chinese delegation should go to Hiroshima on February 1, 1895, to begin the peace negotiations proper.

There were still many in China who argued for not downing arms. The result was a half-measure: China committed to sending a delegation to Japan, yet showing no interest in a ceasefire. But Port Arthur fell soon after, and Weihaiwei in January. With a showdown in the Zhili Plain seemingly imminent, the court must have counted themselves lucky that the offer from the United States had come when it did.

From the Japanese perspective, however, the timing was plainly inopportune. The Beiyang Fleet had not been defeated, and Taiwan and the Penghu Islands were yet to be occupied. The army was mustering its forces in preparation for a decisive battle, with the full support of the public on the home front. It was no time to begin peace negotiations.

Itō called a secret meeting with Mutsu and made the following comment, with which Mutsu could only agree:

After careful analysis of the domestic and international situation, I am persuaded that the time is not yet ripe for peace talks. It isn't even clear how serious the Chinese are. And we need to be careful not to reveal our demands in advance, as it would only invite debate on the validity of our terms, both at home and abroad.

Accordingly, I suggest we not start peace talks until we've taken the measure of the head of their delegation and determined exactly what authority he has. The credentials he presents should be looked at closely.

With Japan to be represented by Itō and Mutsu in the negotiations, China might have been expected to send someone of equivalent importance, such as Prince Gong, leader of the government, or Li Hongzhang himself. Instead, the Chinese delegate was a low-ranking official who didn't even have the prerogative to conclude a treaty. Suspecting that the delegate was there solely to gauge their true intentions, Japan sent him back, arguing that negotiating with someone who wielded so little authority would be pointless.

Meanwhile, the Japanese government had been using its own diplomats to gather information on Western views of the war since November 1894.

By early 1895 it was clear that the West would unanimously oppose anything that might imperil China's existence, although this principle was often expressed only vaguely. The British and German governments, for instance, warned against conditions that could "cripple China" or "topple the Manchurian government."

Itō and Mutsu were confident that these apprehensions could be played down. All they had to do was to make some sort of deal with the Qing court before the army prevailed on the Zhili Plain and captured Beijing.

Russia's attitude was more unsettling. Its leadership appeared determined to wait for Japan to disclose its conditions before deciding on a response. Whatever form that took, vague expressions of disapproval seemed less likely than threats against Japan should it attempt to interfere with Russia's own designs.

For the moment, though, the Russian government's true intentions remained obscure. In fact, it didn't appear to have even formed any at that point, although it ultimately intervened in just the manner its national interest made likely.

Within Japan, the public mood wouldn't tolerate anything less than forcible expansion at China's expense, as Mutsu observes in his memoir:

The army insisted that it should seize the Liaodong Peninsula, calling it a strategic location that controlled access to Beijing where many soldiers had lost their lives already. The navy also coveted the peninsula, in spite of its initial designs on Taiwan. Our financial officials preferred reparations to territory. Finance Minister Matsukata said he hoped to obtain one billion taels [approximately one and a half billion yen].

Among political parties, hardliners insisted on the cession of Shengjing province [southern Manchuria, including Fengtian city and the Liaodong Peninsula] and Taiwan. The Kaishintō and Kakushintō in particular argued that, if the Qing government could no longer maintain control of China, we should be prepared to divide the country into about four hundred provinces and annex Shandong, Jiangsu, Fujian, and Guangdong among them. The Jiyūtō advocated demanding the three Manchurian provinces of Jilin, Shengjing, and Heilongjiang along with Taiwan.

Even diplomats who should have been sensitive to the position of the Western powers had their ambitions. Aoki Shuzō, minister to Britain and Germany, proposed that we demand those parts of Jilin, Shengjing, and Zhili provinces [the metropolitan area, with Beijing at its center] that don't border Russia. Minister Nishi Tokujirō (西徳二郎, 1847–1912) in Russia, drawing on a careful study of local sentiment, predicted that while the Russians would not permit the Liaodong Peninsula to be ceded to Japan outright, neither would they object to our demanding reparations and occupying the peninsula until payment was made.

Mutsu also cites Viscount Tani Tateki, a well-known statesman and army general, who argued against making any territorial demands at all in order to preserve the amity between Japan and China in the long term. Tani's point of reference was Bismarck's magnanimous peace conditions after the Austro-Prussian War, which strategically paved the way for the subsequent alliance between Austria and Prussia and helped in the later war with France. But even Tani was not bold enough to openly defy the general mood, and made his proposal to Itō only by way of a private letter.

The Astute Li Hongzhang

As the outcome of the war became increasingly apparent, so too did the goals of the Western participants. Where once they contented themselves with vague warnings against demanding too much (without specifying where "too much" began), before long the London *Times* was flatly declaring that Japan should not be permitted to seize so much as an inch of continental China.

Recognizing this change in the international climate, Mutsu decided that it would be wiser to move forward with the peace talks. He sent word to the Chinese government through the U.S. minister in Beijing that this time he expected them to send "cabinet-level delegates entrusted with full authority to settle not only the matters of financial reparation and Korea's independence but also the cession of Chinese territory and signing of a trade treaty." This did reveal Japan's goals to an extent, but it was deemed an acceptable loss if it prevented China from sending another inadequate delegation to buy time.

As if in exchange for Mutsu's partial openness, the Chinese government agreed to send Li Hongzhang to the talks with full decision-making authority. All was finally in place for peace negotiations to begin on March 20 in Shimonoseki, a city in western Japan.

Li's speech at the outset of the talks was in typical Chinese rhetorical style:

> Two great empires, of the same race and the same culture [*dōbun dōshu* 同文同種], dominate Asia: China and Japan. Though presently at war, we must restore our time-honored friendship. Indeed, it is my hope that this experience will, if anything, bring us closer as allies.
>
> No one in any nation has greater insight into the position of Asia in today's world than Count Itō.

The great wave of Western civilization is moving toward Asia as we speak. We Asians must join hands in confronting it as it surges nearer.

Japan has achieved remarkable reforms in recent years, all attributable to the good governance of your prime minister. China, by contrast, has been less successful, with my own shortcomings to blame. In this connection, I wish to mention two positive outcomes that the present war has already brought about.

First, in organizing and mobilizing a Western-style armed force, Japan has shown the world that our people are in no way inferior to theirs.

Second, the war has woken China from a long sleep. In this sense, Japan's example and instruction as we march toward the future has been of benefit.

Accordingly, while there are some in my own country who bear a grudge against you, I personally believe we have a number of things to thank our hosts for.

Japan is not inferior even to Europe in scholarship and scientific knowledge. China is richly endowed with natural resources. If our two empires were to stop this altercation and join forces, as brothers, we could compete successfully with the nations of the West, and no longer invite their disrespect.

Mutsu made note of the "astuteness" displayed in this address, "as befitted Li's reputation as one of the greatest men in China today."

It was indeed a well-crafted speech. But, as Mutsu had earlier observed, it was Li who had used every means at his disposal to attract Western support in the first place. Even now, he was planning to report Japan's peace conditions to the West as soon as possible, hoping that the European powers would force Japan to moderate its demands. His appeal for unity in the face of the Western advance into Asia was empty verbiage that failed to move the Japanese side. But it was impressive verbiage, indicative of a mature culture's ability to use words not merely to express one's true feelings, but to win people over for a given purpose.

Attempted Assassination

One of the sticking points at Shimonoseki was the question of a ceasefire.

The standard procedure internationally for terminating a war required a truce between the warring parties before peace negotiations began. Itō and Mutsu, however, hoped to initiate talks while fighting was still going on. "Given the situation at the front, we had no reason to call a ceasefire," Mutsu notes in *Kenkenroku*. "It was always our intention to head straight into peace negotiations." The feeling on the Japanese side, after all, was that the talks had begun prematurely to begin with.

China had also initially preferred to skip a truce, still believing that it might win the war. By the time of the Shimonoseki negotiations, however, the writing was on the wall and China wanted a ceasefire at all costs.

But the Japanese military had no intention of suspending operations with its own reinforcements around the Zhili Plain still getting ready and Taiwan yet to be conquered. Itō and Mutsu, believing that military pressure would help bring the eventual peace more promptly, were not inclined to restrain the army or navy. And with pro-war voices still heard at the Qing court, there was no knowing what China might do to buy time if Japan lowered its weapons.

Because entering into peace talks without even a ceasefire could be seen as a violation of civilized norms—a criticism Japan was determined to avoid—a truce was eventually offered. The conditions, however, were severe. China was to surrender all its troops' weapons, ammunition, and food, and bear all military costs during the ceasefire as well. Japan was to be permitted to occupy Dagu, Tianjing, and Shanhaiguan, none of which had yet fallen in the war itself. Shanhaiguan protected Beijing to the north, while Dagu and Tianjing were gateways to the sea: if China had accepted, Japan would have gained what it hoped for from the Zhili Plain battle without actually fighting.

Li lost his composure on hearing these conditions, repeatedly shouting, "It's too unfair! Too unfair!" This reaction, Mutsu admitted, was perfectly understandable: Japan had made an intentionally unappealing offer in the hope of forcing China to start negotiations directly.

Li had no choice but to do as the Japanese had hoped—only to win his truce by entirely unexpected means.

On March 24, Li was shot and seriously injured by a sniper, Koyama Rokunosuke, a radical member of the Jiyūtō. Koyama reportedly only meant to obstruct the peace talks temporarily, to allow the military to gain more ground, but it was immediately recognized that the incident put Japan's reputation in the international community at risk and would actually make Western intervention more likely, not less, if it delayed the negotiations.

The emperor immediately issued an edict expressing his regret regarding the attack, and sent his personal physician to look after Li. The empress sent a bandage she had sewn for him personally. Public opinion was uniformly sympathetic, and long lines of well-wishers formed in front of his lodgings.

Mutsu paid a visit to Itō to argue that they were now obliged to agree to a truce. Imperial gestures and public sympathy were all very well, but Li would not be satisfied without a concrete concession. In any case, it would be immoral to continue military operations when the incompetence of the Japanese police had brought a temporarily halt to the peace process.

Itō concurred, but had to seek the military's opinion first. He wired Hiroshima, where the cabinet and Imperial Headquarters staff were staying, but found that most were against the idea.

In Mutsu's judgment, however, a truce of two or three weeks would not put any critical military opportunity out of reach. Arriving promptly at a proper settlement was far more important.

Itō traveled to Hiroshima to attempt to persuade the cabinet in person. Addressing a senior civilian/military ministers' conference on March 26, he made his case:

> Until now, we have insisted that matters between Japan and China should be settled solely by us, rejecting all attempts at outside interference. Even when China pleaded for the Western powers to intercede, we gave them no excuse to do so.
>
> But now we have given China an excuse that is quite unparalleled. Li Hongzhang could return home immediately and convince his Western contacts that, despite its claims to be a civilized

country, Japan can't be trusted as a negotiating partner if it harms foreign delegations that arrive at its own request. Sympathy for China would be reason enough for the West to step in at once, and the situation for us would take an immediate turn for the worse.

Our only hope of mending things is to continue the peace talks, and to do this, we must grant China an unconditional truce right away.

Itō's arguments mirrored Mutsu's views exactly.

Their political judgment was given priority over the military's preferences, and the emperor approved the ceasefire. Mutsu immediately drafted a treaty specifying a twenty-one day truce from which only Taiwan and the Penghu Islands were excluded. When the still bedridden Li received the draft from Mutsu, his delight was just visible even with his entire face covered with bandages except for one eye. He even offered to resume negotiations from his sickbed.

The Chinese steamer that had brought Li and his delegation to Japan demonstrated their readiness to return home by maintaining a head of steam throughout the negotiations. Not for the first time, Itō and Mutsu had saved Japan from crisis by a hair's breadth.

The Peace Treaty

Peace negotiations between the two nations then began in earnest. The Japanese side presented its proposal on April 1, and agreement was reached on April 17.

Japan's original demands included:

— Recognition of Korea's independence;
— Cession of the Liaodong Peninsula, Taiwan, and the Penghu Islands;
— Three hundred million taels in reparations;
— Conclusion of a Japan-China commerce and navigation treaty equivalent to those China had with European countries; and
— Opening of additional treaty ports.

The details of the diplomacy between Li and his Japanese counter-parts were fascinating, but space does not permit a full review here. One notable development was China secretly communicating the contents of Japan's proposal to the British, Russian, and French ministers stationed in Beijing as soon as they were presented. Just as Itō had predicted, China called the conditions cruel and the demand for Liaodong in par-ticular completely unacceptable. This appeal to the Western powers was the direct impetus for the Tripartite Intervention.

What China did not mention was the clause on trade, which included numerous concessions that the West had sought for some time from China with no success. China had good reason not to publicize them. If they were accepted as proposed, its other trading partners would expect the same benefits due to most-favored-nation clauses—a development the Western powers would surely welcome. Learning of this careful omission, Mutsu arranged for a British newspaper to publish the clause in full in an attempt to dissuade Britain from opposing the settlement.

After a series of exchanges between the two parties, Japan presented a new, compromise proposal. This reduced the reparations to two hundred million taels and narrowed the definition of the territory in Liaodong to be ceded. The Japanese side demanded that China respond with a yes or no.

From the beginning of the negotiations, Itō had emphasized his "sincere hope" that the Chinese delegation would understand the situ-ation correctly: that Japan is the clear victor in this war. If the present negotiations break down, we will immediately send in reinforcements on sixty to seventy troopships. I hate to think what would happen to the safety of Beijing in that case.

Now, as the talks reached their final phase, Itō urged China to accept the terms presented. "The outcome of a war is never predict-able," he said. "There is no knowing if these terms will remain the same in the future." Recognizing Japan's resolve, China assented at last—all the while, it seems, counting on Western complicity yet to come.

The Treaty of Shimonoseki was ratified by Emperor Meiji on April 20, 1895. Chief Cabinet Secretary Itō Miyoji soon set sail for Zhifu to exchange documents with China.

XX

THE TRIPARTITE
INTERVENTION

An Unavoidable Concession

The Foreign Powers Make Their Move

Not even Itō and Mutsu could fend off the West forever. On April 20, the very day the emperor ratified the Treaty of Shimonoseki, the German minister to Japan expressed a desire to visit the Ministry of Foreign Affairs, accompanied by colleagues from several other countries. The Tripartite Intervention had begun.

Three days later, the envoys from Germany, France, and Russia arrived at the Foreign Ministry to convey their message. Prolonged Japanese occupation of the Liaodong Peninsula, they said, would put unrelenting pressure on China's capital and undermine Korean independence, preventing a lasting peace in the Far East. In the spirit of friendship between nations, they proposed that Japan withdraw from the peninsula altogether.

The Western powers had begun to give serious consideration to intervention on April 1, when China had revealed Japan's terms to them as soon as they were received. Russia had expected Britain to participate in the intervention too, out of concern for China's territorial integrity and regional stability, but in the end Britain abstained.

When the First Sino-Japanese War began, Britain had been viewed as a pro-China force in the region, while Russia was seen as pro-Japan. On January 31, 1895, Japanese Minister to Germany Aoki Shūzō reported by telegram a private remark made by Kaiser Wilhelm II: "It is amusing to see Britain trying to seduce China while Russia tries to do the same with Japan." The young kaiser's understanding may have been superficial, but he was not entirely wrong.

It was true that Britain hoped above all to maintain the status quo in the Far East. It had no wish to see Russia extend its influence by taking advantage of a weakening China.

Three months before the war, Aoki had a lengthy discussion with the British assistant secretary for foreign affairs, F. L. Bartie, in which he inquired about Britain's view of the political situation in East Asia. "Britain seeks nothing from Korea," Bartie replied. "We are only concerned that Russia should not occupy the peninsula. Accordingly, we are privately glad that China maintains its authority there."

Nor should it be forgotten that the moderate British proposals presented around the outbreak of war were more accommodating to China than Japan.

At about the same time, Russia suggested to Mutsu through Minister Khitrovo that the two governments should conduct an exchange of views to prevent involvement by other foreign powers.

Russia was intent on securing at least the northern part of Manchuria so that the Siberian Railway could run straight to Vladivostok instead of making a long detour via the northern bank of the Amur River. To acquire a port that didn't freeze over during the winter (as Vladivostok did), Russia also had to either excise China's influence in the Korean Peninsula or occupy southern Manchuria. Since it expected fierce opposition from China and Britain if it attempted to realize these goals, to have Japan as an ally would probably be advantageous. Japan's insistence on Korean independence was also convenient, since giving Korea greater autonomy would fit in with Russia's hope of ending China's suzerainty there—the Japanese could always be driven off the peninsula later. And, of course, Japan's weakening of China benefited Russia too.

Developments show that the situation in the Far East before and after the First Sino-Japanese War evolved exactly as Russian leaders had calculated. Once a debilitated China had abandoned its claim to Korea, Russia was able to secure advantageous positions there and in Manchuria with ease.

Russia and Anglo-Japanese Relations

Yet Japan's hopes lay more with Britain. Russia's posture was inherently contradictory. It might be proposing an informal alliance to thwart Britain's efforts to preserve existing conditions, but its interests would obviously clash with Japan's, in both Korea and Manchuria, once China was out of the picture. Everyone in Japan expected an eventual confrontation with Russia to take place.

As a result, it was only natural that Japan should pin its hopes on Britain. From the British perspective, too, if China was no longer able to block Russia's southward advance, it would be helpful if Japan could play that role instead. In fact, Aoki made this very point during his dialogue with Bartie. The Anglo-Japanese Alliance would not begin until 1902, but Japanese diplomacy had already begun to move in that direction.

When Russia made its attempt to intervene before the war, Itō wrote to Mutsu three times in as many days. On June 30, he said, "I don't think it would be unwise to rely on Britain." The following day, he had a more detailed suggestion:

I hear that the British fleet presently at anchor in Yokohama is bound for Hakodate.... For the purpose of restraining Russia, it would be far more convenient for us if it went to Korea or Shanghai instead, or even remained in Yokohama. I doubt that Acting Minister Pasett has the authority to change the fleet's itinerary, so I suggest that you wire Minister Aoki and have him bring this to the attention of the British foreign minister.

Finally, on July 2, he wrote, "I'm sure you need no reminding, but it would be a good idea to occasionally contact the British acting minister to keep him unofficially abreast of the situation," all but making explicit his plan to rely on Britain's help in containing the Russian threat.

Some years later, on the eve of the Russo-Japanese War of 1904–05, Japan would be faced with a choice: either negotiate a divided occupation of Korea and Manchuria (although, as it turned out, Russia had no intention of abandoning its plans to capture the entire peninsula itself), or resist the Russian incursion through an alliance with Britain.

As seen above, however, Japan faced exactly the same choice in 1895. There was one difference: during the First Sino-Japanese War, Britain had low expectations of Japan as a partner, consistent with its low regard for Japan's capabilities in general. Nevertheless, the pragmatic British were happy to accept Japan as a buffer against Russia's southward advance, just as they had accepted China in that role. As a result, a British cabinet meeting on April 8 concluded that the Japanese peace conditions "would not adversely affect British interests to an extent justifying the use of military power by us."

It was obvious to anyone that seeking aid from Britain and the United States was one of Japan's options in the face of Russian pressure. Mutsu was no exception. His decision to agree to the American offer of mediation was a step in that direction. But the United States never had any intention of intervening militarily, and Mutsu expected little from Britain either. As he wrote in an editorial for the monthly magazine *Sekai no Nihon* (Japan in the World) after the war:

> Many people have high hopes for the Anglo-Japan Alliance. But Britain is not Don Quixote—identifying with others' suffering. Any alliance that requires Britain to guarantee Japan's security must guarantee Britain's security in return. Is Japan capable of helping it defend its endless lines of defense across the empire? Britain doesn't think of us as an ally capable of fighting wars on the continent or dispatching our fleet beyond Singapore. If they had only referred to Japan as their ally during the Tripartite Intervention, the Itō cabinet might have made the historic decision to tie the nation's fate to an alliance with the British. But they didn't, and we were left with no choice but to accept the intervention instead. . . .

Once again, Mutsu's judgment proved sound and prescient. Indeed, when Britain eventually proposed an alliance with Japan around the turn of the century, it was only after Russia and France's combined naval power had finally caught up with its own, leaving it unable to send ships to the Far East lest it lose command of the seas around Europe.

At the time of the Tripartite Intervention, Japan's only battleship was the badly damaged *Zhenyuan* captured from China at Weihaiwei. But Japan would soon acquire more, expanding its fleet ship by ship until it had become a naval power of such consequence that Britain thought it necessary to rely on Japan to protect its interests in the region. This marked the end of Britain's own century of "splendid isolation."

In 1905, when the Anglo-Japanese Alliance was renewed and expanded to a full offensive and defensive agreement, Japan committed itself to the defense of India and the Indian Ocean, a British colony a long way from its own territorial waters. Things had proceeded exactly as Mutsu had predicted.

After the war, at the ninth session of the Imperial Diet (1895–96), Itō proposed expanding the navy by more than 200,000 tons and the army by thirteen divisions. According to journalist Sakazaki Sakan, the impetus for this was Mutsu's argument that Britain would not agree to an alliance unless Japan was powerful and influential enough to justify one.

Japan's military expansion during the postwar *gashin shōtan* period ("persevering for redress") was remarkable. The wartime naval budget for 1895 was thirteen million yen, but this was tripled in the 1896 peacetime budget—and then doubled again in 1897 to reach seventy-six million.

Along with the revenue from a massive tax increase, the government devoted almost ninety percent of the three hundred sixty million yen received from China as reparations on a military buildup. In a sense, the margin that China had not spent on the war was instead used by the Japanese government to prepare for war with Russia—which ultimately preserved the territorial integrity of China.

Today's map of the Far East might well look very different if this military consolidation and the Anglo-Japanese Alliance had not kept Russia from moving further south.

Russia and Germany

To return to the time of the First Sino-Japanese War, however: Japan was still a minor power with little room for diplomatic maneuver. Fundamentally, all it could do was accumulate gains in battle and wait and see how the Western powers would behave.

It was only natural for France to go along with Russia on the intervention.

In 1890, Bismarck fell from grace with the newly installed Kaiser Wilhelm II and was forced to resign as prime minister. Before doing so, he attempted to renew the secret Reinsurance Treaty with Russia as his last service to the long-term security of the German empire, but the kaiser and his entourage blocked it, and Russia sought a clandestine alliance with France instead. (This, in fact, was the beginning of the German tragedy that would culminate in the First and Second World Wars.)

The Franco-Russian Alliance was signed in 1892, and relations between the two countries were still in their honeymoon phase when Russia decided to intervene in the Sino-Japanese peace talks. France had nothing against Japan; it was simply supporting its ally.

The third member of the Tripartite Intervention, Germany, deserves closer attention. Japanese Minister to Russia Nishi Tokujirō once said that without Germany's participation there might not have been an intervention at all. Certainly opinions were divided within the Russian court, which didn't reach a decision until it was almost too late. The main reason for this, however, was a reluctance to involve the country in Far Eastern affairs with the rising threat of Germany on its western front; as a result, German participation in the intervention undoubtedly made it easier for Russia to sign on as well.

Nevertheless, Russia might have made a last-minute decision to intervene unilaterally in any case. To quote an abbreviated passage from the memoirs of Sergei Witte, Russian prime minister during the war:

> Far Eastern affairs at the time were solely in my hands. Tsar Niko-lai II had no particular political interest in the region, though I sensed a vague desire on his part to expand Russia's territory in

that direction, and naturally I could not ignore the tsar's intentions once I was aware of them.

After careful consideration of the options available to us with regard to the Far East, I concluded that it would be best for Russia to block Japan's occupation of the Liaodong Peninsula and permit a lethargic China to survive intact.

Thus, during the ministerial conference, I agreed to support Japan's demand for reparations but insisted on warning the country that Russia would not tolerate a treaty proposal that could damage China's territorial integrity. If Japan ignored this warning, I continued, Russia would have no choice but to take aggressive action against it. While the details of this action would have to be worked out, I submitted that we should be prepared to do something in the nature of a limited bombardment.

Only the army minister agreed with me. The chief of staff in particular was concerned only about contingencies in the west. However, my proposal was adopted at the cabinet meeting held in the presence of the tsar. The foreign minister sent the projected warning to Japan once he had obtained agreement from Germany and France.

Japan had no choice but to accede, although naturally it demanded a vast amount of money in exchange for ceding the Liaodong Peninsula. As long as our demands regarding China's territory were respected, we decided to refrain from commenting on lesser matters in case it was interpreted as over-interference.

Although some doubt the credibility of this memoir, seeing it as Witte's attempt to take all the credit for the Tripartite Intervention himself, it seems plausible enough. It is in perfect agreement with the natural choices for Russia in terms of Far Eastern strategy now that progress had been made on the Siberian Railway project.

Even if Germany had not joined Russia and France in the intervention, Witte's proposal would have been adopted in the end, barring an emergency like a sudden deterioration in relations with Germany. The other cabinet members were unable to make up their minds only because, as Witte rightly observes, they were simply ignorant about the situation in the Far East. So long as Witte had the tsar on his side, he would have prevailed eventually.

A Last-Minute Partnership

Russia's intentions aside, why did Germany decide to take part in the intervention at all? This has been exhaustively debated in other publications, so I will not go into it here.

Various German objectives have been proposed: to restrict rapprochement between Russia and France; to draw Russia's attention eastward and reduce the threat it posed to Europe; and—more fundamentally—to fulfill Germany's own ambitions in the Far East, driven by the kaiser's obsession with the "yellow peril." There is something to each of these ideas, but none of them seem urgent enough as an issue to make German participation in the intervention unavoidable. The sense that Germany acted on the spur of the moment, even carelessly, cannot be dispelled.

In the final analysis, Germany's participation in the Tripartite Intervention was attributable to a foreign policy infrastructure dominated by an inexperienced kaiser and his cronies since Bismarck's retirement in 1890. There seems little harm in leaving matters at that and moving on.

Mutsu's Discernment

And so the Tripartite Intervention went forward as planned.

Mutsu's health had taken a turn for the worse shortly beforehand, and the news reached him as he was recuperating in Maiko, Hyōgo prefecture. He immediately wired Itō in Hiroshima to ask for instructions, saying "This is just the delayed arrival of something that could have come much earlier had we informed the Western powers of our peace conditions then. Now that it's here, I believe it worth the risk to resist as much as we can. Please let me know Your Excellency's opinion."

As seen earlier, Mutsu had originally suggested laying the groundwork for a peace treaty with China through consultation with the Western powers beforehand. Itō, however, had preferred to begin with exclusively bilateral negotiations, in order to prevent other countries meddling in the process before it was completed. Mutsu had assented to this judgment, and presumably now felt that, with only the signing of the treaty and the exchange of documents remaining, allowing themselves to be intimidated by the intervention made the decision to proceed without consulting the Western powers meaningless anyway.

Mutsu realized that Japan would probably have to make concessions at some point, but was uncertain whether domestic public opinion would tolerate acceptance of the Tripartite Intervention itself. Initial resistance would allow the government both to gauge the true intentions of France, Germany, and Russia and see how the Japanese public would react.

Yamagata Aritomo and Saigō Tsugumichi were the only cabinet members in Hiroshima aside from Itō, but a meeting with the emperor was hastily convened anyway. It was agreed that while meekly accepting the intervention would make Japan appear weak, rejecting it entirely would be impractical: the country's military capacity was too extended for a confrontation with the Russian navy. Settlement of the Liaodong Peninsula issue, it was decided, should be entrusted to an international conference of concerned nations. The idea had a worthy ring to it, but inviting further foreign involvement in the peace process simply to save face was a real risk, even if necessary to appease public opinion.

In the early morning of April 25, Itō visited Mutsu in Maiko to discuss the meeting's outcome.

At first Mutsu stuck to his original position: the government should hold out until the intentions of the three participants could be more clearly discerned. Itō, with his characteristic realism, pointed out that Russia's intentions were already obvious, and that flatly rejecting the tripartite recommendations would be too risky at that point. The others present, including Matsukata, concurred.

Mutsu agreed to accept the group consensus, but remained apprehensive about the proposed international conference. Two or three additional countries would need to join France, Germany, and Russia to convene such a conference, and he was concerned that the preparations necessary would prevent Japan and China from exchanging signed documents in time. He was also worried that the conference might trigger new demands by the nations that attended.

Here was another example of Mutsu's firm conviction that interventions lead to more interventions. By contrast with China, which had been quick to invite foreign involvement, Mutsu's prudence was commendable. Permitting interference, he felt, only led to the latecomers taking a share of the spoils. It was an outcome to be avoided wherever possible. In this attitude, he showed how well he understood the practices of imperialism.

Itō understood Mutsu's concerns about the conference. Those attending the meeting at Maiko finally decided that, while the government would have to be prepared to make some concessions in the end, it should first (1) buy time to assess the domestic and international situation by bargaining with the interventionists—appealing to both logic and compassion—for the withdrawal, or at least modification, of their recommendations; and (2) urge China to promptly complete the treaty process as planned. Itō and Mutsu's views were once more in alignment.

Subsequently, telegrams were sent to the Russian, German, and French envoys in Japan to dissuade their countries from pressing their demands. At the same time, the British and American governments were sounded out on the possibility of providing assistance. But while they were sympathetic to Japan's position, it soon became apparent that both intended to uphold the principles of neutrality and non-interference.

The Japanese government also suggested a reduction of the area to be ceded on the Liaodong Peninsula, hoping to obtain a concession from Russia, but to no avail.

The aims of the Western powers having become clearer, the Japanese had no further moves to make. At the same time, public opinion in Japan had quietened down in recognition of the gravity of the situation, making it less of a concern. The process of buying time to take the measure of things both at home and abroad had been useful.

At a cabinet meeting as well as a conference at Imperial Headquarters on May 4, it was officially decided to adopt a basic policy of accepting the tripartite recommendations. The decision was recorded that very day in a succinct memorandum delivered to the three intervening parties. "On the advice of the governments of France, Germany, and Russia," it stated, "the Japanese government declares that it will abandon permanent occupation of the Liaodong Peninsula."

Before sending the memorandum, some argued for demanding

additional reparations in exchange, or attaching other conditions, but Mutsu insisted that sending a clear message with no room for uncertainty was more important. Details could be worked out later—and, as it turned out, he was correct.

The Russian minister in Tokyo replied as early as May 9, offering congratulations from the Russian government "on the discernment the Japanese have shown in the interests of world peace."

"I Do Not Believe Any Alternative Was Possible"

In this way, the crisis passed.

The Chinese appeared to want to somehow postpone the exchange of signed documents, but the Japanese commitment to returning the Liaodong Peninsula left them with little excuse for stalling—not to mention the prospect of Japan resuming a full-scale offensive the moment the truce expired. Documents were exchanged on May 8 as planned.

To close this chapter, Mutsu's remarks in the final chapter of *Kenkenroku* are appropriate:

> The Tripartite Intervention put the Japanese in a panic. Fear that we could be attacked by these three countries at any moment was widespread, and not a single person seemed to have a solution to the situation.
>
> To take one example: when Prime Minister Itō met with a group of hardliners at the time, he declared that, rather than listen to their usual opinions, he would prefer to hear what they thought could actually be done concerning the threat of naval and military action by the Western powers. Uncharacteristically, the hardliners, who were usually highly argumentative, offered neither complaint nor workable solution. A while later, however, once things had been settled, the same people leveled a storm of criticism against the government. But the crisis itself left them completely at a loss for words.
>
> This being a work on diplomacy, it is no place to pick an argument with them. I merely wish to establish for a fact just how

intensively the Itō government deliberated on the domestic and international situation, as well as our long-term national interests, and how scrupulous were the measures it took in order to protect Japan and its people.

Given our military preparedness back then, we had no choice but to accept the Tripartite Intervention. Nobody was to blame.

The intervention arrived as the date for ratification of the peace treaty was rapidly approaching. The government did its best to handle both China and the intervention simultaneously, and ultimately managed to prevail over the former and fight its way through the latter.

Japan went as far as it could without overextending itself. I do not believe any alternative was possible, no matter who was at the helm.

Mutsu's assessment has the ring of truth.

Japanese diplomacy during this period was a tightrope walk. A single misstep in either direction could have had devastating consequences.

The government was forced to be totally self-reliant, handling all manner of problems without a partner to confer with or provide relevant information. There was no Anglo-Japanese Alliance like the one that backed Japan during the Russo-Japanese War.

And yet Japan survived, weathering the Tripartite Intervention to enter a half century of prosperity.

It is true that luck and enemy errors played a part in Japan's success during the First Sino-Japanese War. Even so, the country could not have achieved as much had the Itō–Mutsu leadership faltered for even a moment.

XXI

MUTSU'S DEATH

Fighting for Democracy to the Last

Saionji Kinmochi

From the July 1894 revision of the unequal treaties to the outbreak of the First Sino-Japanese War a year later, Mutsu physically pushed himself to the limit, resting very little and putting his duties above his health.

The tuberculosis he had contracted in his twenties had ravaged his lungs in the decades since. The disease was all but untreatable at the time, and Mutsu's prospects were bleak. The slightest overexertion caused severe coughing, expectoration, and fever. Surviving more than a year after the war ended was testament to sheer willpower.

After the stress of peace negotiations with Li Hongzhang, Mutsu went to Maiko to recover—only to be faced with the Tripartite Intervention. The demanding days that followed left him drained. On May 13, 1895—the day that the imperial edict on the return of the Liaodong Peninsula was issued—he moved to Ōiso, a seashore town near Tokyo.

Before withdrawing to Ōiso, Mutsu appointed Deputy Minister Hayashi Tadasu as the new minister to China, giving him responsibility for overseeing postwar affairs. Hayashi's old position at the head of the Ministry of Foreign Affairs was filled by one of Mutsu's confidants, Hara Takashi. Finally, Mutsu entrusted his own duties at the Foreign Ministry during his leave of absence to Saionji Kinmochi, appointed acting foreign minister.

Saionji had been Japanese minister to Vienna while Mutsu was studying there with Professor Stein, and the two had been close ever since. Now, at the ministry, he still received instructions from Mutsu, who told family members on his sickbed that "only a trusted friend would accept a job like that, taking full responsibility while actual power was held by someone else."

Saionji was a bright, enterprising individual, but concealed these qualities beneath an aristocratic manner, augmented in later years by a cultivated stoicism. Born to one of the noblest of noble families, he came to understand the Western concept of freedom and political liberalism through direct experience during a ten-year stay in Paris.

Returning to Japan in 1880 at the height of the Freedom and People's Rights Movement, he became president of the daily *Tōyō Jiyū Shimbun*, where he was a prominent advocate of moderate liberalism. Despite the relative mildness of his views, it was embarrassing for the government to be criticized by a guardian of the imperial family, and he eventually resigned from the newspaper at the emperor's request.

He was unafraid both by nature and as a result of his upbringing. He did largely as he pleased and spoke the truth without hesitation. Only someone as open-minded as Saionji could have recognized the abilities of a man like Mutsu, the enemy of the *han*-based oligarchy, and unreservedly recommended him for government posts.

After Mutsu's death, followers such as Hoshi Tōru, Hara Takashi, and Okazaki Kunisuke were naturally drawn to Saionji instead. With their support, he became head of the Seiyūkai and, eventually, prime minister. He was not responsible for any remarkable achievements during his term in office, but history views him as a good head of government who personified the period of the Anglo-Japanese Alliance, considered an era of orthodoxy in modern Japanese diplomacy.

As the last surviving elder statesman of the Meiji period, Saionji played a central role in bringing in the Taishō Democracy of the 1920s and helping to rein in the militarists in the 1930s. But even he couldn't hold back the current of the times forever. He was kept at arm's length during the negotiations involved in the Tripartite Pact between Japan, Germany, and Italy, and on hearing the news of its completion in 1940, he made an accurate prediction of Japan's future in a comment to his mistress: "I don't think you will be allowed to die peacefully in your bed now." He passed away himself two months later, a year before the attack on Pearl Harbor.

Completing Mutsu's Diplomacy

During his recuperation in Ōiso, Mutsu applied the finishing touches to his diplomatic legacy with the help of Saionji and Hara.

The revision of the remaining unequal treaties was simply a matter of time. Following the example of the Anglo-Japanese Treaty of Commerce and Navigation, revised treaties had been concluded with the United States and Italy even before Mutsu's withdrawal from public life. Now that it had won its war with China, no country could refuse to recognize Japan as a significant sovereign state. The treaties with other Western nations were indeed revised in quick succession, starting with Russia. Tariff autonomy depended on the lapse of the Ansei Treaty (安政条約) of 1858, which had hitherto been permanent but under the new treaty was set to expire in twelve years. The way had been opened to complete tariff autonomy by the end of the Meiji period.

Progress was also made on the postwar settlement with China. Li Hongzhang and Minister Hayashi's negotiations on compensation for the return of the Liaodong Peninsula had ended with China finally agreeing to pay an additional thirty million taels to Japan in October 1895.

The following year, Japan concluded a Treaty of Commerce and Navigation with China. These talks had proceeded smoothly, since the peace agreement had already stipulated that China sign a treaty with Japan comparable to the ones it had with the Western powers. From the Chinese point of view, however, parts of the process made painful reading. On one occasion, Li asked Hayashi whether he still regarded "China as an independent nation," to which the reply was "I am merely following the example of the European countries." This epitomizes the comedown of the defeated nation. Two countries that had been considered twin powers in Asia came to occupy very different positions.

The victor had won recognition as a nation on an equal footing with the imperialistic Western states, while the loser was reduced to a semi-colony no longer treated as an equal.

Beyond Japan's control were Korea's domestic politics. From the Imo Incident and Kapsin Coup to the war with China, Japan's Korean policy had consistently aimed to eliminate Chinese influence from the penin-sula in favor of expanding its own. Now that China had been driven out, however, Japan had no real control over what happened next. If Russia had its own plans for the future of Korea, then the matter was in the hands of the more powerful intruder.

Had Japan and Korea made common cause in countering the Rus-sian threat, history would have been different. But the Korean govern-ment was resentful of Japan's meddling during the war, and actively requested Russia's assistance in freeing it from Japanese oppression.

At a June 4 cabinet meeting, which Mutsu attended during a brief return to the office, he managed to persuade the government to adopt a policy of non-interference in Korea's internal affairs. But he remained con-cerned that the public's "neighborly" (as he put it) interest in modern-izing Korea would not be allayed so easily—and, indeed, after his death, this cabinet decision was more or less ignored.

Miura Gorō (三浦梧楼, 1847–1926), the newly appointed minister to Korea, drafted three possible Korean policies for consideration by the Itō administration. He clearly preferred his first option, which saw Japan take sole responsibility for Korea's defense as well as its political reform.

In point of fact, Japan had no palatable alternatives. Miura allowed that this path might lead to war with one or more Western powers along the way, but predicted that if Japan stayed the course, Korea would be a protectorate within a few years.

Developments proved Miura correct, although it took the defeat of Rus-sia in a war on which Japan staked its very fate to come about. Given Russia's influence over the peninsula, everything Japan had done before the war was nullified, or even became counterproductive.

Less than two months after taking up his post in Seoul, Miura masterminded the assassination of the Korean empress, Myeongseong (Queen Min). This not only ruined Japan's international reputation but also forced the horrified Korean court to take refuge in the Russian embassy. China's influence may have been excluded, but Japan's own misconduct had now driven the Koreans to seek full Russian protection.

The Liaodong Peninsula, which Japan had abandoned under duress following the Tripartite Intervention, was soon leased by Russia. Everything on the continent that Japan had obtained from China in the war Russia snatched away. The Russians also sent a large force into Manchuria during the Boxer Rebellion (1898–1901), establishing a de facto occupation of the entire region.

This was all starkly apparent to the Japanese, allowing a national consensus to form: they would "persevere for redress" until the day came to take revenge in a war against Russia itself.

The Written Record

Back in Ōiso, Mutsu devoted himself to writing his memoirs.

Regrettable as it was that his health prevented further public activities, his infirmity did give him time to complete an account of lasting value. As the quotations liberally scattered throughout this work show, *Kenkenroku* far exceeds other Japanese political memoirs in both lucidity of observation and precision of expression, comparing favorably even with the memoirs of Churchill and de Gaulle.

Saionji contributed the following introductory note to what was then a private piece of work:

> What follows is a transcription of Mutsu's own dictation. It is succinct and clear, with not a word wasted. It could not have been written by anyone but Mutsu, as should be obvious at a glance to anyone with an eye for writing. I have decided to attach this note only to prevent future allegations that this book was the work of some commissioned official.
>
> May 29, 1896
> Tōan [陶庵, Saionji's literary name]

Saionji's purpose in adding this was also to ensure that the artistic value of Mutsu's work would not go unnoticed. Nonchalant though it may seem, he had composed every phrase carefully. "Not a word wasted" appears to be the only compliment he offered, but this is to be interpreted as high praise indeed.

Mutsu's literary activity reached a peak during the last eighteen months of his life. He founded the monthly *Sekai no Nihon* around the time he completed

Mutsu in his later years. Taken in Ōiso residence at the time of writing *Kenkenroku*.

Kenkenroku, and contributed political commentary whenever he had the strength to write. Space does not permit a full review of his opinions on foreign policy toward individual countries, but a few can be summarized. Mutsu thought Japan should refrain from immersion in Korean affairs and adopt a wider perspective on international relations. He was dismissive of calls for the colonization of China, arguing that Japan should establish friendly relations instead by making concessions in the negotiations for their Treaty of Commerce and Navigation. Finally, he believed that Japan was not yet powerful enough to enter into alliances with the likes of Britain or Russia or play the game of power politics.

As for Japan's diplomatic activities, Mutsu stated that "what matters in a country's diplomacy is skill. Arguing for a consistently tough or easygoing approach is of no use." In the social climate of pre–World War II Japan, hardnosed diplomacy was favored over more conciliatory attitudes. Mutsu's comment was a reminder that what mattered was the national interest; hawkish and dovish approaches could be adopted and discarded as the situation required.

This realism was echoed by later foreign minister (and prime minister) Shidehara Kijūrō, who wrote:

Nothing is more absurd than drawing a line between autonomous and cooperative diplomacy. Among sovereign nations, there is no diplomacy that is not independent. At the same time, no diplomacy between two or more independent countries is free of the need for compromise. In this sense, the diplomacy of any nation is cooperative by necessity.

Such were the advances made by Japanese diplomatic thinking under Mutsu's leadership. Unfortunately, what came next was a century-long detour through eras of chauvinistic deviation in the early Shōwa period followed by Marxist and pacifist deviation after World War II.

Mutsu continued to write almost until his death, freely criticizing contemporaries like Ōkuma and Matsukata. He used various pseudonyms, but his style was readily identifiable, and he dispensed so much disparagement that he probably had nothing more to say when he did pass on.

The quality of these articles suggests that Mutsu could have been a successful critic. A skilled administrator of state affairs, his pen alone could have made him a significant opponent of the government had his desires for office been frustrated. As Mencius wrote:

> To sit in the broad places of the world and stand in the right places of the world ... if given state responsibilities, to practice one's principles for good governance, and, if not, to practice them alone; to be neither degraded by riches and honors nor cowed by power and force: these are the characteristics of the truly great man.

A Lasting Influence

The outlines of Japanese foreign policy over the next fifty years were laid down during the Mutsu era.

First, Japan succeeded in revising its treaties with the Western powers and becoming a fully independent nation. Considering that other Asian and African nations suffered under such treaties for fifty more years, the benefits of this were considerable.

Next, Japan broke China's suzerainty over Korea and secured a free hand on the peninsula. By undermining the already ailing Qing empire, however, it disturbed the traditional balance of power in the Far East. This invited the Tripartite Intervention—Japan's firsthand introduction to the dog-eat-dog age of imperialism. After Mutsu's death and the *gashin shōtan* period, Japan defeated Russia and set to work expanding its empire.

Japan's trajectory through to its defeat in the Pacific War was thus in many ways the continuation of what Mutsu had begun. It was a tragedy for the country that it failed to produce a single statesman during this period with either his penetrating analysis of international politics or Itō's ability to steer political and military affairs as part of a single broad strategy.

After Itō and Mutsu, most Japanese leaders—with rare exceptions like Shidehara Kijūrō—were either single-minded expansionists or opportunists who pandered to the public. Mutsu, of course, was one of the first statesmen who truly understood the power of popular opinion. He had the judgment to calculate how far the public needed to be accommodated and the determination to implement unpopular policy when necessary. Japan has yet to produce his equal in this area.

It is no overstatement to call Itō and Mutsu both the first and the last politicians to shoulder responsibly the burden of Japan's imperialism.

In the realm of domestic politics, Mutsu's work remained incomplete. Cambridge in the mid-1880s had convinced him that "sooner or later" Japan too would have to implement an Anglo-Saxon type of parliamentary democracy, party politics and all. But this was accomplished only after a few years' worth of twists and turns following his death, partly driven by the dedication and lifelong efforts of Mutsu protégés like Hoshi Tōru and Hara Takashi.

According to Sakazaki Sakan, on his deathbed Mutsu said the following to his former brother-in-law:

> My real desire was to revise the treaties with the Western powers and establish constitutional democracy in Japan. I managed the former, but am not even halfway to the latter. This will bother me beyond the grave.

Tellingly, Japan's historic victory over the Chinese empire went unmentioned. Sakazaki interpreted Mutsu's words as a declaration of his pre-eminent goal: to realize democracy in the form of a party cabinet system.

Toward a Parliamentary Democracy

We don't need Sakazaki to confirm that Mutsu ultimately hoped to see representative government of this sort in Japan. Of course, it took a lot of ideological exploration before Mutsu himself narrowed down his goals to this degree.

The fiercest of his struggles in the first half of his life all turned out to be in vain. His attempt to establish a powerful military state in Kishū to rival Satsuma-Chōshū was crushed when the Meiji government abolished the domain system in favor of prefectures. The *Genrōin* (Council of Elders) that he created to add "checks and balances" to the *hanbatsu*-dominated government was soon nullified. His subversive dreams during the Satsuma Rebellion ended in a prison sentence.

After brooding on different sociopolitical systems during his imprisonment and comparing the modern political orders he encountered in Europe and the United States, Mutsu became determined to work with Itō to realize constitutional government in Japan and, in the course of that effort, gradually establish a parliamentary democracy.

The first step toward this target was taken during Mutsu's lifetime.

Support for the First Sino-Japanese War by the anti-government parties was unanimous. The Jiyūtō in particular favored an aggressive Korean policy from the beginning. This party had a longstanding relationship with Mutsu, and communicated and collaborated frequently with him, as well as with Itō, from the first treaty revisions through the war proper. Afterwards, there were calls within the Jiyūtō for the party to align itself further with the government and support its policies.

In the wake of the Freedom and People's Rights Movement in the 1870s–80s, the Jiyūtō had become the largest anti-oligarchic party in

Japan, recruiting respected figures from various parts of the country. Beginning with the very first general election, it had established itself in every constituency as a political force all but immune to government intervention.

The Kaishintō and its affiliates, by contrast, were led mainly by former bureaucrats and journalists, none appearing to be as deeply rooted in individual constituencies as the Jiyūtō.

Itō was a founder of constitutional government in Japan, as well as the most powerful figure in the *hanbatsu*-dominated regime. He understood the importance of a party system far better than others in the Satsuma-Chōshū clique like Yamagata Aritomo, Matsukata Masayoshi, and Kuroda Kiyotaka.

The partnership between enlightened officials like Itō and Saionji and the influential anti-oligarchic force that was the Jiyūtō made party politics in Japan viable. But it was Mutsu who connected the two sides and enabled their collaboration. It is impossible to imagine how Japan's parliamentary democracy would have turned out without this partnership.

The two sides did not find common ground immediately. Itō was an ardent admirer of Bismarck, overconfident in his ability to steer a political party. The Jiyūtō, on the other hand, had proudly defied severe government repression since the days of the Freedom and People's Rights Movement. Persuasion from Mutsu protégés like Hoshi Tōru and Okazaki Kunisuke was needed before they became true partners.

Thus, when the Kaishintō and four other opposition parties began the 1896 Diet session by submitting a bill denouncing the return of the Liaodong Peninsula and the failure of the Itō government's Korean policy, the Jiyūtō united to defend Itō and defeat the motion by 170 votes to 103. After Mutsu's death, the same combination resulted in the formation of the Seiyūkai.

With parliamentary support secured, Japan was ready for the great increase in military spending during the period of *gashin shōtan* leading up to the Russo-Japanese War of 1904–05.

In April 1896, when Mutsu had recovered enough to return briefly to work, Itō appointed Freedom and People's Rights Movement leader Itagaki Taisuke to the office of home minister. For roughly a month, Itō, Itagaki, and Mutsu "bonded" in the cabinet. It was Itagaki's first time in government, and Mutsu made a point of meeting with him almost daily to brief him on the system's inner workings.

It was also during this brief period that Mutsu made Deputy Foreign Minister Hara the new Japanese minister to Korea and, in his final action as a member of government, appointed Komura Jutarō to the Foreign Ministry as Hara's replacement. All was now in place for the passing of the diplomatic baton from Mutsu to Komura.

The alliance between the cabinet and the Jiyūtō—the first ruling (or "government") party in Japanese political history—proved convenient for both sides. The government found it easier to work with the Diet, and the Jiyūtō had finally realized its longtime goal of independently administering state affairs. Government posts for party members were another welcome outcome.

But the Kaishintō was not about to let the Jiyūtō reap all the benefits of the new order, and found its own ally in the government's Satsuma faction, which was keenly aware of the lack of its own supporters in the Diet.

As a result, when the second Itō cabinet resigned in September 1896, it was succeeded by a coalition cabinet led by Matsukata and Ōkuma of the Satsuma faction and the Kaishintō respectively.

Amid these changes, Mutsu apparently concluded that the time was finally ripe for party politics.

All of the parties, Jiyūtō and Kaishintō included, were entering a period of turbulence. The Matsukata-Ōkuma alliance was one of pure convenience, not rooted in shared history. Even the Kaishintō's support for the government was uncertain, and so the Satsuma clique tried to undermine the solidarity of the Jiyūtō and tempt its supporters to abandon the party.

But these attempts to split the Jiyūtō only added to the factors driving a series of party realignments in which each saw its accumulated internal dissatisfaction break out into the open. Even the Jiyūtō experienced a string of defections largely attributable to antipathy toward the intra-party hegemony enjoyed by the Tosa contingent since the days of the Freedom and People's Rights Movement. In March 1897, Itagaki was forced to resign as party president.

Mutsu had already been receiving a steady stream of Jiyūtō-affiliated visitors at his sickbed in Ōiso, since various factions within the party hoped to see him as president eventually. After Itagaki's resignation, the stream became a flood, sufficient to actually delay his recovery.

But Mutsu's thinking was evolving as well. The clearest expression of this can be found in a treatise entitled "The Power of *Rōnin* (unemployed samurai)" that he contributed to the March 1, 1897, issue of *Sekai no Nihon*, which includes this passage:

> I hereby declare to my fellow gentlemen out of office who were advocates of freedom and people's rights: we may encounter opposition and obstacles along the way, but we will prevail in the end.

Never had Mutsu proclaimed his support of the Freedom and People's Rights Movement so explicitly. The boldness of the language shows his confidence that Japan was ready to move openly toward democracy.

Given the political situation at the time, it was only natural for him to reach this conclusion.

There is no doubt that he would have become head of the Jiyūtō had he survived his illness. He had the endorsement of Itagaki and the Tosa people as well as members of the Kantō faction affiliated with Hoshi Tōru.

Mutsu would also have been the natural successor to Itō as president of the Seiyūkai, although this was formed three years after his death. Even if Saionji had been appointed instead as a temporary buffer against opposition by the oligarchy, the marquis would have known what was expected of him and handed the reins to Mutsu as soon as possible.

That Saionji secretly hoped for a Mutsu cabinet seems almost certain. He all but regarded Mutsu as a brother, and was so desolated by the older man's death that it was painful for those around him to watch. "Mutsu is dead, but the clique seems almost immortal...," he was heard to murmur. It is not hard to imagine how keenly Saionji felt Mutsu's absence during the upheaval of the decades to come.

Forming a Mutsu cabinet would not have been easy. Getting Emperor Meiji's approval would have been difficult, and the Satsuma faction would have resisted. But eventually it would surely have happened—most likely on the demise of the emperor in 1912.

Mutsu's unceasing efforts, combined with the natural course of politics following the promulgation of the Meiji constitution, paved a broad, level way for Japan's democracy. The attainment of a goal pursued for thirty years—the defeat of the Satsuma-Chōshū clique—no longer seemed a dream.

In his final months, Mutsu appears to have become increasingly convinced that the end of the oligarchy was near. From May to June 1897, he seriously considered becoming president of the Jiyūtō. He even planned to travel to the northern provinces if his health improved, instructing *Sekai no Nihon*'s chief editor to prepare an itinerary and a list of sympathizers there.

But his condition took a rapid turn for the worse at around the same time, and his dream of a party cabinet remained unfulfilled when he passed away in August.

Mutsu's Final Days

In June 1896 Mutsu went to Hawaii for a two-month stay—a last attempt to restore his failing health.

Before leaving, he told friends of his hope of returning reinvigorated and, since the current cabinet did not seem likely to hold out much longer, fulfilling a long-term goal by becoming prime minister. But it was clear that his health had already deteriorated beyond any hope of recovery, and those around him couldn't meet his eyes as he spoke of these unattainable plans.

As expected, Mutsu's time in Hawaii failed to help, and by August he was in critical condition. Hara Takashi visited his sickbed almost daily, describing these visits in minute detail in his *Hara Takashi nikki* (Diary of Hara Takashi). The entry of August 24, the day of Mutsu's death, contains an emotional recollection of an exchange with Mutsu a few days earlier:

> Usually, I would tell him interesting stories during his meals. Knowing this might be our final meeting, though, I couldn't go on talking

as if nothing was wrong. It was unbearable, too, to see Mutsu endure great discomfort in order to speak with me.

It seemed to me that he wanted to continue our conversation, and it was obvious from his expression that he would have liked me to stay.

I wanted to stay longer as well, but I said goodbye because I couldn't hold back my tears any longer. I was also worried that his family would be unhappy about my spending so long with him.

Nakajima Nobuyuki offered the following account of his final visit to Mutsu on August 20:

I was unwell myself, but decided to pay him a visit because I knew I had to say goodbye. Mutsu was uncharacteristically tearful.

"My friend," he said, "I am resigned to leaving my wife and children behind. I'm not concerned about my household at all. What saddens me most is taking my leave of you and all my other colleagues in politics. Please tell Itō this when he returns from Britain [where he was attending a ceremony in honor of the sixtieth anniversary of Queen Victoria's reign].

"I feel better having told you. I know that you're unwell too. There's no need to be polite—go home."

We shook hands, and I left the house.

On August 22, two days after Nakajima's visit, the emperor presented Mutsu with some confectionery as a token of imperial sympathy. With the help of his family, Mutsu managed to receive this honor on his feet. But he became visibly weaker afterwards, and on August 24 he no longer had the strength to spit out the phlegm that obstructed his throat.

He fought death to the last, as fiercely as he had fought for his principles in life.

Hearing of Mutsu's death, Katsu Kaishū composed the following lines:

One of the paulownia's leaves has fallen
I sense that many others will follow.

The departure, one by one, of the historic figures of the Restoration obviously moved him, though many of them had come in for scathing criticism in his memoir *Hikawa seiwa*. Mutsu was the only one who received an elegy.

Katsu himself died two years later, like the last leaf falling from the tree of the shogunate and the Restoration.

Mutsu's Dream

Mutsu's dream of party politics in Japan was technically realized less than a year after his death with the formation of the Ōkuma-Itagaki cabinet (隈板内閣)—the first party government in Japan—in 1898. Two years later, in 1900, the Seiyūkai was established with Itō Hirobumi as its president, and the Seiyūkai cabinet soon followed.

Both cabinets were led by men who had been senior statesmen since the Meiji Restoration and were familiar to the oligarchy, with whom power still rested. In a sense, these were trial runs, under sufferance. True democracy was still a while off, but its arrival could not be postponed forever.

Hara, inheritor of Mutsu's aims for democracy, finally formed the first authentic party cabinet in 1918, twenty-one years after his mentor's death. Six years later, in 1924, Katō Takaaki's (加藤高明, 1860–1926) new cabinet was nicknamed the *Goken Sanpa Naikaku* ("cabinet of the three pro-constitution factions"). These events marked the unveiling of what came to be known as Taishō Democracy.

Within a mere eight years, however, the public would lose confidence in democracy due to the political and economic turmoil of the Great Depression that began in 1929. After Katō's cabinet, the country lapsed into autocratic rule by militarists and bureaucrats. And yet, eventually, the resurrection of Taishō Democracy became the central pillar of occupation policy after Japan's defeat in World War II.

The empire of Japan that Itō and Mutsu helped to create collapsed in just fifty years (1895–1945), brought down by a series of misjudgments by subsequent generations of leaders. But the Jiyūto, with which Mutsu entrusted his hopes for democracy in Japan, remained the core of the country's parliamentary system for a century, first evolving into the Sei-yūkai before becoming the postwar Jiyūtō and then the Jimintō (Liberal Democratic Party).

The tradition of pure "samurai democracy" was sabotaged almost at once by Satsuma-Chōshū's crude interference, but the system that Mutsu worked to realize—"the worst form of government except for all those other forms that have been tried from time to time," as Churchill said—survived, developing into the parliamentary democracy still seen in Japan today.

References

Bitō, Masahide. 1983. *Ogyū Sorai*. Tokyo: Chuokoronsha.

Date, Jitoku. 1926. *Date Jitoku-Ō zenshū* [Collected works of Jitoku-Ō]. Tokyo: Ujunsha.

Date, Munehiro. 1848 (1972). "Taisei santen-kō" [Study of three eras]. In *Rekishi shisō-shū* [Collection of historical thoughts], edited by Maruyama Masao et al., vol. 6 of Nihon no shisō [Japanese thought]. Tokyo: Chikuma Shobo.

Hagiwara, Nobutoshi. 1997. *Mutsu Munemitsu*. Tokyo: Chuokoronsha.

Hirano, Mineo. 1938. *Okazaki Kunisuke den* [A biography of Okazaki Kunisuke]. Tokyo: Bankokai.

Imperial Japanese Army General Staff Office. 1995. *Nihon no senshi: Nisshin sensō* [A military history of Japan: The First Sino-Japanese War]. Tokyo: Tokuma Shoten.

Itagaki, Taisuke, ed. 1910. *Jiyūtō-shi* [History of the Liberal Party]. Tokyo: Iwanami Shoten.

Itō, Chiyū. 1931. *Mutsu Munemitsu*. Vol. 3 of Itō Chiyū zenshū [Collected works of Itō Chiyū]. Tokyo: Heibonsha.

Itō, Hirobumi, ed. 1967. *Kimitsu Nisshin sensō* [Classified documents on the First Sino-Japanese War]. Tokyo: Hara Shobo.

Itō, Masanori. 1981. *Dai-kaigun o omou* [Remembering the great navy]. Tokyo: Kojinsha.

Itō, Takashi, and Sakeda Masatoshi. 1985. *Okazaki Kunisuke kankei bun-sho: Kaisetsu to shōden* [Documents on Okazaki Kunisuke: Commentary and brief biography]. Wakayama: Jimintō Wakayama-ken Shibu.

Kajima, Morinosuke. 1970. *Jōyaku kaisei mondai* [Revision of unequal treaties]. Tokyo: Kajima Kenkyusho Shuppankai.

Kissinger, Henry A. 2009. *Kaifuku sareta sekai heiwa* [*A World Restored*]. Translated by Itō Yukio. Tokyo: Hara Shobo.

Koike, Ryūkitsu. 1937. *Bankō Okazaki Kunisuke*. Wakayama: Shounso Bunko.

Matsumoto, Masazumi. 1894. *Kin Gyokukin shōden* [A biography of Kim Okgyun]. Tokyo: Koseido.

Mutsu Munemitsu-Haku 70-shūnen Kinenkai, ed. 1966. *Mutsu Munemitsu-haku: Shōden/nenpu/furoku-bunshū* [Count Mutsu Munemitsu: Biography/chronology/appendices]. Tokyo: Mutsu Munemitst-Haku 70-shūnen Kinenkai.

Mutsu, Munemitsu. 1929. *Hakushaku Mutsu Munemitsu ikō* [Literary remains of Count Mutsu Munemitsu]. Tokyo: Iwanami Shoten.

———. 1941. *Kenkenroku* [*Kenkenroku: A Diplomatic Record of the Sino-Japanese War, 1894–1895*]. Tokyo: Iwanami Shoten.

Okamoto, Ryūnosuke. 1912. *Fū'un kaikoroku* [A memoir of troubled times]. Tokyo: Bukyo Sekaisha.

Okazaki, Kunisuke. 1912. "Mutsu Munemitsu-Haku." *Taiyo* 18 (9).

———. 1935. *Kensei kaikoroku* [Memoir on parliamentary government]. Fukuoka: Fukuoka Nichinichi Shimbun Sha.

Saiga, Hiroyoshi. 1927. *Ōe Tenya den* [A biography of Ōe Tenya]. Tokyo: Ōe Futoshi.

Sakazaki, Sakan. 1898. *Mutsu Munemitsu*. Tokyo: Hakubunkan.

Seki, Yoshihiko. 1979. Bensamu: J.S. Miru [Bentham: J.S. Mill]. Tokyo: Chuokoronsha.

Shimizu, Shin. 1971–1973. *Meiji kenpō seitei-shi* [History of establishment of the Meiji constitution]. Tokyo: Hara Shobo.

Shinobu, Seizaburō. 1938. *Mutsu Munemitsu*. Tokyo: Hakuyosha.

Tabohashi, Kiyoshi. 1951. *Nisshin sen'eki gaikō-shi no kenkyū* [Study on diplomatic history around the First Sino-Japanese War]. Tokyo: Toko Shoin.

————. 1963. *Kindai Nissen kankei no kenkyū* [A study of modern Japan-Korea relations]. 2 vols. Tokyo: Hara Shobo.

————. 1979. *Kindai Nisshisen kankei no kenkyū* [A study on modern Japan-China-Korea relations]. Tokyo: Hara Shobo.

Takayanagi, Mitsutoshi. 1942. *Dai-Nihon senshi, dai 6-kan* [Military History of Japan, vol. 6]. Tokyo: Sankyo Shoin.

Takekoshi, Yosaburō. 1902. *Heishū josanki* [Tales of great people from the Meiji era]. Tokyo: Kaitakusha.

Toriumi, Yasushi. 1982. *Meiji o tsukutta otoko-tachi* [The men who built Meiji Japan]. Kyoto: PHP Institute.

Tsuda, Michitarō, ed. 1917. *Kohi: Tsuda Izuru shōden* [Kohi: Short biography of Tsuda Izuru]. Tokyo: Aoki Tōsaku.

Wang, Yunsheng. 1936. *Nisshi gaikō 60nen-shi* [60 years of Sino-Japanese diplomacy]. Tokyo: Kensetsusha.

Watanabe, Ikujirō. 1934. *Mutsu Munemitsu den* [A biography of Mutsu Munemitsu]. Tokyo: Kaizosha.

————. 1937. *Nisshin-Nichiro senso shiwa* [Historic tales of the First Sino-Japanese/Russo-Japanese War]. Tokyo: Chikura Shobo.

Watanabe, Shūjirō. 1897. *Hyōden Mutsu Munemitu* [A biography of Mutsu Munemitsu]. Tokyo: Dobunkan.

Witte, Sergei IUl'evich. 1921. *The Memoirs of Count Witte*. Translated by Abraham Yarmolinsky. Garden City, N.Y., and Toronto: Doubleday, Page & Company.

APPENDIX

Chronological Table of
Mutsu Munemitsu's Life and Accomplishments

Year	Japanese Era	Age*	Life Events	Domestic/Overseas Incidents
1839	Tenpō 10			First Opium War (1839–42).
1841	Tenpō 12			Tenpō Reforms (political reform promoted by Mizuno Tadakuni in 1841–43).
1844	Kōka 1	1	Munemitsu born in July, son of Date Tōjirō Munehiro, retainer of Wakayama *han* with annual stipend of 500 *koku,* and Masako. Born as Ushimaro, given name changed to Kojirō when he came of age. Subsequently, family name changed to Mutsu, while given name went from Kojirō to Genjirō, to Yōnosuke, and, finally, to Munemitsu.	Western military equipment introduced.
1848	Kaei 1	5	Munemitsu's father, Munehiro, assumes office of *kanjō bugyō,* or finance minister—top post in *han* bureaucracy.	Revolution of 1848 in France.
			Munehiro completes *Taisei santen-kō.*	Karl Marx publishes *The Communist Manifesto.*
1852	Kaei 5	9	Munehiro's annual stipend raised to 800 *koku.*	
			Entangled in intra-*han* feud, Munehiro ousted in December and exiled to Tanabe.	

Year	Japanese Era	Age*	Life Events	Domestic/Overseas Incidents
1853	Kaei 6	10	Munemitsu's older brother, Muneoki, purged from Wakayama domain, while Munemitsu and other members of family move around villages at foot of Mt. Kōya and along Kinokawa River. Munemitsu becomes house guest of bookstore owner in Yamato-Gojō and studies textbooks on civil administration.	U.S. Commodore Mathew Perry's East India Squadron arrives in Uraga to demand that shogunate open up the country.
1854	Ansei 1	11		(U.S.-Japan) Convention of Kanagawa concluded. Anglo-Japanese Friendship Treaty concluded.
1855	Ansei 2	12		Russo-Japanese Treaty of Shimoda concluded.
1858	Ansei 5	15	Munemitsu goes to Edo and studies rigorously under renowned scholars such as Yasui Sokken and Mizumoto Seibi.	Treaty of Amity and Commerce (U.S.-Japan) concluded. Japan concludes Treaties of Amity and Commerce with Netherlands, Russia, Britain, and France. Ansei Purge (1858–59).
1860	Man'en 1	17		Sakuradamon Incident (*Tairō* Ii Naosuke assassinated by *rōnin* samurai of Mito and Satsuma *han*).
1861	Bunkyū 1	18	Pardoned in June, Munehiro returns to Wakayama with annual stipend of 35 *koku*. Munemitsu reunited with father but leaves for Edo. Joins *sonnō jōi* movement (revere the emperor, expel the barbarians), and visits Chōshū's Katsura Kogorō and Tosa's Inui Taisuke to become their apprentice.	
1862	Bunkyū 2	19	Munemitsu goes to Kyoto. Father and older brother desert Wakayama *han* and move to Kyoto.	Ikedaya Incident in Fushimi, Kyoto. Namamugi Incident.

Year	Japanese Era	Age*	Life Events	Domestic/Overseas Incidents
1863	Bunkyū 3	20	Munemitsu makes acquaintance of Sakomoto Ryōma and enters Katsu Kaishū's Kobe Naval College.	Shogun Iemochi goes to Kyoto to pray for expulsion of foreigners. Height of xenophobic *jōi* movement. Chōshū *han* fortress bombards foreign vessels passing through Kanmon Strait. Anglo-Satsuma War. *Jōi* advocates brought down by coup undertaken by *kōbu gattai* faction (Union of Imperial Court and Shogunate).
1864	Ganji 1	21		Hamaguri Rebellion. First Chōshū Expedition. British/French/Dutch/U.S. allied fleet's bombardment of Shimonoseki fortress and capture of Chōshu *han* fortress.
1865	Keiō 1	22	Moves to Nagasaki to follow Sakamoto Ryōma.	Second Chōshū Expedition.
1866	Keiō 2	23	Joins Sakamoto Ryōma's Nagasaki Kameyama Shachū to engage in shipping and trading.	Satsuma-Chōshū alliance formed after mediation by Sakamoto Ryōma. Shogun Iemochi dies, resulting in dissolution of Chōshū Expedition forces. Emperor Kōmei dies.
1867	Keiō 3	24	In April joins *Kaientai* established by Sakamoto Ryōma.	Emperor Meiji ascends to throne. Tokugawa Yoshinobu offers to return power to emperor, but imperial order to overthrow shogunate given to Satsuma and Chōshū. Sakamoto Ryōma and Nakaoka Shintarō assassinated. Declaration of restoration of imperial rule.
1868	Meiji 1	25	Appointed official in Secretariat of Foreign Affairs in January together with Itō Hirobumi. Appointed judge in Yokohama in March, but fails to assume post due to pneumonia. Marries Suita Renko.	Meiji Restoration. Battle of Toba-Fushimi. Surrender of Edo Castle as result of negotiations between Saigō Takamori and Katsu Kaishū. Charter Oath promulgated.

Year	Japanese Era	Age*	Life Events	Domestic/Overseas Incidents
				New government-regulated organization comes into effect (separation of power/public election of public officials).
				Edo renamed Tokyo.
				Name of era changed to Meiji (beginning of one era name for one reign).
1869	Meiji 2	26	Appointed governor of Settsu in January.	Satsuma/Chōshū/Tosa/Higo *han* to return *han* registers to Emperor Meiji.
			Appointed governor of Hyōgo in June. In consultation with Itō Hirobumi, writes recommendation on abolition of *han* system and establishment of prefectures.	Capital relocated to Tokyo. Kōgisho (lower house) established. Hakodate Goryōkaku falls, ending Boshin War.
			Participates in political reform of Wakayama (including financial and military systems).	Emperor allows domain lords to return their *han* registers and appoints them governors of their respective *han*.
			Oldest son, Hirokichi, born in March.	Ōmura Masujirō dies of wounds incurred in assassination attempt.
1870	Meiji 3	27	Travels to Europe in March to purchase weapons on behalf of Wakayama *han*.	Restrictions on *han* regular troops announced.
			Second son, Junkichi, born in October.	Franco-Prussian War (1870–71).
1871	Meiji 4	28	On return from Europe in May, appointed acting military commander/vice-governor of Wakayama *han*.	Abolition of *han* system and establishment of prefecture system.
			Appointed governor of Kanagawa in August where devotes himself to financial reform.	Government dispatches ministers to France, Germany, and United States.
				Iwakura Mission (including Kido Takayuki, Ōkubo Toshimichi, and Itō Hirobumi) departs for United States and Europe.
				Sino-Japanese Friendship and Trade Treaty signed.

Year	Japanese Era	Age*	Life Events	Domestic/Overseas Incidents
1872	Meiji 5	29	Wife, Renko, dies in February.	Ministry of Military replaced by Ministry of War and Ministry of Navy.
			Proposes reform of farmland tax in April.	Solar calendar adopted.
			Appointed director of tax collecting agency in June.	Japanese consulates opened in Shanghai and Hong Kong.
			Resigns as governor of Kanagawa in July.	
			Remarriage, to Kaneda Ryōko.	
1873	Meiji 6	30	Appointed third-class officer/director of tax collecting agency in May.	Conscription ordinance promulgated.
			Appointed deputy director-general of Ministry of Finance in June.	*Seikanron* (advocacy of punitive expedition to Korea).
			Oldest daughter, Sayako, born in July.	Iwakura Mission returns. After debate on expedition to Korea, Saigō resigns from government positions in protest.
				(In Korea) Heungseon Daewongun forced to retire by Min clan, which takes over government.
1874	Meiji 7	31	Writes treatise *Nippon-jin* (The Japanese) and submits it to Kido Takayoshi. Tenders resignation from government post.	Iwakura Tomomi assaulted by advocates of invading Korea (*Seikanron*).
				Itagaki Taisuke and Gotō Shōjirō submit written petition requesting launching of popularly elected (not appointed) parliament.
				Saga Rebellion.
				Japanese troops dispatched to Taiwan under pretext of murder of Ryukyu residents.
1875	Meiji 8	32	Appointed member of Council of Elders (*Genrōin*) in April.	Osaka Conference of 1875 (compromise between Ōkubo Toshimichi and Kido Takayoshi). Kido and Itagaki Taisuke join cabinet.
			Appointed executive secretary of *Genrōin* in November.	*Genrōin* sets up local officials conference.

Year	Japanese Era	Age*	Life Events	Domestic/Overseas Incidents
				Treaty of St. Petersburg concluded between Japan and Russia.
				Ganghwa Island incident.
				Conscription ordinance amended to promote general conscription.
1876	Meiji 9	33	Accompanies Chancellor of the Realm Sanjō Sanetomi's inspection tour of Hokkaido in July.	Japan-Korea Treaty of 1876 concluded.
				Shippuren Rebellion (Kumamoto), Hagi Rebellion (Yamaguchi), and Akizuki Rebellion (Fukuoka) erupt.
				Imperial Japanese Naval Academy established.
1877	Meiji 10	34	Receives provisional appointment as vice president of *Genrōin* in January and proposes reform of local autonomy.	Satsuma Rebellion.
			Father, Munehiro, dies in May at age of 75.	Kido Takayoshi dies.
			Appointed member of criminal law drafting committee in December.	Segment of Tosa-Risshisha, including Ōe Taku, plots overthrow of government.
				Saigō Takamori commits suicide.
				Indian empire established.
1878	Meiji 11	35	Arrested in June for involvement in Tosa-Risshisha's plot.	Ōkubo Toshimichi assassinated.
			Sentenced to 5 years imprisonment in August and confined in Yamagata prison in September.	Imperial Japanese Army Academy established.
				Takebashi Incident.
				General Staff Office of Imperial Japanese Army established (autonomy of military command).
1879	Meiji 12	36	Yamagata prison burned down. Transferred to Miyagi prison in Sendai in December.	Gustave Emile Boissonade starts drafting Japan's Civil Code.

344

Year	Japanese Era	Age*	Life Events	Domestic/Overseas Incidents
1880	Meiji 13	37	Completes treatise *Menpeki dokugo* (Monologue Facing a Prison Wall) in March and continues to write *Fukudō dokugo* (Mutsu's Monologue), and *Shiji seiri-dan* (The Principles of Governance) while imprisoned.	Japanese legation opened in Seoul, Korea.
				Li Hongzhang builds up Chinese navy.
1881	Meiji 14	38	Finishes translating Jeremy Bentham's *The Principles of Morals and Legislation* and writes *Sashi jirei ippan* and *Fukudō shizon*.	Hokkaido Colonization Office Scandal of 1881.
				Ōkuma Shigenobu dismissed as result of political upheaval of 1881.
				Imperial edict on establishment of parliament in 1890.
				Jiyūtō established (Itagaki Taisuke, president).
1882	Meiji 15	39	Released from prison under special amnesty.	Itō Hirobumi leaves for Europe to study constitutions.
				Rikken-Kaishintō established (Ōkuma Shigenobu, president).
				(In Korea) Imo Incident (riot of Korean soldiers in Seoul; raid on Japanese legation).
1883	Meiji 16	40	Heads for Tokyo in January, then leaves for Wakayama.	Iwakura Tomomi dies.
				Itō Hirobumi returns from Europe.
			Translation of Bentham's *The Principles of Morals and Legislation* published in two volumes.	Army War College founded.
				Rokumeikan opened.
1884	Meiji 17	41	Departs for political study in Europe in April. Arrives in London in July.	Sino-French War (until 1885).
			Mother, Masako, dies at age of 76.	Jiyūtō dissolved and Kaishintō broken up.

Year	Japanese Era	Age*	Life Events	Domestic/Overseas Incidents
				Kapsin Coup (Kim Okgyun and Japanese minister to Korea Takezawa Shin'ichirō lead Japanese troops to occupy Korean royal court).
1885	Meiji 18	42	Leaves London for Continent in March. Starts studying under Lorenz von Stein in Vienna in June.	Convention of Tianjin concluded between Japan and China, stipulating simultaneous withdrawal of respective troops from Korea and mutual prior notification on deployment of troops.
			Returns to London in September and heads home toward end of year.	Dajōkan abolished and replaced by cabinet system. Itō Hirobumi becomes first prime minister of Japan.
				British naval ships occupy Port Hamilton, Korea, until 1887.
1886	Meiji 19	43	Returns to Japan in February.	Foreign Minister Inoue Kaoru convenes first conference on revision of unequal treaties.
			Appointed to Ministry of Foreign Affairs in October.	Fierce debate on Foreign Minister Inoue's Westernization policy.
1887	Meiji 20	44	Appointed deputy chairman of Ministry of Foreign Affairs' law investigation committee in April.	Movement to oppose revision of unequal treaties on the rise in Japan. After announcing termination of treaty revision negotiations to delegates of participating countries, Foreign Minister Inoue resigns.
				French Indochina (federation of three Vietnamese regions) formed.
				Hoan Jōrei (regulations for preservation of law and order) established.
1888	Meiji 21	45	Assigned as minister in Washington, D.C., in February.	Privy Council established. Resigning prime ministership, Itō Hirobumi becomes president of Privy Council. Kuroda Kiyotaka cabinet formed.
			Signs Japan-Mexico Treaty of Amity, Commerce, and Navigation (Japan's first equal treaty with Western country) in November.	(In China) establishment of Beiyang Fleet.
1889	Meiji 22	46	Signs revised trade treaty with United States in February.	Promulgation of Constitution of the Empire of Japan and Imperial Household Law of 1889.
			Heads home in December.	Minister of Education Mori Arinori assassinated.

Year	Japanese Era	Age*	Life Events	Domestic/Overseas Incidents
				Foreign Minister Ōkuma Shigenobu injured by member of group opposing revision of unequal treaties.
				Kuroda Kiyotaka cabinet steps down. First Yamagata Aritomo cabinet formed.
1890	Meiji 23	47	Returns to Japan in January.	First general election of House of Representatives.
			Appointed minister of agriculture and commerce in first Yamagata cabinet.	Rikken-Jiyūtō formed (renamed Jiyūtō in following year with Itagaki Taisuke as president).
			Runs in first general election of House of Representatives from Wakayama 1st District in May and wins seat.	Civil Code, Code of Criminal Procedure, and Code of Civil Procedure promulgated.
				Genrōin abolished.
				Imperial Rescript on Education signed by Emperor Meiji.
				First session of Imperial Diet.
1891	Meiji 24	48	Joins first Matsukata cabinet as minister of agriculture and commerce in May.	First Matsukata Masayoshi cabinet formed.
			Resigns as member of House of Representatives in September.	Ōtsu Incident (Tsuda Sanzō's assassination attempt on Tsar Nicholas of Russia).
			Okazaki Kunisuke elected to House of Representatives in by-election.	China's Beiyang Fleet makes port call in Nagasaki.
				Kabayama Sukenori, minister of navy in Matsukata cabinet, makes reckless speech.
				Shimose powder invented.
				Naval Arsenal established.
1892	Meiji 25	49	Resigns from post of minister of agriculture and commerce in March and becomes councillor to Privy Council.	Second general election of House of Representatives (bloodshed due to election interference by Home Minister Shinagawa Yajirō).
			Appointed foreign minister in second Itō Hirobumi cabinet in August.	Matsukata cabinet steps down, replaced by second Itō Hirobumi cabinet.

Year	Japanese Era	Age*	Life Events	Domestic/Overseas Incidents
1893	Meiji 26	50	Submits draft of revised treaty and negotiation plan to cabinet meeting in July regarding unequal treaty with Britain.	House of Councillors rejects budget for building naval ships.
			Makes historic speech denouncing proposal for stricter enforcement of existing treaties at House of Representatives in December.	Itō cabinet weathers crisis by obtaining imperial edict asking for people's support for construction of battleships in return for voluntary cut of 10 percent in private expenses of imperial family for next 6 years, as well as 10 percent salary cut for all government officials.
				Budget for building naval ships passes.
				House of Representatives dissolved.
1894	Meiji 27	51	Oldest daughter, Kiyoko, dies in January at age of 21.	Kim Okgyun assassinated in Shanghai. Donghak Peasant Rebellion in Korea. Itō cabinet decides to dispatch composite brigade to Korea.
				Imperial General Headquarters established. Japanese government proposes to Chinese government that troops dispatched by both countries should cooperate in suppressing rebellion in Korea and promoting reform of Korea's domestic politics. Proposal rejected by China. Japanese government makes announcement it would not withdraw troops from Korea until latter's political reform implemented.
				Anglo-Japanese Treaty of Commerce and Navigation signed, marking first step toward revision of unequal treaties.
				Japanese fleet attacks China's fleet off Pungdo (Battle of Pungdo); Japanese army occupies Seonghwan and Asan (Battles of Seonghwan & Asan); Japan declares war on China (First Sino-Japanese War).
				Japan's Second Army wins Battle of Port Arthur (Lüshunkou).

Year	Japanese Era	Age*	Life Events	Domestic/Overseas Incidents
1895	Meiji 28	52	Peace proposal submitted to emperor at Imperial General Headquarters conference in January.	Shangdong Operation. Beiyang Fleet surrenders. China's delegate to peace negotiations arrives in Japan. Japanese government sends back delegate as lacking authority. Peace negotiations start in following month in Shimonoseki between Japanese side and Li Hongzhang.
			Together with Prime Minister Itō, starts peace negotiations with China in March.	Li Hongzhang injured by Japanese radical. Sino-Japan armistice signed. Treaty of Shimonoseki agreed (approval of Korea's independence; cession of Liaodong Peninsula, Taiwan, and Penghu Islands; and Qing to pay war reparation of 200 million taels).
			Recuperates in Ōiso in June. Education Minister Saionji Kinmochi serves as acting foreign minister in his absence.	Tripartite Intervention by Germany, France, and Russia. Cabinet meeting decides on return of Liaodong Peninsula to China. Exchange of documents of Sino-Japanese Peace Treaty.
			Completes *Kenkenroku* in December.	Korean Empress Myeongseong (Queen Min) killed by Japanese assassins in Seoul.
1896	Meiji 29	53	Returns to Ministry of Foreign Affairs in April.	Komura-Waeber Memorandum on Korean affairs signed.
			Resigns from post of foreign minister in May.	Yamagata-Lobanov Agreement on Korean affairs signed.
			Goes to Hawaii for recuperation in June, returning home in August.	Itō cabinet steps down, replaced by second Matsukata cabinet.
			Founds monthly *Sekai no Nihon* (Japan in the World) under editorship of Takekoshi Yosaburō, and contributes political articles.	
1897	Meiji 30	54	Dictates *Gotō-haku* (Count Gotō), his last written work, in July.	Currency Act (adoption of gold standard) promulgated.
			Dies in August. Funeral takes place at Kaizenji temple in Asakusa, Tokyo.	Office of Japanese governor-general of Taiwan established.
			His remains buried at family grave site in Yuhigaoka, Osaka, in November.	Shangdong Rebellion. Germany occupies Jiaozhou Bay.

Year	Japanese Era	Age*	Life Events	Domestic/Overseas Incidents
				Joseon (Korea) renamed Korean empire. King Gojong becomes Emperor Gojong.
1898	Meiji 31			Germany obtains lease of Jiaozhou Bay from China; Russia obtains lease of Lüshun (Port Arthur) and Dalian; Britain obtains lease of Weihaiwei and Kowloon Peninsula. Japan secures promise from China not to sell any part of Fujian (Japanese sphere of influence).
1899	Meiji 32			Boxer Rebellion (until 1901).
				United States declares open door policy toward China in September.
				France obtains lease of Guangzhouwan from China.
1900	Meiji 33		Wife, Ryōko, dies in August at age of 45.	Japanese cabinet meeting agrees to dispatch composite brigade to suppress Boxer Rebellion.
1901	Meiji 34			Qing court compelled to sign Boxer Protocol (peace agreement between eight-nation alliance and China).
1902	Meiji 35			Anglo-Japanese alliance signed.

*According to traditional age counting system.

（英文版）陸奥宗光とその時代
Mutsu Munemitsu and His Time

2018年3月27日　第1刷発行

著　者　　岡崎　久彦
訳　者　　野田　牧人
発行所　　一般財団法人出版文化産業振興財団
　　　　　〒101-0051 東京都千代田区神田神保町3-12-3
　　　　　電話　03-5211-7282㈹
　　　　　ホームページ　http://www.jpic.or.jp/

印刷・製本所　　大日本印刷株式会社